EMERSON ARTS PRESENTS:
THE STAGE LIGHT FLICKERS

CREATED BY: MASON MICEVSKI
PRODUCED BY: EMERSON ARTS
PUBLISHED BY: PANDAMONIUM PUBLISHING HOUSE

Emerson Arts   The Stage Light Flickers   Pandamonium Publishing

Copyright © 2021 Emerson Arts and Collaborative Artists

The opinions, views, and values expressed in this book reflect those of each individual performer, and do not necessarily represent that of Emerson Arts or Pandamonium Publishing House. All rights reserved. No part of this publication may be reproduced, distributed, or transmitted in any form or by any means except in the case of brief quotations embodied in reviews.

ISBN: 978-1-989506-46-2

Cover Design: Alex Goubar

Ig: goub_art

Published by Pandamonium Publishing House

www.pandamoniumpublishing.com

pandapublishing8@gmail.com

This book is dedicated to my grandmother, Bora, who showed and taught me unconditional love. To Emily Bolyea, for holding me up as the world around me crumbled and for providing me love and a safe space. To Pagé & Ava, Emily's daughters, for their endless love and support. And to all the artists who felt alone, disconnected, or less than everyone else. This book is a magical compilation that would not have been possible without each of the artists willingness to share their stories. This book is for you- for everyone- these stories are here to help lift your spirits, to let you know you are not alone, and help reconnect us all, to our feeling of community!

I dedicate this book to John and Kathryn Bolyea, my mom and dad, for always believing in and supporting me – always. To Page and Ava Kyere, my talented, beautiful daughters, who motivate me through their own greatness. And finally, to Mason Micevski, my whatever-is-better-than-a-best-friend. Your unwavering love and support has allowed me to dream bigger. Thank you for reintroducing me to me. I love you, all.

Emerson Arts   The Stage Light Flickers   Pandamonium Publishing

CONTENTS

Allison, Thom	1
Atanackovic, Vasilisa	6
Blackwood Marques, Pamela	18
BRAINBREAK	25
Bolyea, Emily	26
Bowrin, Shanice	38
Churchill, Carley	45
Eddy, Madeleine	54
Garneau, Linda	61
Gillard-Bentley, Paddy	67
Gokhale, Nupi	84
BRAINBREAK	96
Hall, Dana	97
Hu, Pheobe	108
Jones, Julianna	120
Kangas, Mikael	124
Khan, Rami	126
Kween	137
Lacas, Matt	142
BRAINBREAK	149

Lange, Heidi	150
Magrath, Melly	155
McGinnis, Caitlyn	169
McFarlane, Anita	176
Micevski, Mason	180
Ng, Timothy	201
Pierce, Erin Bree	206
Pinto, Christabel	209
Porter, Jensen	211
Shields, Tré	217
Spencer, Darlene	234
Wilson, Tom	239
Wincza, Vitek	244
Wyder, Holly	252
Zammit, Ann-Marie B.	266
Group Discussion Questions	272

YOU ARE NOT ALONE!

The Stage Light Flickers... What the hell does that mean?

It is said that a theatre stage should never be left dark. That when the last person leaves the theatre, they are to leave one light on. A single stage light. This is to appease the spirits and illuminate their performances. Every theatre has a ghost and when the spirits are happy, the next evenings' performance is blessed.

This light, the constant, tip of the hat to the tenacity of performers, is something very meaningful to us at Emerson Arts. Our logo, the light bulb, is a direct symbol of this. That no matter what, art will continue, in this life and the next.

The pages to come are filled with emotion, experiences, and LIFE. Over 100 performers were contacted to help on this project. Before you now, are 32 individual experiences from performers of all types that have stripped down their personal stories to provide insight into our world during COVID-19. Each performer was provided a list of prompts and was directed to work from the heart. No matter how artsy, out of this world, or completely unpredictable, we share with you the authentic stories, thoughts and feelings of performers, from national rock n' roll stars, to Broadway choreographers, to a knight at Medieval Times, this is what I wanted to share with you. None of the authors knew who was involved while they were writing. We asked that they keep their involvement a secret. This was so none could compare their stories or edit their experiences. We wanted only the truth. The raw emotion and real narrative of genuine experiences.

There's no people like show people. Sharing these stories will help to create hope, give advice, and let other performers and those struggling to make it work during a global pandemic, know they are not alone.

We have created a series of 'brain breaks' to allow the reader time to decompress and reflect on what they have read. Group discussions and considerations can be found at the back of the book to help guide meaningful discussion.

> *"The stage light may flicker, but it always stays on."*
> -Mason Micevski

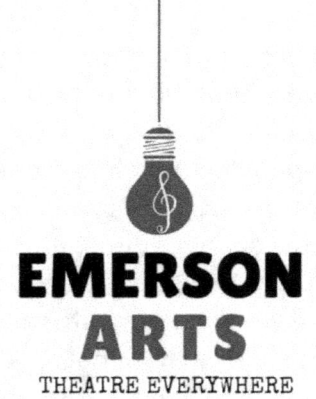

ALLISON, THOM

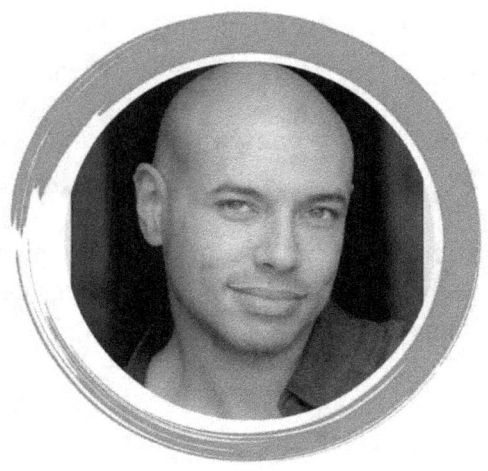

Canadian Screen Award winner, Thom Allison, played "Pree" in the hit series, KILLJOYS. Thom has appeared on Broadway in Priscilla, Queen of the Desert and in the original Canadian companies of Miss Saigon, The Who's Tommy, and Rent. At The Stratford Festival: Romeo and Juliet, My Fair Lady, The King and I, King Henry VIII, and Into the Woods. At the Shaw Festival: Ragtime, Wonderful Town, A Little Night Music and Follies: In Concert. Some other credits include: The Wizard of Oz (Young People's Theatre), Cabaret (Theatre Calgary), Annie (Grand Theatre), Evita (Theatre Calgary/Royal Manitoba Theatre Centre) and The Drowsy Chaperone (The Vancouver Playhouse, The Citadel, National Arts Centre, Royal Manitoba Theatre Centre). Directing: Seussical, Mary Poppins (YPT), A Little Night Music, Wonderful Town (Randolph Academy) TV/Film: Frankie Drake, Hudson & Rex, Murdoch Mysteries, Kim's Convenience, CBC's Over the Rainbow, I Me Wed, Road to Christmas, Leaving Metropolis. His CD, "A Whole Lotta Sunlight" is available on iTunes.

Visit his website: www.thomallison.com

Who among us under 50 has had to live through a world trauma? There have been no world wars in our lifetime, no event that has affected all nations of the world simultaneously that we have yet had to live through and then here comes COVID-19 and we are all thrown into a life-altering experience. There was no guidebook for what to do or how to survive. And our own experiences and life-views were the only things we could draw on for inner guidance. I watched many friends struggle emotionally, physically, mentally, and spiritually.

But I will say right here that I didn't have the hugely negative experience that others had due to several factors… and I'm about to lay them out for y'all.

First this is the way I'm built. I've got a very clear sense of inner fortitude. My parents (black father, white mother) were funny, large personalities who survived poverty, racism, and 56 years of life's ups and downs together with a sense of humour and the motto of "Onward!".

Second, my partner of 12 years and I realized how great we really were together. Our love got deeper, and we became more protective of it. We fostered it and cared for it. We made sure we had clear and loving ways to communicate so we didn't add hurts or slights where there didn't need to be. We knew we were good being in the same space for long periods of time and we realized we were great existing in a small apartment without getting on each other's nerves. That alone was a miracle.

Third, my partner and I actively sought ways to take advantage of the situation to know each other and ourselves more, to grow individually and together. We both were ready for change, and this seemed like the moment to take advantage of the quiet in the world, to look inside and explore the quiet within ourselves. Life is so busy; it can be hard to hear what we want from the universe. Sometimes what we want is just whispering to us because it's afraid to express its "want". So, having the chance to get quiet, we both started listening to these whispering voices - mostly without fear. But even when there was fear, we knew there was no better time to sit inside the fear and see what it's made of. Plus, we had the luxury of each other - a loving partner to lean on and trust. Now I will say here that I am built to move forward with or without a partner.

What is more important than having a partner is that you have to know that you will push yourself to move forward with or without someone else being there. If I can't move forward without someone else in my life, I need to re-establish who I am as a person at my core. The only way I want to move forward is knowing that I am determined to survive and find my joy as a solo being no matter what. Then I know I have all that good mojo to share with my partner (who is mega-awesome, btw).

Which brings me to the next point. Joy. Choosing Joy. That does not mean just being happy all the time. Joy does not mean happy. Happiness comes and goes. But we, as individuals, can choose Joy as a way of walking through life. Joy in the small details - a good night's sleep, a favourite park, a favourite breakfast every day, a colour of a building you pass that makes you smile. Small Joys add up to a life of optimism, which begets a joyful attitude, which begets a positive energy surrounding you, which begets more positivity swirling into your future. We have so much power to create the energy that happens in our lives, but most people accept an idea of powerlessness. That is an illusion. Every human being can create the life they want. We have choice. We can't control all of what comes at us, but we can control how we react after it happens. We can control whether we let a moment crush us or we take it as an opportunity to grow - leaning in to make a different choice, choosing to seek help, if need be (physical, emotional, mental, spiritual), etc. I make a choice to choose Joy. Learn whatever the lesson is and be happy to have the lesson - it makes us stronger.

But the biggest factor in my pandemic experience happened before the pandemic began. Within a 2 1/2-year period, I lost my father, my mother, and my only sibling - my older brother - to cancer, ending with my mother, who had died 9 months before lock-down in March of 2020. My father's death of gastric (stomach) cancer was gradual, but not painful, and it was over the course of 2 years. My brother's death of Lung/bone cancer was 22 months later; the last 16 months of which he was in constant agony. I won't go into detail here of what I witnessed him go through, but I will say this: there were multiple surgeries just to keep his bones from breaking and paralyzing him. If a new nurse (one who had not tended to him before) was sent to give him his meds, she would go and check with the head nurse that the dosage was right because it was so high, she was afraid it was a mistake and that she would kill him. Even with that high a dosage, it was a good day if they could get his pain down to a 6 on a scale of 1-10 (10 being the most painful). And my mother's death which was rather quick (5 weeks from when she seemed to go downhill) was 8 months to the day after my brother's.

What I had to witness in those 2 1/2 years was full of so much heartbreak and sadness. But through it all, there was laughter and connection and support. So much beauty existed in so much pain.

So far, I haven't lost anyone I know or love to the pandemic. Even if I had, the people I loved the most in the world - who knew me, loved me unconditionally, raised me, protected me, taught me to love and be generous and respect others - were already taken. I had to watch my mother lose her husband of 56 years, then watch her listen as my brother told her that he was just given 3 months to live, then watch her watch him die in unimaginable pain for the next 8 months, then watch her move into a retirement home, then die 3 months later, worrying about how I'm going to be left alone to emotionally carry all of this.

After that, this pandemic was in no position to take me down. I am the last of my dad's and mom's direct line. I am left alive to make the most of this life and be the best and brightest version of me and them, to represent the strength and joy and fortitude they instilled in me. I'm made to bring joy to people, to lift them. And I've been using this time to reinvent and expand how I do that as an artist.

Everything "bad" that happens to us is an opportunity to learn. Lessons are hard, y'all. If they were easy, they'd be called "triumphs". And that's the key, turn them into opportunities for "triumphs". I've learned 2 things from my family's mass exodus. 1. Even if you live to be 90, life is still too short. Don't waste a moment. And 2. You can only be taken down by what you allow to take you down.

    Onward!

Thom admits that his COVID-19 experience has had many benefits. How have lockdowns affected you positively?

ATANACKOVIC, VASILISA

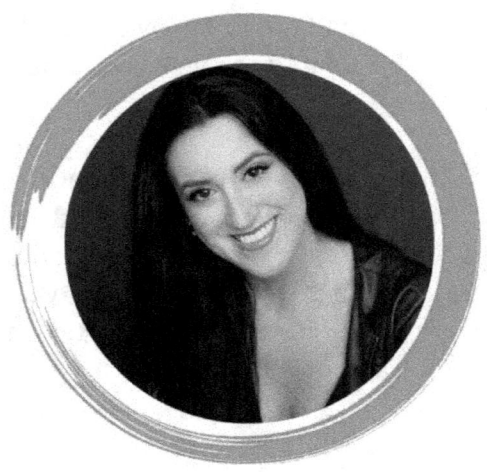

Vasilisa Atanackovic is a dancer, singer, and actor from Toronto, Canada. She began performing at the age of 6 at the Hamilton Conservatory for the Arts where she later graduated with a diploma in Vaganova Technique Classical Ballet under the teaching styles of Vitek Wincza and former Bolshoi Ballet prima ballerina, Olga Krymchanska. She then went on to train at Ryerson University's prestigious Performance Acting program, where she graduated with a Bachelor of Fine Arts degree and award for 'Best Graduating Actress.' Vasilisa has performed around the world, including Canada, Europe, and The United States. As an actor, she has performed in many productions, from the works of Shakespeare (Romeo & Juliet, Richard III, Macbeth, Hamlet, Twelfth Night, Othello, A Midsummer Night's Dream) to hit Musicals (The Addams Family, Cinderella, Hairspray, The Wiz, Chicago, Phantom of the Opera, Annie, Ragtime, Cabaret). She has worked with some of Canada's leading stage directors such as Peggy Shannon, Judith Thompson, Soheil Parsa, Ian Watson, Perry Schneiderman and Sheldon Rosen. Coached by Polish Soprano Marta Greda-Kicek, Vasilisa is a classically trained operatic soprano. Vasilisa has been classified as as a 'true dramatic soprano' and 'a voice that comes around once in a lifetime' by renowned musical director David Gowland, soprano Nelly Miriciou and coach Jack LiVigni. She portrayed Helen of Troy at the LA Opera with conductor and composer Nathan Wang. In the summer of 2016, Vasilisa performed the title role in Puccini's Suor Angelica in Sicily under the direction of Maestro Leonardo Catalanotto. In 2017, she reprised the dramatic role of Suor Angelica with the Berlin Opera Academy. In the summer of 2018 Vasilisa was invited by AVA's musical director, Ghena Meirson, to Philadelphia to portray the lead role of Tatyana in Tchaikovsky's 'Eugene Onegin.' In November of 2020, Vasilisa was the lead role in a TV Series called "The Stranger Experiment" produced and aired on 'CRAVE TV' in Canada where she portrayed herself as an opera singer.

An Evening at the Opera

I love what I do.

Simply put, I believe I was put on the Earth to tell stories to the public, whether that's through song, dance or spoken word. To share stories that everyone can relate to in one way or another. That's my purpose.

And I love my purpose.
To create, recreate, and speak the truth.

I love the feeling that I get right before I'm about to sing a note so high in an opera, that it feels like that note is a portal to another dimension, something that isn't earthly, and we go on that journey together, the audience and me.

Isn't that the artist's purpose? ...To lift the music and words and story off the paper or out of the choreographer's mind onto a blank canvas...the stage.

I always believed so.

My goal of stepping on stage can't be to revel in my ability to cry on cue, or to sing a perfect high C...if that's my goal then I've failed at my job. My goal is to give a fresh perspective to a room full of people that are vastly different from one another, to allow them to let their guards down and perhaps, if I'm lucky, look at life a little differently than they have been.

Ideally, to open their hearts and understand the journeys of the characters in front of them.

*** Now what does it mean to be an artist?

A very cliché question.

I'm sure all artists ask themselves this at one time or another, and they try to come up with whimsical, inspirational, almost poetic answers to this timeless question. It means a lot of things, but I guess what most artists are still trying to discover is...what out of all those things is MOST important in this equation? Does it mean a person is talented at something in particular? Does it mean that they're constantly creating? That they see the world in a different way? Do they work harder than anyone else around them to make their dream a reality? ...Or that they can empathize with countless different viewpoints at a time?

Do you ever stop and think about why artists working on their craft are so frowned upon? No matter the decade, setting or surrounding, artists are looked at as lower-class citizens. Isn't it odd that when a law student finishes law school, he is automatically called a lawyer, but when an actor finishes theatre school, he is called an "aspiring actor?"

There's nothing aspiring about my art.
It is professional.
It has been professional since I was 5 years old.
Blood, sweat, and tears went into creating the performer I am

today.

I didn't spend 15 years training as a competitive dancer, 10 years in countless acting programs, including a university program, and 10 years brutally perfecting my voice so that I can reach the pinnacle of operatic perfection in one bar of one Puccini aria, to be called aspiring.

I am as real as they come.

I think we're a special kind of people. We represent a strong, passionate, open-minded, and rebellious sort. The way I see it, it's ALL this that makes the artist. The passion, the talent, and drive, but also the criticism and the doubts of the people around us. Those things push us to be better.

We Matter...
And not just when we've made it onto the big screen or the top 10 hit list, but while we're giving every ounce of ourselves and our work to get to that point. When we're openly vulnerable with audiences to have them either absolutely love it or tear us to pieces. That's what we are. We give 120% of ourselves in our work, in our day-to-day life, and in our relationships. We aren't satisfied unless we can live and see the world not in 3D, but in 5D. Like I said, I love being an artist, but I don't love what this pandemic has turned so many artists into.

Art is not mindless compliance for empty validation. If you ask me, validation and art should not be in the same sentence. The best art arises when the artist knows exactly what they want to say and cannot be swayed by "likes" or to conform to the majority.

There are some ugly human traits that this pandemic has brought to light, and I believe that the constant need for validation is one of them.

In art, like in life, disagreement is inevitable. It's perfectly normal to disagree on a subject, with the billions of people on our earth it is unavoidable and even healthy. However, when we start using those differences to hurt or devalue someone, it becomes much more problematic. I never thought I'd see the day when artists, are the ones doing the demeaning instead of the lifting.

Throughout this last year and a half, I've been trying to find the motivation and drive to get back into my music and create but seeing how the world is reacting in this difficult time is creating an even more strenuous setting for me.

***The coronavirus had brought out the worst in so many people. Watching our society become so torn and split is hard, but watching fellow dreamers and creators have such little tolerance and understanding for different opinions has been even harder. Where is the empathy that we've been nurturing and growing during our artistic journeys? Where is the big world view and tolerance for someone who thinks and speaks differently? We as performers, singers, actors, movers, and creators, are supposed to be leaders.

We artists have been ostracized for being different for a long time, but now we have a society full of artists doing the exact same thing.

As the effects of the coronavirus begin to ripple around the globe, the arts are hit painfully hard.

Agitated
Peaceful
Confused
Anxious
Content
All valid feelings, but all different feelings. These are the feelings

that came over me, an opera singer...a performance artist, during the weeks which turned into months of the coronavirus pandemic. The fear and confusion came from the unknown. That made sense to me. We're all in this weird limbo-like state where we don't know what's up and what's down, what's next and what happens if we get sick? I could comprehend this thought process but at first, I couldn't understand why the slight glimmers of happiness and mental clarity? It is excruciatingly hard as an artist to allow yourself these moments of calmness. My brain has been programmed to, as the youth would say, "constantly hustle." I hate that phrase, by the way. It makes me feel like a worker ant that spends most of its day carrying heavy morsels of food above its head from point A to point B, with no regard to the other workers around me. In this "hustling" mentality we are constantly conditioned to believe that the more intensely we work, the more successful we will become, especially artists. While this may be true to a certain extent, there is only so much "hustling" a person can do before they completely burn out. Ideally, it wouldn't be complicated to get into a worker's "groove" and focus only on your "hustle." It shouldn't be complicated when you have no distractions around you, but we have social media, we have access to everything and anything with the click of a button.

You didn't get the role? No worries...here's a post about all the people that were cast in the show and why they're better than you.

Haven't booked a gig in a while? Tough luck, here's Jess from university posting about the tenth gig she's booked this month!

...This information hurts the hustle.

As heartbroken as I was, to know that coronavirus had ruined all my gigs in the near future, all my auditions and chances to sing magical operatic roles, however, (as bad as this may sound) I was also secretly happy that other artists were simultaneously having their gigs cancelled. It gave me peace to know that even for a brief moment, the universe was focused primarily on ONE thing, and additionally, I wouldn't have to see any more "look at me performing in this role!" posts. It had nothing to do with not wanting my fellow colleagues to succeed, but the mental clarity came from feeling like I was free to not compete for those so-called, two weeks. I was free to not "hustle" for a role and get discouraged if I don't get it, free to not compete with the hundreds of incredible singers and actors going for the role(s) I so desperately wanted.

At some point, I had lost myself, I knew what I loved to do but I lost that feeling of why I loved to do it.

WHY I loved to perform.

No matter how many great things I accomplished, or how many roles I sang, even while on vacation I would feel tremendous guilt for not sending out my resume to opera houses, for not being able to audition for projects while I was away.

More, More, MORE.

Well, the beginning of this pandemic felt like the whole world was on a vacation together, and I didn't have to worry about another singer stepping in on my role while I was off tanning on the beach.

Now, we were all collectively tanning on the beach.

At first, the clarity and peace of not auditioning outweighed the fear and anxiety of this coronavirus. As the days turned into weeks, and weeks turned into months, I began singing a different tune. Literally and figuratively.

The more time I spent singing in the confines of my own bedroom or living room, the more I craved a stage and audience, and I mean a real audience. Putting on at-home concerts for my husband and family was nostalgic and cute in the beginning, but by week 10 I longed for a proper proscenium stage.

As things were settling down ever so slightly, and people were moving around more, I began to run into fellow artists, colleagues, and performers again. The more time I took to really listen to their stories and their struggles, it was obvious that I wasn't the only one feeling the sting of not performing. I had realized that the more we wanted to get back on stage, the less patience people were having for one another. Our society is split right down the middle and struggling desperately to understand each other. I had heard colleagues say things and I had seen them write comments about those whose opinions differ from theirs, comments that made me sick to my stomach and question, "What kind of artist are you?!"

I would never wish harm upon anyone. As they say, not even my worst enemy.

I thought, "Is this what artists had become? But how? We'd been made fun of, excluded, and told our life choices are not good enough…we know how badly this stings. So why in God's name are we doing this to others now?" I didn't know whether I wanted to be called an artist, to be honest. No matter what your beliefs are on this pandemic and what the best way to end it is, I didn't want people thinking "Oh she's an artist so she must be a huge snob, I can't speak my truth around her."

NO! Quite the contrary! Tell me your truth! Explain why you feel the way you feel, I would love to listen to you and hear what made you, YOU. In return, I'll do the same! Let's learn something about each other. Maybe we can help each other?

I was scared that these horrible, close-minded creatures are what artists had become. I didn't want to be associated with that.

I was losing myself.
I was losing my favourite thing about me, my voice.

My hope is that we can all remember a time in the theatre, when we're working on a role and a character's story, there's absolutely no judgement.

There's reading and writing and watching and learning different literature and different people to be able to understand how to approach the role with respect and an open mind, because all good artists know that's the only way to give an honest and relatable performance.

I hope that we can remember that feeling, that pre-pandemic feeling, and apply it not only in our work when we get back on stage, but in our everyday lives. The people who walk amongst you and think differently have a story, they have something to say, but you must put your "self-righteousness" away for long enough to listen and understand their struggles. As a performer, this golden rule is what has helped me find my passion for my art and music again. What kind of artists are we if we don't practice what we preach? The countless times artists have fought for justice, freedom of speech, and fair representation for everyone, but all it took to shake this system is the fact that someone believes something slightly different? I understand fear, I understand we all want out of this mess, but what I can't understand is that as artists, we spend an immense amount of time (quite literally) putting ourselves in other people's shoes, but we're so incredibly quick to judge people the last 16 months regarding their approach to this pandemic?

To my colleagues far and wide, I've often wondered what happens when this pandemic ends, and someone writes a piece of theatre or a screenplay based on our experiences.

Imagine, up for grabs is the role of Mark the immune-compromised deli-owner who can't get any sort of COVID-19 vaccination because he's got West Nile Virus and it could potentially be fatal to him. Mark spends his time avoiding crowds, because in addition to his inability to get this jab, he's twice as worried about the virus itself.

Now, judging solely based on most reactions I'm seeing in the community, the role of Mark will be vilified, and that actor will deem him/herself to be a righteous fighter for the people by vilifying Mark.

How will you, the performer, be able to find justification for Mark's actions if you're so consumed by your own arrogance? Forgive me if that sounds harsh, but arrogance is what it is. And no, to give this role a proper portrayal you shouldn't be looking down on him and his decisions, you shouldn't be playing the role as a someone you "feel bad" for. To properly portray Mark, you have got to let go of that NEED for validation, that hunger for doing a certain thing purely so you don't rub someone else the wrong way. To properly portray Mark, you've got to listen to the Marks of the world right now. They may be going through things you couldn't have imagined possible.

That, to me is an artist.

Someone that has their own belief system, knows what they want to say, but who can also make room in their mind for the experiences and thought process of someone else.

Nobody believes themselves to be the villain, and in the words of a brilliant author, Simon Sinek, "Our reputations don't come from how we talk about ourselves, our reputations come from how others talk about us."

My beautiful, brave, intelligent artistic community, if you let anything guide you, let it be this quote: "Be careful not to dehumanize those you disagree with. In our self-righteousness, we can become the very things we criticize in others, and not even know it."

Life imitates art, and if we can have compassion for one another in a theatre, we should very well be able to translate that into our day-to-day lives.

Then it dawned on me. The more I listened to people's struggles, talked to them, and truly heard what they were saying to me (be they an artist or not) the more I started to feel the life coming back to my art, my singing, my passion.

Throughout this journey of being a pandemic singer, singing to keep my voice in shape, then not having the motivation to sing, then singing to find my motivation, I realized that my motivation lies in my ability to empathize. A situation as complicated as the coronavirus pandemic is not, nor can it be black and white. There is so much gray area that the only way we can work through it is to accept the black, white, and gray.

My competition was no longer another singer or another actor. I related to their struggles, and I understood that they just wanted to get back on stage as eagerly as I did. My competition was and will always be myself. If I can strive to be a better version of myself each and every day in life, then I can safely say that will translate to being a better, stronger, and more capable artist...one that doesn't "hustle," but rather one that has a healthy, and grateful work ethic, appreciating all the artistic journeys around me.

It is a difficult pandemic, but ultimately, I learned more than I ever have about myself, my singing, and the world around me. For that, I am thankful.

For that, I am ready to take on every stage by storm, singing my way back into the hearts of a beloved audience waiting to be taken on a journey.

Vasilisa was candid about her feelings towards the success her actor friends and colleagues while she was struggling. In what ways has the pandemic affected you negatively where it affected friends and/or family positively?

BLACKWOOD MARQUES, PAMELA

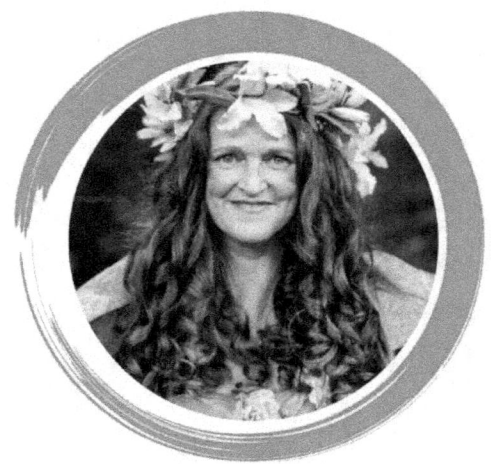

Pamela's stand-out roles have been Mrs. Kendal in The Elephant Man, Edith in Pirates of Penzance, and Carmen. She has performed with Celine Dion, The Three Tenors, and the late Michael Burgess. For the last two years, she has been costuming and acting in the film industry. She recently completed her first horror which has been adapted for film and stage. She is blessed to have a supportive husband and family.

Memories of Pamela Blackwood Marques

Hi, my name is Pamela Blackwood Marques and I am... wait let me take you back, way back, 53 years back. "What do you want to be honey, when you grow up?" Pammie's reply, "A Bare Naked Dancing Lady." Well, that went off really well I thought. What I really meant was a performer with style and dignity that just so happens to, maybe, sometimes, get naked. Dreams change but never die. I studied violin, ballet, gymnastics, synchronized swimming, piano, voice, trombone, piccolo, xylophone, tympani, and recently guitar.

My childhood was amazing I had a loving and supportive family. All sugar coated with icing and whip cream and chocolate ice cream. I kept a horrible secret from all of them for 53 years. I was sexually abused by a family friend and was terribly bullied all through every stage of school. But that is not what this story is about.

Despite what happened to me, it does not define me. Just like what we do for a living is not who we are. When people ask me what I do for a living this is what I tell them: First I get to play with cats and dogs, bath them, care for them, fix them, save them. Then I sing whenever my heart wants to sing. Maybe I play a little guitar ditty or pound one out on the piano. And then I am blessed to share those things with whoever will have me. Lastly, I get to play dress up whenever I want.

The performer's career is always in constant flux and being ready for change is essential. Unfortunately, we are not always prepared for what faces us. I have always thought that to be successful you need to have these four things: Diversity, never put all your eggs in one basket; Flexibility, if you cannot bend then you will break; Sustainability, how long can you be effective; Talent; do what you are good at.

Streaming along, my talents blossomed, and I began to shape a career in the arts that my mother and father would have been very proud of. Many of the aspects of the talents I possess are self-taught or at the very least self-developed from a basic skill set that was taught to me. My father was an Anglican Priest, so he performed every Sunday in front of an audience. My mother was a musician extraordinaire, and she performed and taught her six children and about half the province, (well, maybe not that many) so, performing was in the blood. My father was an accomplished seamster making all his own church vestments and countless other priests' as well; he taught me how to hand sew and the creative process.

My career both in Costume Design and as a musician was really starting to take flight and then all flights were grounded. I was in demand in both fields and began tip toeing in the film industry with costumes, acting, composing, and modelling. My life was exciting and scary all at the same time. Maybe I could be that bare-naked dancing lady. Most people know I have taken my clothing off for Opera and Broadway, was film next?

Life in the performing arts came to a halting screech.

My rooms filled with contracts, gone breach.

Clothing, costumes everywhere, suffocating in the mounds of forgotten actors.

Hanging on, month after month, depending on factors
He yells why do you hang on so, can't you let go?
Do something, anything, to extinguish defeat
I pick myself up, dust myself off, learn a new song, wash, rinse, repeat.

A lot of firsts for me came because of this viral infestation that has devastated humanity. I have acquired a drive to push myself beyond what I thought was possible. Going beyond my comfort zones. Reaching for perfection. Embracing technology even though it drives me mad. Purging my home of things that were really impeding my true success. Let us face it, no one really wants to clean. It would be great if we were Bewitched and could just crinkle our nose and *poof* everything has a place and everything is in its place. I gave myself challenges and fulfilled those challenges. We bought a house and flipped it.

I found the courage to put myself out-there and it paid off. If you are too afraid to ask for something, then you will never have something. I took what I did and made it better, having that time that the virus gave us could be a blessing for some. This makes me think that if I could have this attitude when I was younger how things would have been different right now. My profound words of wisdom, "Do it now, don't wait, don't hesitate."

The most heartbreaking of changes for me would have to be the loss of the mentorship position I had at Glendale For the Performing Arts. For the last 8 years helping, guiding, and costuming the students has been an integral part of my life. Expanding my creative wings and helping students do the same has been truly rewarding and the friendships I have received from that, remarkable. I had already experienced losing this part of my artistic life once before when I worked with Westmount High School students for years under the leadership of Cynthia Knowles; it came to an end with her heaven bound journey. I will always be grateful for that opportunity she gave me, but sad nonetheless for its end. So again, history repeats itself and COVID-19 rules determine my fate as a mentor. Not being an actual Hamilton School Board teacher, my services were no longer permitted. This was a hard one to swallow; the rejection comes with real feelings of worthlessness, and you would think that someone in this field should be used to rejection, but it just isn't so. It hits hard every time.

A positive that did come from that was a culling of sorts. My presence could still be felt through my donations of period costumes to the school, most of which were from the Arts performance of Fame couple years prior to COVID-19. I also donated much of my modern-day costumes which I had come to the realization that period costuming is my jam. I'll do modern day but not my first love. (Dirty Rotten Scoundrels with Willard Beaudreau and Gary Smith at Drury Lane would need to be excluded from the modern-day downer as that was a great show

and worked alongside some great actors).
Although I can't interact directly with the students, I have helped organize and sort through the costume department so that when (not if) things improve, I can step right back into that role.

But I will always look forward
Not dwell on what was
What could be
Only what is
No one is going to discover you
You discover you
Never sit and wait
For something to happen
Make it happen

I am grateful for meeting Paula Penton, another drama teacher that prior to COVID-19 ran an amazing theatre called Connect Theatre, that gave young performers opportunities to shine. We had great plans to encourage, teach, and help shape youth and young adults in the arts, so I am praying that that will continue when our world repairs itself. I am grateful that Paula was still able to reach kids through her position at school.

This process has made me pinpoint parts of my costuming business that I love and parts that I do not love. Having that extra time to reflect on our process is so vital. In a busy world we just don't or are not able to dissect our process in order to be more effective.

Was I frustrated, sad, depressed, angry? You're fucking right I was. I started drinking again, thought I could handle it this time. Thought "I could do that on my own" and I couldn't. 8 years of sobriety and *poof* it was gone. I drank for 8 months, and a light bulb went off. "What the fuck, Pam?" Oh, by the way, this was in the second wave. I do not think I handled it as well as the first wave. Probably because no one thought it was going to last this long.

Do not even get me started on my body and the state of affairs which is my waistline or lack thereof. I want my Cabaret body back, "has anyone seen it?" It has only been five years I'm sure it's lurking somewhere.

Happy Thoughts! Happy Thoughts!! Happy Thoughts!!!

The second wave, one thing did happen; Mr. Ford decided that dog and cat groomers were essential, so there's that small morsel to chomp on.

Music was still. Well, at least the music groups I sang with were still, stagnant, empty. I had a large event planned in April 2020 with over 30 performers and 10 artists, gone. Shrek, gone. Numerous charity events planned with Gary Santucci, gone. One feature film, gone. Handful of small indie movie projects, gone. Two more Broadway productions, gone. After each gone, there should be a very, very, dramatic pause.

I really think that Facebook saved me. Wow, did I just say that? Really it has been an amazing tool for networking and exposure. I need to thank Helen Graham and Father Doug Moore from Laidlaw United Church, Gary Santucci, John Laing and Sue Hawthorne from Church of the Ascension, and my husband Roger. They have been my rocks, and God my comfort. My spirituality is very important in my life and without that there is no pathway to true joy.

I have been blessed to share my voice with these two congregations mentioned above. Father Doug Moore, Steve McRae, John Laing, and Sue Hawthorne are such talented musicians and Father Moore, and Father John Stevenson are both brilliant pastors.

I have managed to dibble and dabble in the film industry with very cautious COVID-19 protocols. Costuming a handful of indie shorts and composing music for one of them. I participated in some online Zoom script readings which got me very excited about throwing together a project that could be almost entirely rehearsed remotely and then a performance outdoors. I put together a Mid-summer Nights Dream Team and presently working through the steps towards success.

This further prompted me to develop an entire Virtual Theatre Experience Program which I intend to launch in the Spring of 2022 with enrollment beginning in January 2022.

I thank my daughter and granddaughter for guiding me through computer processes. They are truly patient with me and that is exactly what us non-computer-literate human beings need. More patience, more compassion, more of those skills which can help you further yourself in today's climate.

Am I tired? Am I weary?
Do I want to stay in bed, a query?
I struggle every day,
I struggle in every way.
But I push myself!
Think to self!!
Note to self!!!
Push without delay.

For Pamela, Facebook was an effective tool for networking and exposure. How did social media help you or hinder your experience during this global pandemic?

THE STAGE LIGHT FLICKERS

```
P A N D E M I C I T S T D U C M U L
T C O V I D G N M K I T R Y A L R I
P F L I C K E R A V A M A I C O G G
P E R S E V E R A N C E E G T Y K H
J U F M A S K S R E S I L I E N T T
H A X I V A C C I N A T I O N Q P H
S O C I A L D I S T A N C I N G A A
K B W T A L E N T L C R E A T E I P
I F O R U S T R A T I O N S A D P
L U R X Z H A R T I S T E W A X K Y
L Q K V L A O O D A N C E F B R V U
D J A C T S I N G V M B H J I H B H
```

Find the following words in the puzzle.
Words are hidden → ↓ and ↘ .

ACT	LIGHT	SKILL
ARTIST	MASKS	SOCIAL DISTANCING
COVID	PAID	STAGE
CREATE	PANDEMIC	TALENT
DANCE	PERSEVERANCE	TIME
FLICKER	RESILIENT	TRY
FRUSTRATION	SAD	VACCINATION
HAPPY	SING	WORK

BOLYEA, EMILY

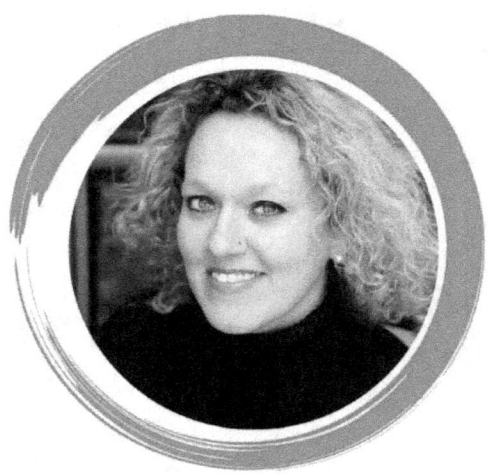

Emily Bolyea brings years of passion, knowledge, and experience to her role as Co-Founder and Co-Artistic Director of Emerson Arts. She is a humble country girl planted in Hamilton, ON and has performed and taught all over the world, including Korea, Ghana, U.S.A & Canada.

Early in her career, Emily developed her skills as a communicator and educator while working as an English teacher in South Korea. This led to her fronting an 80's Funk & Rock n' Roll cover band, and a series of children's CDs sold nationally. That country will never be the same.

Upon her return to Canada, she raised two talented young daughters, Page and Ava, (Emerson Arts' Social Media Gurus). Emily developed her grant writing and event planning skills when she hustled as director of program and special events for a national Canadian non-profit, working in conjunction with the Toronto Film Festival and Maple Leaf Sports Entertainment (MLSE).

A board member for Hamilton Theatre Inc since 2016, she is an active member of various local theatre companies such as Theatre Ancaster and Flush Ink Productions.

EmersonArtsCanada.com.

MAKING THE BEST OF IT – EXTREME EDITION

It was the best of times, it was the worst of times, but one thing was for certain...there was a lot of newly experienced time! Time to think, reflect, learn, and grow. Time to appreciate what you have and time to plan for the future. My COVID-19 time was full of emotional ups and downs. But I'm grateful for the time I had to be with the ones I love, doing the things I love to do. This word-art seems to represent my COVID-19 experience.

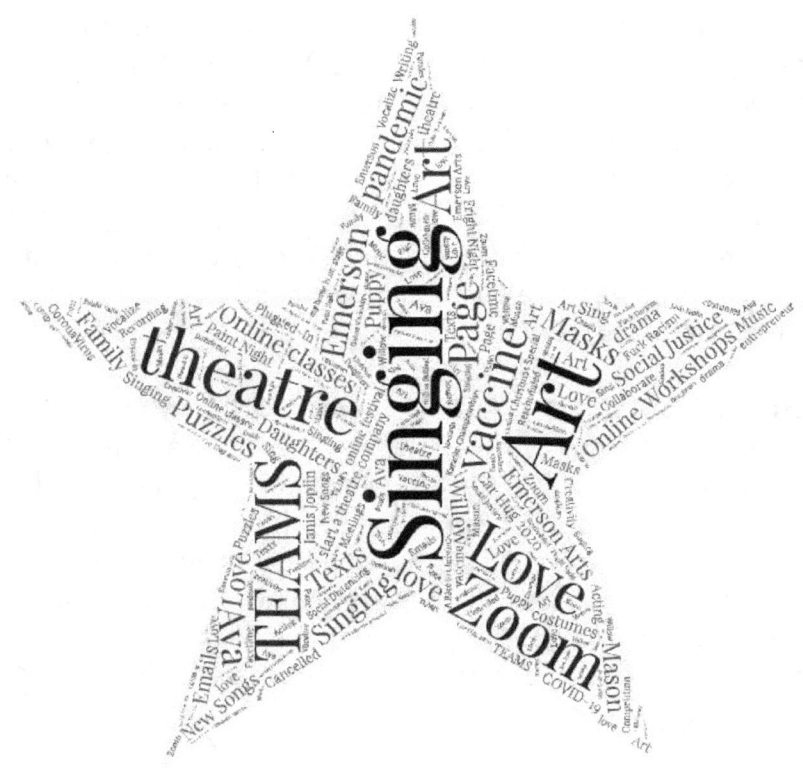

Maybe?

THE COVID-19 ASSESSMENT
For me, living through COVID-19-was like listening to a musical under water. You're kind of there, you kind of hear the music but it's muffled, you can feel the big musical numbers around you, but you can't really see the characters. You can hear their conversations, but you're not really part of it. You're on your own, and you're in control – but the stage is out of reach. At least the water is clean and warm. It's not so bad.

I LOVE THE STAGE
I love to perform. Give me a stage and I'll sing and dance and act the fool, or the nun, or the whore (LOL). But, without a stage, what is an actor to do? I'll tell you what... we create our own stage. THAT's what we do. We make things happen. We push and build and try – because we thrive in adversity. That's what our lives consist of. It's our normal. Overcoming challenges. From auditions to strenuous rehearsals, to back-to-back shows, to public criticism, on-stage bloopers, and the notoriously gruesome 'Tech Week' (a week of technical rehearsals, fine tuning costumes, lighting, make-up, sound cues, etc., usually long, long nights that lead-up to the dress rehearsal and then, the very next night – it's opening night). We leave our blood, sweat and tears on the stage and that is no exaggeration.

THERE'S NO SUCH THING AS SMALL PARTS ONLY SMALL ACTORS
For me, theatre is like a drug. I tried it, I liked it, I want more and more and more – my appetite for performance is insatiable. It's like I can't live without it. I can't say no. If there is an opportunity, I grab it. I want to try it all. Ask me to be in a show and I'll say yes. I'll play any character, try any movement, wear any costume. Every role is a challenge. Every experience is valuable. I've been hung, whipped, kissed, slapped, murdered, and kicked. Just call me, Yes-And. I love it!

THEY CLOSED THE PLAYHOUSES
But when COVID-19 turned our lives upside down, the playhouses closed, the stages went dark. Performers were left with few options. And it became illegal to sing and dance, at least in public spaces.

CANCELLED SHOWS CANCELLED DREAMS
I was smack dab in the middle of rehearsals for 'Spring Awakening' an incredibly cool show with an incredibly cool cast. As corona crept into our lives, we attempted a Zoom rehearsal or two and then stopped. It was over. The show must go on – but this one didn't even get started. That was sad. It's hard when you work on some kind of thing, and it doesn't come to fruition. Like going to a call-back and not getting the part but worse by 500 times. But then, I was cast in a big show intended to kick-off the re-opening of the theatres. I'd be hosting and singing...but I think it didn't take very long before organizers could see that this pandemic was here to stay. That show was also cancelled – because although we were optimistic and had high hopes, the virus was out of control, our lives were full of unknowns and this show, too – was just something that could have been.

It COULD HAVE BEEN WORSE
I was lucky. Lucky to be in lockdown with those I love the most. My daughters became young women right before my eyes. My best friend in the whole entire world, my ride or die, spent the first lockdown at my house and essentially never left. It has been awesome. Everyday is like a party! I missed my mother, nephew John, sister Natalie, and the rest of my extended (too many to name) family more than they'll every know. One of the most tragic experiences took place at the beginning of coronavirus, when it was still so much more unknown than now. My grandma passed away. We never had a funeral. We never had a memorial or a proper send-off. And that really sucks. But at least my mom and her family could be close and provide comfort to my grandpa and each other.

NEW FUN WAYS TO PERFORM
It was only a few days into the first pandemic lockdown before my talented friends started morphing and adapting to fit into the new 'theatre at home only' situation. They found new, unconventional but totally awesome and unique projects to keep themselves fulfilled, me busy doing what I love and in turn – entertaining the masses.

JUST BE QUIET
Do you want to know what the hardest part of pandemic lockdowns was for my family – myself, my best friend, Mason, my talented daughters, Page and Ava, and our adorable new puppy, Willow? Being quiet. We just can't shut up. We are cooped up in a small home filled with great big, giant voices and personalities. We all sing. We are all dramatic. And we all think we are quiet and moderate and appropriate. We're not.

SILENCE IS BORING
If I had a nickel for each time one song was playing on the radio and two people were singing two completely different songs…I could retire…or at least have a really good night out! This makes me feel so grateful.

SOCIAL BUTTERFLY STUCK IN A COCOON
"Emily is a social butterfly." These words were written on my third-grade report card and are tattooed on my heart. I love to meet new people, hear their stories, share a laugh, and make new friends. It's hard to do when you can't leave your house – but I made connections with actors and directors from across North America participating in anything I could get my hands on. I made it work.

BUSY DOING NOTHING
Now, you might think that time off from lots of life's pressures might motivate someone to do all the things they ever wanted to do – but the truth is – the closing of everything and forced

staycation allowed me to slow down and relax for the first time in my life. I loved it. I appreciated every opportunity to watch a re-run of Michael Scott and the Dunder Miflin gang. There was a time when I never had a minute to do something for no good reason. I never had the luxury of having time to do nothing. I was go-go-go! Now, I was slow, slow, slow!

A WHOLE NEW ME
Suddenly slowing down seemed a whole lot easier. I was still a bit of a last-minute Linda, but I took my own time to do the things I wanted, and the things I didn't want to do, I just didn't.

WORLD'S BEST BEST FRIEND
Anyone who knows me, knows how much I love my bestie, Mason. He is the most thoughtful, kind, and loving person I have ever known. We met four years ago doing a show and have been inseparable ever since. He boosts me every chance he gets. He is proud of me and loves me with a pure and strong love that gives me all the confidence in the world. If I am half as great as he thinks I am, I must be okay. He encourages me to push myself harder. I have spent every day of this pandemic with him. I am so grateful. Mason is hilarious and talented – but like…on a whole other level. He is artistic brilliance with a never-ending stream of excellent ideas that only need the right backing to be successful. He is inspiring, dedicated, and beyond his years. I am so excited for him and his own performance-future. I know he's going places. We all know he is.

MOTIVATING MASON
Having my best friend and business partner at my full disposal was wonderful. We could plan, organize, and create together at all hours of the day or night. EMERSON ARTS was born and nurtured in the mass confusion of an unknown virus. We were motivated, excited, and using all our creativity to put together a show during a pandemic. Who puts on a show during a pandemic?
WE DID!!!

CAN'T STOP WON'T STOP
It was awesome. We were fortunate that crowds of up to 50 people could meet at an outside gathering. Our audience members were theatre-starved theatre-folk who just wanted to be dazzled. And that's just what we did. Fright Night: An Evening of Horrors became Hamilton's newest annual October must-see. Our audience members wore masks, respected social distancing, and were so grateful for the experience. Our actors were unhinged, excited, and willing to do what it takes to make a show a show. We stayed within government guidelines, and all worked together to bring together a spooky night-time, outdoor, site-specific show with the backdrop of Dundurn Castle in Hamilton, ON. It was magic.

A DIFFERENT KIND OF SCARY
While we thought we figured out the mystery of how to put on a show during a pandemic, we also knew when to stop. Fright Night was the perfect show at the perfect time. Our next planned show: RACE TO CHRISTMAS was cancelled within a couple weeks of announcing auditions and play submissions. COVID-19 casualties were increasing and getting closer and closer to home. Broadway lost Nick Cordero and local theatres close to home lost important community theatre members who left legacies of grace and excellence.

BLACK LIVES MATTER and EVERY CHILD MATTERS
Being an empathetic Caucasian woman sucks. I am so disgusted with how white people have treated every other race. Slavery, residential schools, internment camps, etc. all bring me shame and sadness. It's frustrating to hear how others can justify our actions and mistreatment of others with a variety of bullshit excuses I will not give a platform to repeat. Black Lives Matter activists now had more time to protest for positive change. And just when it seemed like we were making some headway, announcements of children's bodies in unmarked graves on the properties of dozens of former residential schools are reported

across North America. Statues of Canada's first Prime Minister and historic-businessman, Egerton Ryerson (who both orchestrated the cultural genocide and continued systemic racism of native people) were defaced and toppled. Within months of the discovery, Ryerson University announced it will now be changing its name. At the time this book was published, the new name had yet to be announced. Canadians don't want to honour the evil used to build this country. We choose to document and archive it in museums and books. Statues are for the glorious. There is no glory here. I'm glad anti-racism and effective social activism was at the top of every Facebook newsfeed and news story on the radio and headline in the newspapers. The physical and mental exhaustion that people of colour must endure is unfathomable to me. Yet they continue to create and do great things while pushing for representation. When I get to write, they must advocate first. As an artist with a theatre company, I will forever provide a platform for racialized artists. I am humbled.

ANOTHER ONLINE EVENT
We attempted to keep the momentum of FRIGHT NIGHT going with EMERSON ARTS PRESENTS Plugged-In – an online show that features local artists, including interviews and performances. On Valentine's Day we organized a paint-night with a local painter and local musicians – it didn't go as planned. We created contests and challenges online. One thing is clear – people are over doing anything online. We are stuck in front of screens for work all day long, then rush home to plug-in again for another Zoom-style event. Even when you love the content, staring at a screen can be torture. I detested it. At work, I have three screens and a cellphone, at home we have three TVs, everyone has their own cell, there are a couple of tablets...everywhere I turned...SCREENS! This has made everything that I WANT to do...like writing for Emerson, or writing grants, donation letters, etc. a horribly unattractive task. Or maybe I'm lazy?

DONE COMPLETE FINISHED HAPPY

Throughout the pandemic, I did my best to keep myself busy, when I wanted to be busy. Like most people, I completed projects I had been working on and never got around to finishing. I did a 1000-piece puzzle of Super Girl that now decorates my living room. That's the biggest puzzle I've ever done. My favourite COVID-19-creation was a conversation piece I created. I've collected cool, tiny trinkets, like broken jewelry that was just too beautiful to throw away, or a pair of red, sparkly lips that used to decorate my keychain in high school, to a *Jem and the Holograms* Barbie-sized phone from my childhood. It used to fill a giant pickle jar from when I worked in a sub shop in university (I swear I'm not a hoarder!!) that was my bedroom doorstop. I took all those pieces and glued them onto to the glass frame of a macramé framed picture I found curbside. Now, it's the centrepiece of my home that has so many memories and good times associated with it, that it warms my heart everyday. It was a simple project that turned into a sort of magic decoration. Every time I look at it, I feel happy.

THE KIDS ARE OKAY
My kids ebbed and flowed in their day-to-day activities. They TikToked a lot. My youngest, she did a lot of experiments from the sciencey-side of the app. My oldest was on 24/7 video-chat with her friends. It was cute. For a lot of the time, they were disinterested in anything that had to do with me. LOL! And I'm so proud of them because, for all the time they had to fill, I barely heard them say, "I'm bored". I know they spent a lot of time on their phones, but I'm glad they have learned to entertain themselves. That is one positive that has come from this global emergency. When the artists aren't there to do it for you, many people can now entertain themselves. I love my girls and am so proud of them both. Page and Ava, you give me life.

MY COVID-19 EXPERIENCE
- Started a new company
- Created a new show/Sold-out our first run

- Multiple online play readings with actors from across the world
- International online play festivals that didn't exist before the Pandemic
- Online concerts
- Multiple musical collaborations

All of this and
- We got a puppy!
- My Best Friend moved in with me and everyday was a party and every night a slumber party
- Watched all 20 Marvel Movies in chronological order
- Watched 'The Office' season 1-9 x10!!!
- #carhug2020 – a European-city tour of southwestern Ontario. (London, Paris, Brussels, Dublin, etc.)

And we learned about new words and phrases that are now embedded in our daily lives
- Social Distancing – Stay six-feet away
- Zoom – online video-chat/meeting platform
- Flattening the curve – slowing the spread of the virus to a manageable number for the healthcare system
- COVID-19-respiratory disease caused by a new coronavirus
- 14-day quarantine – stay isolated as carriers of the virus can be asymptomatic for 14 days
- Pandemic – an epidemic out of control, infecting or affecting the entire world
- PPE -Personal Protective Equipment (masks, hand-sanitizer, disinfectant wipes)
- Face Mask – gets its own mention because these are mandatory in most places, are fashionable, and cause controversy because after more than a year, people STILL don't know how to wear them effectively (insert eye-ball roll)
- Herd Immunity – when we're mostly vaccinated, we can protect those who can't be vaccinated due to real, medical reasons
- Vaccinations – a magic potion created by scientists, that protects you against deadly illnesses...this one is extremely

controversial because some feel the roll-out was too fast, not enough testing, conspiracy theories about government control and that the vaccine is not perfect or 100% - but the best we can do with what we've got at this time. The scientific regulations continue to develop and be shared and modified with and for the world, but some see these things as negative and now...
- The World is Divided – pro-vax or anti-vax
- Anti-Vaxer – someone against vaccinations for a number of reasons ranging from- vaccinations are made from poisonous ingredients to they are a money-makers for Big Pharma, to the government is poisoning us and trying to control us
- Pivot – the term use to describe rolling with the punches. There is so much unknown that we all have to be ready to change the way we do things for the safety of others
- Isolation – having to stay away from other people until your scheduled 14 days of quarantine is complete.

There's just so much to think about. Mason often catches me staring off into the sky...or the ceiling...I'm usually just thinking...like, I don't know how I feel about so many things because everything seems so extreme now – thoughts, feelings, actions...there is no subtlety anymore...it's black or white, yes, or no...but I am just one big gray area with strong, passionate feelings about what I know...and a million thoughts streaming through my head of complicated things I don't know. And that's normal. And I'm thinking about how to run a business that is notoriously under-paid, under-appreciated, under-funded, and misunderstood. It's a lot. But one thing is for sure, I am a work in progress. I am my own art.

YIN AND YANG
This past year and a bit could have been worse. Aside from the death of my beautiful grandmother, I gained more than I had lost (especially on the scale, but who cares about that???) Although I didn't get to see my mom – we talked on the phone a lot!! I didn't get to do 'Spring Awakening', but I started Emerson Arts

with my very best friend. I didn't get to see my kids on stage, or on a soccer pitch, but we had dinner together at a reasonable time, almost every night. I loved how things slowed down. I could breathe. Working my day gig at home was awesome – I loved it. For everything that was bad there was a bit of good in it. I'm grateful for all my COVID-19 experiences. The best part about having all this extra, available time is that it has allowed people to get to know themselves better, the yin and the yang. And it's no secret, the world could never have gotten through quarantine as well as we did, without the hard work, perseverance, openness, and talent of the artists of this world. When we were working, you were watching and listening. We were there for you! Let's hear it for the artists, performers, and the dreamers!

Emily welcomed the break from the busy day to day life that had become her norm. How did the forced slowdown affect you? Were you able to adapt to the abrupt swing from chaos to calm?

BOWRIN, SHANICE

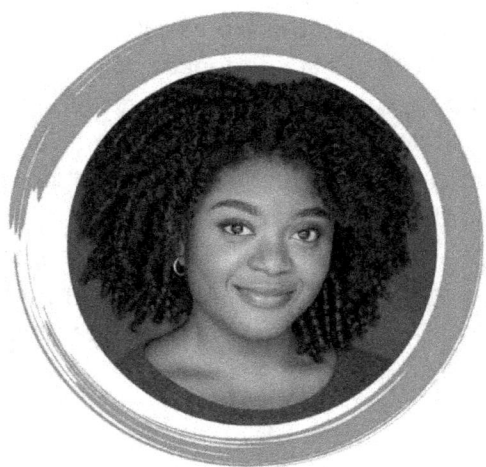

Shanice Bowrin is a Montreal-born bilingual actor and voice actor situated in Hamilton, Ontario. She has studied improv fundamentals at Theatre Staircase and trained with LB Acting Studios in Toronto. Recent credits include "Best in Venue" award winning play, The Butler: A Superhero Detective Story (The Hamilton Fringe), and sold-out performances of Mamma Mia (Theatre Ancaster). Shanice is featured in the positively reviewed web series Sofa Queens on YouTube and has worked as a voice actor with Microsoft Office, Synapz Productions and Valnet Studios specializing in narration, animation and e-learning.

When the news broke, I remember being on the phone with one of my best friends. We were joking about how these were "the end times" and how anti-climactic it all seemed. As we joked about the end of the world, I was pacing in my living room. An increasing sense of dread tied up like a knot in my stomach, the urge to sob rising into my throat. We've all seen 'end of the world' movies and how they begin. It would start with a rogue incident here or there, whispers of a disaster coming then turn into a full-blown catastrophe. Morbidly enough, the movie Contagion about an airborne pathogen infecting the world was just released and heavily advertised on Netflix around the same time. Ironic.

It was March 2020. Earlier that year, I remember proclaiming confidently at the annual Christmas family dinner, "This is my year, I can feel it!" Not knowing just three months later, we would be ushered into our homes with little sense of normalcy for months to come.

Just before everything changed, my proclamation was starting to come to life. My new career as an actor was starting to rev up, my day job was finally starting to balance with my dream job, and I felt sociable and well-connected. Very quickly though, the world I created for myself... disappeared. We were promised that in two weeks, things would be better. It was just a tiny little lockdown. How bad could it be?

Then the two weeks came... and went. More weeks pass by, then months. Hope dwindled with every extension on stay-at-home orders, with every cancelled plan, with every phone call to a loved one far away that couldn't be visited. We were nowhere close to being out of the woods. And with the fear, isolation and changed sense of 'normal'... I started to go mad.

I became self-destructive; I slept and smoked for most of the day. I became apathetic to the world around me but also incredibly bitter. I was mad at everyone. At the people who were checking in on me, at the ones who weren't, at the ones who didn't take the pandemic seriously and at those who couldn't talk about anything else. I snapped at everyone. Every call, text or glance at a screen was draining any energy I had left. I was tired constantly. I cried more often. I didn't like the person I was becoming.

I was starting to think that my dream to be an actor was over before it even began. That all I've worked for was just a waste of time.

This wasn't how my story was supposed to end.

After weeks of spiraling and self-loathing, I finally had enough. I knew if I didn't put myself on a routine or give myself tasks and direction that I would've completely lost my mind. I started to look at the entire situation as a glass half full scenario. I was always too busy to focus on growing myself properly, so this was a great opportunity to develop myself as an artist and do all the things I've been putting off. So, I kicked my butt into gear.

I researched ways to develop myself. I joined just about any workshop, Facebook group, and networking site I could get my hands on. I attended weekly script readings to stay sharp and I read books on voice acting and the art of performance. I started looking at my other creative friends not as competition or as a reason for why I wasn't doing enough, but as inspiration. I built my own home recording studio from scratch, practiced my audio producing skills, and even booked some jobs! I made genuine connections with people online and got the chance to reinvent how I performed. I wrote and starred in my first virtual theatre experience, co-created my own short film, and perfected my ability to improvise. I felt unstoppable.

I took better care of my body and my mental well-being too. I went on daily walks. I would jam out to my favourite music and go. And each time I went out, I stayed out a bit longer. I learned how to take my time and to be mindful. I even took to taking therapy online. I reflected on my dreams and aspirations and started to make concrete plans on how to achieve them.
 Finally, in the midst of all this chaos, I was able to take control of my life and grow into the person I wanted to be. COVID-19 gave me fear, hopelessness, and panic, but it also gave me space to

breathe, to reflect, and the space to grow. It made me appreciate the small moments; like dancing in your living room on a warm sunny afternoon or sipping that first cup of tea in the morning or staring out your window feeling the coolness of the evening air on your skin as you gaze out in the dead of night, surrounded by the comforting but eerie sound of silence.

I felt accomplished, motivated, and scared as hell. I loved it. It felt like a new page was turning in my life and like I was getting back on track.

Then the video was released.

When the news of George Floyd's death flooded my social media feed, I didn't know what to feel. It wasn't the first time a Black person being the victim of police brutality went viral. I mean, it happens nearly every month. The cycle begins, people are outraged, they protest, protestors get vilified in the news, very little to no change happens, and we move on once it phases out of the news cycle. I wish I wasn't so callous about this. But when something happens often enough, you run out of rage or sadness. You just feel empty.

But this time was different, more people were talking about it and Floyd's story quickly became a hot topic with the barrage of black squares on Instagram and out of context Martin Luther King Jr. quotes. Friends and peers started to care about the effects of white supremacy in society and how it affected all of us. People were speaking out and finally trying to understand what their friends of color go through.

My DMs were flooded with acquaintances, friends and colleagues checking in on me to see if I was okay with the news and offering help in any way they could. They were trying to create a space to feel supported, listened to and understood. For some, it was a blessing. For myself, I felt mixed emotions.

Some people were genuinely trying to help. But from conversations, it seemed like the interactions were out of guilt rather than out of compassion. I felt forced into conversations about race where Black people would have to teach what was right and wrong. Most of that time would usually be spent reassuring the person that they were a "good ally". Other conversations were from people that hadn't spoken to me in years; some as long as 10 years. Their only purpose was to prove how anti-racist they were or to commiserate on something that's been going on unknowingly to them for years.

I felt used. Like contacting me contributed to some subconscious woke point system.

So, I shut down. I didn't know how I was supposed to feel. Was I supposed to be grateful that people were paying attention? How about all the times my friends and peers had done something racist in the past? Was I supposed to just forget about that? And what about the people who were my friends and said nothing? Just pretended like it wasn't happening because it was uncomfortable for them to talk about? How was I supposed to navigate that?

I also looked inwardly at my own habits. Was it my responsibility to teach non-Black people about racism? What have I done to help the cause? What could I have said to make things better?

I fought with a few close friends and lost a few during that time. I realized that growing up, I let a lot of crap slide because I didn't want to lose my friends by creating a scene. It brought to light the ways that I shrank myself to make others comfortable. That my comfort didn't matter. It made me think of all the ways I've internalized racism and colorism to myself and to the people who looked like me. Since the video of George Floyd's passing, it made me realize that I could have done more. Said more, donated more, make change in ways that I could do best. And I knew that that would have to start internally, with who I chose to surround myself with and how what I chose to surround myself with.

I marched at the rallies, I posted informative and helpful resources on social media and donated to organizations that helped Black people. But for me it wasn't enough, I still felt like there was more I could do.

So, I thought about being an artist and how I could use that to work toward a more equitable and inclusive future. During this time, the entertainment industry was being told to look within themselves and confront the lack of diversity in the industry. People in the industry were finally looking to create a more inclusive space for all types.

Then I had a revelation. The start of the COVID-19 pandemic forced me to take ownership of my career and to work hard at achieving the goals I set for myself. But that wasn't enough. It was great to have the drive, but what I was missing was a purpose. A raison-d'etre, a reason why I was trying so hard to make it as an actor.

Growing up, little black girls on screen came few and far in between. Most protagonists were blonde or brunette with blue eyes.

The few movies with representation I did watch were Rodgers and Hammerstein's Cinderella starring Brandy and Whitney Houston and Studio Ghibli movies with independent female leads. It made me think about how hard Black and actors of colour had to work just to have a seat at the table. And I didn't want to do that.

I didn't want to be the sole black face in a sea of white. So why not set out to make my own damn table? I want to rise in my career and bring my friends with me. I want to enrich television and movie screens with images of black joy, black adventure, black love, black life, without the sole scope of the movie being about black suffering. I wanted that and so much more. And in that, I found my purpose.

As an actor, I was going to create projects where little black girls could see themselves fully on screen. Where Indigenous stories can be told worldwide and where we see that love is love, no matter what. I was going to create stories that looked like real life did. Full of color and experiences. COVID-19 was a terrifying time but out of everything, I found a silver lining. It wasn't much but it was mine. For me, creating, acting, and writing gave me back the passion I lacked and reminded that above all else, things will be okay. Even if it doesn't seem like it right now.

In times of tragedy, we go through moments of despair, moments of fright and hopelessness. But no matter how dire the situation, humans have an incredible ability to get back up and rebuild even better than before. I believe out of this experience along with mourning and healing, there's hope. Hope for a better future, hope for a better time. And I think each of us has that ability to rebuild in times like this. During this pandemic, I found that ability and I hope for those reading this, you do too.

Shanice found it difficult to maintain typical day to day activities at the beginning of lockdown, though soon changed her outlook and behaviour after examining her situation. Did you have an 'aha' moment during the pandemic where you adjusted your behaviours and changed your lifestyle?

CHURCHILL, CARLEY

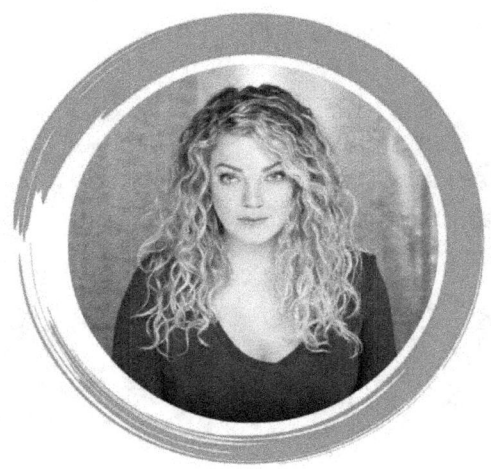

Carley Churchill (she/her) is a queer identifying Toronto based performer, director, writer, creator, and body positivity activist. She is a graduate of Randolph College for the Performing Arts Triple Threat Program. Her credits include Smokey in The Polar Express (Warner Brothers), Shirley in Priscilla Queen of the Desert (LOT), Mama in Dogfight (First Act Production), and Caitlin in the site-specific series Straight Up! (SBM Productions). Carley is also an emerging director working on projects such as: Saucy Jack and the Space Vixens (Director, Small but Mighty), Call it a Holiday (Ass. Director, Call It a Day Productions), and On the Rocks (Ass. Director, Small but Mighty). She recently released the teaser season of the web series she co- writes and co-stars in called Straight Up! Check out the first three episodes on the Nebulatte YouTube channel. She is thrilled to be a part of this project and cannot wait to have the opportunity to share.

Part One: Stagnation

It's dark down here
Not pitch black
But it's as if a dark lens is placed over my eyes
Clouded

The sun doesn't quite reach
The particle filled rays filter in
Showing where each single speck lays
But never showing me

There is a smell
Not one you'd expect…
Like a cave or a hole or a basement
But something else

Stagnation

As if nothing has moved from its exact spot in years
Nothing comes, nothing goes
Thick stillness

I hear people upstairs
Footsteps come and go rhythmically
An occasional cough
They sound far away

Music fills this space
A steady beat and melodic tune
Her voice floats softly above
It makes me feel less alone

My mouth tastes bitter
Cold stale coffee
Hinting for me to wake

Me or my heart?

This dark place
Mirrors the same place within me
I feel stuck here
No escape

No light
I can breed no more light
So, I'll continue to struggle
Continue to fight.

Part Two: Anyone Else

I am here to acknowledge that I am an asshole.

It's got to be true. No matter how much I try to hide it, or push it down, or deny it completely, that label just comes creeping right back in like the little asshole IT is.

I am an asshole.

Now at this point, you're probably saying to yourself, "But Carl, you're probably being too hard on yourself, I'm sure you're not really an asshole." Well, I'm here to tell you that you are wrong. I'm here to say, nope...

I am an asshole.

You might also say, "Come on Carl. We can all be asshole-ish at times though." My rebuttal to that would be, but what if it's most of the time?

I am an asshole.

And now I bet you're wanting to say, "Ok, I concede, you are an asshole then. But why, Carl? Why are you an asshole?"

Here it is-I can't be happy for other people. And to be clear, I'm talking about those people who are booking jobs, being accepted into mentorship programs, and all around killing it in the industry somehow during a global pandemic while I am not!

Ya you! I saw your Instagram post while you were on set last week. I commented, "OMG! You deserve it!" But in my head, I was like eff you. Now, I won't deny that you definitely deserve it, your determination is astonishing, but I still can't be happy for you.

And you. Another human who posted a selfie on Facebook with the caption, "I got my own trailer." I'm pretty sure I commented "How amazing!" But in my head, I secretly wanted that trailer to burn down. And honestly, it is amazing that you have your own trailer, you've been working your ass off and it's finally happening, but I still can't be happy for you.

And finally, to my best friend booking most things coming their way these last few months while I struggled to pay rent... I am proud of you; you have so much talent, but I want to punch you in the face. And while I beam with pride and cheer you on endlessly, I still can't be happy for you.

So, to everyone booking the roles they deserve, sharing their immense talent, and finally seeing their hard work pay off, I still cannot be happy for you.

-Petty, Asshole, out of work Actor

Part Three: Who gets hired then fired three times?

This is kind of the story about how I booked then lost all three of my gigs (for the same company) throughout the first year of the pandemic. It sounds like a really sad story, but I think there are some funny bits and I've really learned that I need to laugh at myself or I'm just gonna cry all the damn time.

I'd also like to preface this story with the acknowledgement that other people/actors/peers of mine have booked, and then subsequently lost some pretty sensational opportunities, so in no way do I want to compare my experience with anyone else's. We've all lost out as an industry. We've all been taken out at the knees. We've all suffered. I can only hope that my little ridiculous story can make someone smile or even laugh a little.

We can probably all remember with intense clarity the moment this started to feel real. For myself, I was at my serving job, and we were watching the news as it was reporting that the NHL was cancelling the 2019/2021 season. We were told that all our shifts were getting cut for the following week and that in two weeks, we would get our shifts back. Remember when we all thought it would only be two weeks? At this point, I was already struggling financially. This serving job that I'd had for four years had already cut my shifts back to once a week, so earlier in the year, I had to get a new bartending job. It abruptly ended one month later when the bar closed for good, because of course, that was my luck. I then got another serving job at a very swanky restaurant one week before everything shut down. So, from January up until March 17th, I was already not doing well financially, and on top of that I was not booking any gigs. So, when there were no opportunities to work in either industry any longer, I felt like my world was coming crashing down. Visa maxed out, no way to make money, and with rent in Toronto being an absolute bitch, what was I going to do? Those first few months were tough.

Then the first light at the end of the tunnel - Casa Loma: Legends of Horror! I had friends who had done it the year prior, and while not the most glamorous gig in the world, it was performing, and more importantly, it was paid. I was cast in the role of Zombie (along with about 8 other performers), and I was ecstatic because I am a massive geek for anything zombie related (The Walking Dead, anyone?). We went in for orientation, everyone was excited to be working, and even just to be around other people again. We got to try on the ridiculous costumes, I couldn't believe my luck with how comfortable mine was! It was basically torn up pajamas, but we did get stuck wearing masks that were quite tight. The night before we were supposed to do our dress rehearsal show, the city of Toronto cancelled the event as we headed into our first full-fledged emergency lockdown. We did, however, end up getting to do one show for the owners, some friends, and a film crew.

Obviously, I was very disappointed when the full event was cancelled, but also happy to be invited to the filmed walkthrough that we did for promotional purposes. Certain actors couldn't make the one-night gig work, and things had to be shuffled around, so I was recast as a Camo Jumper. The outfit was ridiculous, but again, super comfortable, so I was a happy actor. I was wearing overalls and a jacket in dark green camo, and instead of a mask (like the zombies had to wear), I got a helmet with a breathable mesh camo veil. I was basically a blob of camo, a very sexy blob of camo if I do say so myself. One other woman was cast as a Camo Jumper with me, and our role was to hide in the Casa Loma bushes down near the south retaining wall and shake leaves, make noises, and jump out at people walking by before they would enter the zombie pit. Now, before the actor zombies did their jump scares, there was this animatronic zombie cage that would shake and make zombie noises at different intervals. And it is at this point that I have to say - I should have known. I really should have predicted what would happen. Anyone who has ever watched a scary movie with me could have predicted what would happen but, of course, I didn't think twice about being all alone in the woods, next to zombie noises. I did not have the logical foresight.

Well, it turns out I was TERRIFIED. I was convinced that the zombies were real - I started hearing noises all over the place in the woods (if we can even call them that). I started to think I was surrounded by zombies that would attack me. I ended up finding this little hiding spot under some thick tree roots, where I was kind of camouflaged (the irony is not lost on me). I could not keep the camo mesh veil over my face, because it obstructed my view and I needed to be prepared for when the real zombies came to attack. Now, intellectually, I understood that my anxiety was playing tricks on me, but I just kept coming back to this thought: it would be just my luck to be working in a haunted walk while the real zombie apocalypse happened. I kept looking around at my surroundings obsessively, straining to hear any strange sounds closing in on me, and checking my phone to try and distract myself from the fear. At one point, one of the roaming goblins came super close to me in the south wooded area and I almost screamed at the top of my lungs and went into fight-or-flight mode. I bet that actor was wondering what the hell was wrong with me. I was counting down the minutes until the manager would come to say the night was over. I bet it was no more than 2 hours, but it felt like 2 days! All the while, I was preparing for my stand against the very real zombies that were surely coming to get me. Finally, she came, followed by all of the actors featured earlier in the walk, and let me tell you, I was so damn relieved. They were basically the only jump out scare I did the entire evening and I jumped out very early and very quickly so that my nightmare would be over even faster. I had to experience the rest of the haunted walk, which was no picnic, but at least I was surrounded by other humans who could band together and fight with me. After the whole evening was over, safely tucked into my bed, in the security of my home with my guard cat at the end of the bed, I realized that it might have been a blessing that the haunted walk was cancelled, for the sole fact that I am a scared little baby and may not have been able to survive 5 nights a week of scaring the shit out of myself instead of other people!

The second gig I booked with Casa Loma was the Christmas show. I was stoked to be given another opportunity to work, and I was even more excited because I was cast as a Caroler. At this point, I hadn't performed or sung in public for an entire year, and I was itching to get out there and play. We were all just gearing up for our roles when we all received the dreaded second shutdown email about 10 days before we were supposed to start.

My third opportunity came in the form of the Imagine Dragons, the medieval spring forest walkthrough, where I was going to get the phenomenal opportunity to be cast as an Archer. Obviously, I was beyond excited - who wouldn't want to play with a bow and arrow for 5-6 hours a day 5 days a week? I hadn't done archery in some time, and I was ready to sharpen my skills. I was nervous we were going to get shut down again, so I tried not to get my hopes up too high. Key word here: TRY. I couldn't help but have the whole "third time's a charm" mentality, and I ended up getting way too hopeful that we would all get to come together to perform again. But alas, this program didn't even come close to opening up. It was postponed first and then we went into our third lockdown so t'was not meant to be.

Although every time I was let go from a job because of the pandemic, it was difficult and disappointing, I look back on it with a laugh - who gets hired and fired 3 times in a year from the same employer because of an unprecedented global pandemic? I also recognize my privilege in being able to look back and find some laughter in it - not everyone has that opportunity. Not everyone had the small amount of responsibilities that I did - I didn't have children to worry about, and I didn't have school to worry about. If what I went through with losing those jobs was the worst I had it during the first year of the pandemic, I think I got off easy. It definitely didn't feel like it at times, but the truth is that so many people had it so much worse, and I'm grateful that I was still able to survive somewhat comfortably.

Carly was let go from her employer three times due to three different lockdowns. Was there a time, in 2020, when you chose to be hopeful and optimistic, even when the situation seemed bleak?

EDDY, MADELEINE

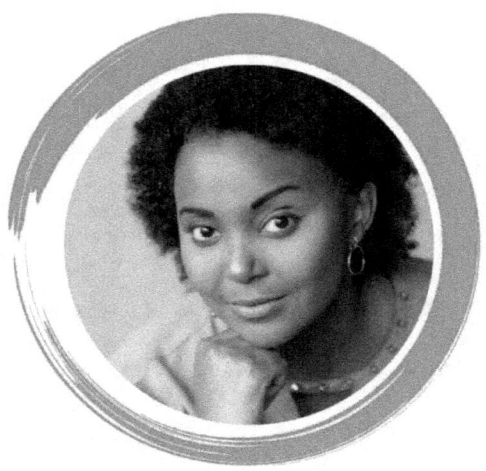

Madeleine has performed at various note worthy venues in Canada and internationally that include Carnegie Hall, NYC, as a featured soloist; the REX Hotel Jazz & Blues Bar, Toronto as a regular performer; and Motor City Casino, Detroit as a regular performer. Some other credits: Dreamgirls (Lower Ossington Theatre), Ragtime (Toronto Centre for the Arts), Wahala Dey O! (Isabel Bader Theatre), Motherhood (The Medley). Madeleine has appeared on CBC 's The Coroner, and True Dating Stories as the title role of Phelisha that you can find on CBC Gem. She also is a graduate of Toronto's Humber College Jazz performance Program.

An artist in a Pandemic

2020. You feel like yesterday, but I can't believe we are closer to 2022 than to you. I still remember the first hearings of the virus but thinking "this will never hit us" or if it does "its not that serious".

See, I'd be laughing at myself, but instead it'll just turn into sobbing. My life as an artist got completely shut down however a new passion was birthed within a few looooooooong months in 2020. Let's start from the beginning.

I had just finished up a contract that required us to be on a train performing Christmas tunes and get this, the train was PACKED and full of people...WITHOUT. MASKS. *shocked* And let me just say I can't even think about being on a full train without a mask now because that is the new norm.

I remember turning on the news and hearing about what was happening in China in regard to the virus after that contract around January or February (the months just mold together) and again thinking this shouldn't hit us, we will be fine. Cut to the next month when I couldn't have been more wrong. I received email after email saying the production I was supposed to be in got shut down due to COVID-19.

It was a troubling time because my art was how I made my money, it was my life and passion, so to have it all taken away was again, a time.

So, my new passion was a few things that you all should know: Netflix, Disney+, and the Uber Eats app. They became my only outlet because the internet felt so loud and scary. Spent countless hours watching Friends for the 100th time and The Office, and of course, every Marvel movie on a loop. It was a routine I would wish for when I was super busy and overwhelmed, but when that's all I could do, it turned me into a couch potato, which ain't cute.

But there was nothing else to do.

After a while, I started playing the piano wanting to do covers and post them on Instagram, but it felt even more sad even because I missed performing LIVE. Still, it helped pass the time.

I also did what any singer does with free time and learned new songs for the auditions that will happen in the next 50 years because of the constant lockdowns. Found some good ones, attempted some bad ones, but again I felt trapped and unfulfilled. I mean, I can only sing YouTube karaoke to my upstairs neighbours so often (they weren't happy about late-night karaoke).

However, I still was trying to find things to keep my spirits up because again the world was LOUD. We, on top of a deadly virus and pandemic, also had an orange Cheeto as president yelling on Twitter and on the news 24/7 so yeah, the world was chaotic. I did find myself getting into writing, which was something I always wanted to do, but with my annoying case of ADHD and being a professional procrastinator, that was short lived (for now). A TV show about my life that someday will get made, but 2020 sure made it hard for inspiration.

Now, after months and months of trying to just keep my spirits up and trying my best to ignore the upset in the world and it being on literal FIRE, something happened in May of 2020 that I couldn't ignore.

The world and I saw the murder of George Floyd. Now, for my profession I never really liked to post political or social issues on my pages because I dedicate those to my art; however, seeing what happened to him awakened something in me that I kept quiet. I became vocal for change.

It started out as a post about what happened and how awful it was, but then turned into something bigger. I was using my platforms solely to spread awareness about what was happening with minorities in regard to society and the justice system. Again, I wasn't a person to speak out about these topics for fear I'd be shut down or it wasn't my place (adopted with two white parents aka privileged), but seeing firsthand how we (black people) are treated I couldn't be silent anymore.

I took pride and made it a mission to share as much as I could i.e., which emails to use or to contact and which phone numbers to call, which people to ask for, who to complain about etc. etc. etc. At first, it was just me posting about specific cases; however, it also turned into me speaking on those and speaking about my own personal black experience that I never would bring up. Like I mentioned before, I wanted to get into writing, and this was a great outlet for me to let out feelings, and observations, and comments that I was too scared to do before.

That became my art. An 'Actor-vist' if you will. I was a person people turned to for information, and it started to feel like a responsibility; however, it was one I was happy to take on. That was before I started to receive my first ever "Online Hate". It started at first with people on my profiles who came from the small town I grew up in, but quickly turned into "friends" and "family" and then internet trolls from all over, because I made my posts public.

Now, on my profiles I have my agents, directors, producers, managers, and countless industry people who I used to filter all my posts for fear I'd get dropped; however, those were some of the more supportive people which helped me feel safe in being authentically honest when dealing with my posts. But, back to the trolls.

I found myself engaging with negative comments so often that I was on edge 24/7. Lots of sleepless nights and I was barely eating, but the friends and family I had who supported me, started shielding me and going after the negative comments. I received such great support which was needed so I could focus on continuing to post and raise awareness on these issues.
It all sounds intense, I know, but so was 2020! However, I was struggling as an artist to find something that kept me going through that dark year and activism did. It became my routine.

What started picking back up were these Zooms I used to do in person; I would go through schools in the GTA and be a storyteller. Through song and acting I would tell black history and stories and have Q&As with students and teachers. It's fun but exhausting. So, when that started back up I still was heavily into being an activist, so through Zoom and being in my safe place, my story telling changed from when I did it the year before. I became more real, open, and honest with these students and teachers because even though some of these stories I was performing happened in the 1950s, we still in 2020 are fighting for basic human rights. I wasn't putting on a Disney performative performance where I was shielding; I became more real with them, which was received very well. That opened deeper conversations after and that also worked into me doing Zooms for peoples' families for private sessions.

This became my routine which in 2020 I was thankful to have. My activism I could bring into my art, and it helped me feel full. Because before, when I wanted to speak up, I never did. And in 2020 I said goodbye to that.

Now, when auditions started rolling in, I also remembered during 2020 the many discussions with black actors in my city about how frustrated we felt only being seen as the best friend or there aren't roles for us vs white roles. But with how the world became vocal for BLM and equal rights we started noticing how many BIPOC roles were being created and stories. And I even remembered thinking "performative or not they're bringing us in" and giving us a chance to be seen. Now I know what you're thinking..." did she really say BLM pertains to actors not getting roles or auditions?" What I am saying is we are finally being seen and heard and thought of because before we were either thug #1, ghetto chick or bully, sassy best friend, etc. We are being considered as leads and other roles that before we wouldn't have been thought of. And luckily, I landed a few great projects in in 2020 which was a triiiiiiiip. Being on set was scary because we were still in a lockdown, but film was one of the first art forms to come back. Someone's job was to yell MASKS ON or MASKS OFF because of COVID-19 procedures. It was tense however there was a feeling on each project I was apart of that "we're lucky to be doing this, so let's make the most of it" which was a motivating feeling...

Especially during those long and sometimes very early calls. I felt lucky to be working during this time, but also realized how unvalued art really is. How many theatres got shut down permanently, yet art was how people even got through the pandemic. Friends of mine doing online shows, porch performances they would stream, creating new content, and heck, even watching shows on sites helped pretty much everyone. Yet we were hit and still in 2021 are recovering from the wrath that is COVID-19 and 2020.

But still we kept on; we did what we needed to cope, but also wanted to do it for others. Now, I wasn't as creative as my friends with their streaming, but my activism became my art when the gigs weren't happening.

Now that its almost 2022 and we still all haven't fully recovered, I do thank 2020 for one thing, and that is perspective. The petty little things don't and should not matter because life is too short. Make that change, do the things you've wanted to do, and don't take life for granted because we saw how easily it can be taken away. Take that chance because you never know where it could go.

As I am writing this, I am thinking of one of my favourite actors who passed Aug 28th, 2020, Chadwick Boseman. That was another gut punch of that year, however, I want to end my section of this book with this quote "Purpose is not related to career. It's related to what God put inside you that you're supposed to give to the world."- Chadwick Boseman
Now, I may not be a religious person, but that quote will always

speak to me and I hope it does to whomever reads this book. Lead with kindness and "be the change you want to see in the world".

Madeleine was fortunate to continue working during the pandemic, though she clearly saw how art is undervalued. What can you do to help forward the cause of appreciating artists and their creation?

GARNEAU, LINDA

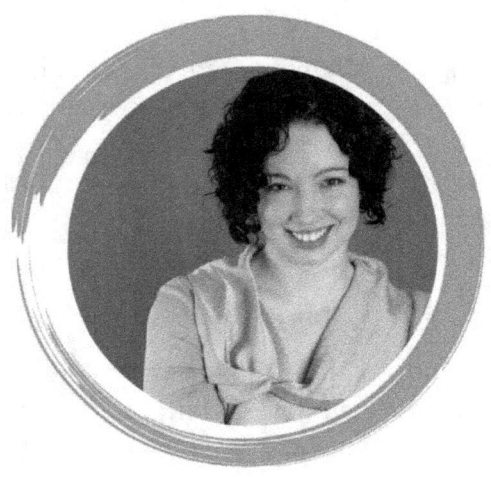

Choreographer, educator, movement coach and PhD candidate in Dance Studies at York U. Linda is the artistic director of the Helix Dance Project, whose works include The Waiting Room, Rain, Unearth, and Integration. Theatre credits include five seasons with The Shaw Festival, as well as productions for Mirvish, Canadian Stage, Charlottetown Festival, Citadel Theatre, National Theatre Centre, Royal Manitoba Theatre Centre, and Sheridan Theatre. Other credits include choreography for Stars on Ice, skating exhibition programs, and music videos. Linda continues to enjoy freelance choreography, teaching both at home and abroad, and discovering new facets of this wonderfully moving craft.

A three-part distillation of moving thoughts; compressed, fossilized, and partially excavated.

Dedicated to Nicolas and Zayla.
We can do hard things!

Part 1: Outside the Lines Here we are.

In the studio/living room/family room/office/rehearsal space/playroom/everything room. Compressed between these walls. Watching the sunlight shift on the floor. Daily. Hourly. Rearranging the room. Re-rearranging the room. Shifting. Staying put. Daily. Hourly.

Here we stay.

Looking out the window. Snow. Rain. Sun. Fallen leaves. Looking at our phones. Watching Netflix. Ordering in. Sleeping in. Working in. Working out. Slowing down. Watching the plants grow. Watching each other grow, fall apart, grow, fall apart. Making rituals. Facetime dinners. Sunday crepes. Colouring inside the lines. Outside the lines. Choreographing our time. Re-choreographing. Solitude like Bitcoin, rising in value by the day.

Here we be.

Anxious, fearful, numb, hopeful, waiting, breaking, adapting, pausing, surrendering, simplifying, screaming, laughing, crying, creating, undoing, breathing, breathing, breathing, longing, loving, discovering, learning, denying, hiding, practicing, procrastinating, pep-talking, real-talking, dismantling, confronting, grieving.

Here we move...

Tentatively at first and then gathering bold momentum. Bumping into furniture. Allowing the smallness of our spaces to squeeze out something new. Something necessary. A hard-won nectar. Movement excavations ensue. Out come the chisels, the scaffolding, the toothbrushes. The dust flies about our spaces, we get dirty. We find community in digital portals. We lean in, smushing our faces into the screen. We share our hearts and lay bare our homes. We see and are seen. For a moment our lonely movements find resonance and we connect. We move to undo the knots we have fashioned. We explore alternatives. We celebrate alternatives. Our solitary experiments unearth muffled voices aching to scream out. We dance our screams. We dance our sadness. We dance our forgetting. We allow the movements to dance us. We pretend we are five years old, arms swinging wildly. We withhold our own judgements. We colour outside the lines. Finally. We move to remember something sacred. We move to heal ourselves.

Part 2: A Love Letter to Students
Originally posted on Instagram in the spring of 2021, at the beginning of the third lockdown.

Dearest dancers,

I acknowledge your suffering.
Consider this a virtual (((((hug))))), should you want or need it. When I check in with students at the beginning of a Zoom class, I ask how everyone is doing. Over the year, I've seen countless students give a thumbs up with a brave smile. What has since been dubbed the 'Zoom thumb.' Over the last couple months however, I've seen little shakes of the head during check-ins, forced smiles for both my benefit and theirs. And now the gesture to signal okay-ness with a smiling thumbs up, feels like a veneer – the movement equivalent of 'fine.' I see these shifts and go on to teach a class hoping our moving together brings joy.

I hope these next musings bring you a measure of comfort. That is my wish.

I've been thinking a lot lately about our approach to things, do we close our fist around something we love, or do we hold it with an open hand? I've played with this question in my practice, both personal and when teaching and realized that it's not an either/or answer. Not exactly anyway. Sometimes we need the container that a sense of heldness or tension allows (I'm thinking a hug, daily rituals, stabilizing our supporting leg when balancing on one foot). Sometimes we need to let go with an open hand (surrender our need to get it 'right,' let go of our grasp on being okay, soften into a spinal roll-down or a bend of the knees). Often, however, we need both: my daughter hugs me and I soften, I generate tension in my supporting leg so I can let go in a balancing posture, I close the door to my room so I can cry.

Dancing yesterday reminded me of this paradox.
(((((We let go best when we feel held)))))

Opportunities to feel held can be as simple and profound as lying on the grass and feeling the breeze. Showing yourself kindness by taking a pause, exhaling, and feeling the air rush back in, holding you in a rhythm all your own. I hope this brings you a little comfort in what I imagine are difficult times for you all.

Sending love your way,
Linda xo

Photo: Nicolas Van Burek, 2021. Linda and Zayla Van Burek, Toronto, On.

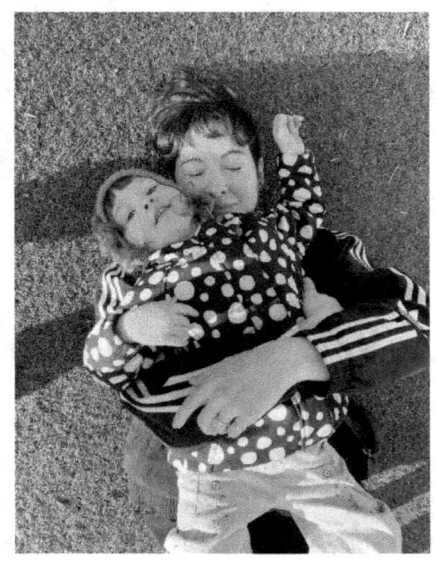

Part 3: still here *

explicit language – try as I might to choose otherwise, I chose to include and wield this language for its physical impact. I decided that my frustration need not be censored or have its sharp edges rounded. So, the cursing remains in its full physicality and energetic imprint. As my literary boxing partner, I ask you the reader to bob and weave as you will.

I am dancing with time. Sensually so. Awkwardly so. Unconsciously/consciously so.

It pulses, swings, sways, it vibrates, it interrupts in ruptures of expectations. Time is a living and elastic force. We lean in and nuzzle into its salty neck. Like an Argentine tango, our dancing is born of listening, subtlety, and fire. I continue to lean in. This dance dances me into being.

Tick, tock, tick...the pendulum keeps swinging.
These days it swings so far to one side that my thirst for the other wakes me up at night. You see, we dancers have been doubly muted. Firstly, in the aesthetic of our craft, and secondly in the digital mosaics of our pandemic communities.

Tick, tock, tick... the pendulum swings.

The movements within these too small walls get louder, they swerve past old self-conscious judgements, and embrace the messiness of their expression. I'm late to this dance party! These new movements are my cursing. I swing my arms and legs with recklessness; fuck my pointed feet. My torso pulses with breathy sounds of expansion and contraction; fuck the constraints and the standards of 'good enough.' Fuck this whole mess of pretending we aren't stuck within these real and imagined walls.

I am leaning in, tasting my own salty frustration.

My movements yell at me to pay attention. There is healing here, in this mess. Within these walls. I watch my three-year-old daughter dance and swing her arms about with wild abandon. I reclaim this for myself. I realize I move to be moved. For no other purpose than to swear/sweat out the frustrations and yield into something new. A new kind of practice. At times this practice yells back at the very craft that rendered me mute in a world riddled with complicit silence.

I continue to lean in. I implore the youth I teach to dance loudly. I quote Rupi Kaur and tell them to be 'mouthy,' to be loud. Behind our surgical masks, we yell.

This time has offered so many points of friction and resistance. So many opportunities to lean in. To listen to the ebb and flow of daily rhythms. I recall my mobility coach reminding me how muscles grow, how strength is earned: "time under tension," she said.

Time under tension. A tango with time.

Tick, tock, tick…

Linda used her experience as a dancer to adapt and communicate through movement during the pandemic. Did you find a secret love language you could use to communicate how COVID-19 made you feel?

GILLARD- BENTLEY, PADDY

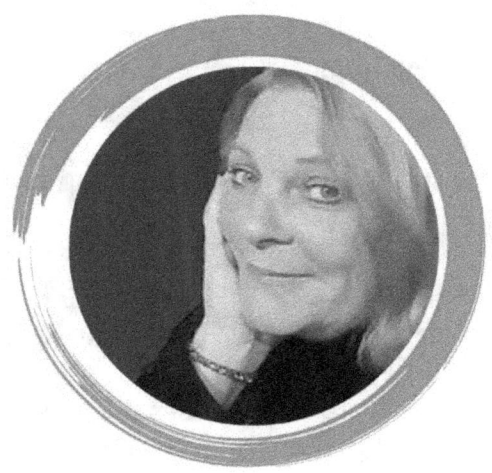

Paddy Gillard-Bentley has been involved in one aspect of theatre or another since her mother, Tessa, was four months pregnant with her, performing in Time Out For Ginger. Her full-length play, Shaking the Dew from the Lilies, debuted in Kitchener, Ont. Canada, in November 2002 and received its American premier in 2005, in Denver, Co. Quantum Entanglement has been produced several times (Philadelphia, Calgary, Kitchener). Her one-acts, White Noise, Sanguine Sonata & Comic Strip, and many shorter plays have been produced in Canada, the US, and UK. Frailty Thy Name is Woe has been published by Meriweather in Volume II of Young Women's Monologues from Contemporary Plays, And Then Full Circle has been published in Mother/Daughter Monologues Volume 4: Urgent Maturity. Paddy is the Artistic Director of Flush Ink Performing Arts and a former President of ICWP (International Centre for Women Playwrights). Paddy's plays online.

A PLAGUE ON BOTH THEIR HOUSES
© 2021 Paddy Gillard-Bentley

Paddy Gillard-Bentley
21-285 Bluevale St. N.
Waterloo, Ontario, Canada
N2J 4L8

INT. DAY. EIGHTH FLOOR OF A CONDO IN FRONT OF THE ELEVATOR

Emma is in her thirties. As an artistic type, she is dressed pretty funky, with a fun mask - as they're in the midst of a pandemic.

She approaches the elevator and presses the down button with her elbow. The 'down' light comes on. She stands in front of the elevator looking up - monitoring the progress of the elevator's approach to her floor from above.
SOUND IN: Ding.

The doors open. Jodi is inside the elevator wearing pajamas, slippers, and a loose-fitting mask. She is much less concerned about social distancing, and her mask often slips off her nose and she adjusts it constantly.

CLOSE UP: EMMA'S EYES WIDEN IN FEAR.

Emma is frozen to the spot. She'd hoped the elevator would be empty.

Jodi sighs.

The elevator doors begin to close. Jodi reaches forward to press the door open button. The door opens. Emma is still standing frozen.

                    JODI
You are allowed two in the elevator, you know.

Emma hesitates.

                    EMMA
Right.

The doors begin to close again. Jodi rolls her eyes, sighs, and presses the door open button - again.

                    JODI
Well? Are you coming?

                    EMMA
Oh, right.

Emma hesitantly enters the elevator and stands in the back right hand corner, diagonally across from Jodi who's still standing at the panel.

                    EMMA
Can you press the lobby, please?

                    JODI
Already done.

The doors close.

INT. CONDO ELEVATOR. MOMENTS LATER.

They stand quietly, looking up at the lights indicating the elevator's progress to the lobby. Suddenly, the elevator jerks to a stop.

                    EMMA
Damn. I thought they were going to get this fixed.

                    JODI
Fixed? It's happened before?

                    EMMA
A couple of weeks ago. That guy on five with the dreadlocks - he was stuck in here for two hours. And Ethel on the 7th last Thursday.

Long pause.

Jodi begins pressing buttons - any buttons. She also seems to be hyperventilating.

Meanwhile, Emma, looking around the elevator sees a sign and begins to read.

                    EMMA
Do these four things if you are stuck in the elevator. Number one. Press the door open button.

Jodi begins furiously pressing the door open button.

Nothing happens.

                    EMMA
Number two. Press the call button. There's a picture of a bell. Is there a button like that?

Jodi begins pressing that.

                    JODI
What's a call button do?

          EMMA
I think it connects to the building's Security Operations Center.

Beat.

          EMMA AND JODI
Donald!

          JODI
He's probably watching porn with his headphones on...

          JODI AND EMMA
Again.

          JODI
Damn! I can't be stuck in here – not now.

          EMMA
I know, right? I have to meet someone in the park for a rehearsal in... *(looking at her phone)* twelve minutes - and, perfect - no bars.

          JODI
Oh. An actor. *(beat)* I didn't even bring my phone with me. I was just...

          EMMA
Where are you going in such a hurry in your *(beat)* pajamas?

          JODI
As I was saying...I just got a notice another Amazon package has arrived for me. It's just like Christmas, isn't it? Ordering stuff and then it comes right to you in a couple of days?

          EMMA
Sure. *(she isn't)* What did you order?

JODI
(proudly) A unicorn head squirrel feeder.

EMMA
Ah.

JODI
It's really cute. I fell in love with it - just had to have it, you know?

EMMA
Sure. *(she isn't)* So you have a dray of squirrels on your balcony that desperately need to be fed from a unicorn head?

JODI
A dray? I think you've got that wrong.

EMMA
Actually...

JODI
Anyway - I don't have any squirrels...just thought it was, you know...

EMMA
Cute.

JODI
Right. *(beat)* And... the hurry is porch pirates.

EMMA
What?

JODI
Porch pirates. They go around and steal packages from people's porches. It's literally a thing now.

EMMA

Shouldn't that be a lobby pirate then?

Jodi just stares at her. Then she forces a laugh that abruptly stops.

Emma continues reading.

          EMMA
Number three. Yell for help.

She barely finishes the sentence when Jodi begins pounding on the door yelling for help.

          JODI
HELP! WE'RE TRAPPED IN THE ELEVATOR. HEEEEEEELP! GET US OUT OF HERE.

          EMMA
(reading loudly from the sign)
Number four. Stay calm. Try to keep a clear head.

          JODI
Right. A clear head. You can do this, Jodi. You've got this.

She does some deep breathing and made-up yoga poses. She glances at herself in the mirror.

          JODI
God my ass looks huge in these pajamas. Do you think my ass looks huge?

          EMMA
Nope.

Jodi reaches for her mask.

          JODI

Do you mind? I feel like I can't breathe. I'm willing to risk taking it off.

Blink. Blink. Long pause.

          EMMA
Actually, the mask isn't meant to protect you, it's meant to protect me.

          JODI
Well, I never get the flu. The only place I go is church on Sundays. Hell, I even have my groceries delivered.

          EMMA
Church, eh? Okay – imagine it like this.
You cough. There's a good chance your germs will remain in the mask. If you cough without the mask, your germs may not go through my mask, but may land on it, or my face, or hands, or all over the buttons you've been just pushing... so... I'd prefer if you kept it on.

          JODI
Ah. That's why they talk about them protecting others. Sorry. I didn't know. *(beat)* Now we're even.

          EMMA
Even?

          JODI
Yeah. You didn't know about porch pirates, and I didn't know that thing about the masks.

          EMMA
Uh huh.
They stand in silence. Jodi pushes the odd button, while Emma watches, making sure the woman keeps her distance.

After a long pause.

          EMMA
So how are you managing?

          JODI
Oh, I'll be alright - just feeling a bit claustrophobic.

          EMMA
I meant - how are you doing through the pandemic.

          JODI
Ah. That. I miss going out to restaurants, shopping, getting my nails done - oh, and this *(indicating her hair)*, haven't seen my stylist in eight months. I'm watching way too much Netflix and YouTube, eating way too much chocolate, and I might be drinking too much Merlot - but my house is immaculate!

          EMMA
So, you aren't working?

          JODI
Oh, I'm working - from home, in my pajamas. I love it.

          EMMA
What do you do?

          JODI
I work in finance. I had to take a pay cut because of this stupid pandemic, which really sucks because I was planning a trip to Europe.

          EMMA
You're probably saving more than your pay cut by not having to buy gas, and eating out...getting your mani-pedi...

JODI
If I didn't have Amazon Prime - maybe. *(beat)* How the hell do those people survive on the governments' thing...what is it...two thousand a month? I'd die. I'd be a bag lady - but with some very interesting bags.

She laughs at her own joke, then stops abruptly when Emma does not join in.

JODI
You know, to be really honest, I hate my job. I would be happy never to see another boring face from the office...ever! Work is such a drag...same thing - like Groundhog Day. I live for Fridays. TGIF!!! Open the Wine!

Emma sits in her corner. Jodi follows suit.

EMMA
That's too bad.

JODI
Oh, it's fine. I drive a nice car - have a healthy stock portfolio – own my own condo - go to a different Caribbean Island every Christmas and shop - a lot.

EMMA
My car's a 2005, I'm not entirely sure what a stock portfolio is, rent and haven't had a vacation since A Plague on Both Their Houses 2016, and yet...

JODI
I'm so sorry.

EMMA
Oh, don't be. I can't wait to get back to work. All the artists I know

are chomping at the bit. So much of the arts were the first things to shut down, and they will be some of the last to resume. Ironically, it's been art that's seen people through, given them hope and joy.

>   JODI

I don't know about that. I haven't had much to do with the arts. I've just been watching movies and music videos and online concerts during the pandemic.

A glance from Emma followed by an awkward silence, unlike those comfortable silences, usually experienced by people in love.

>   JODI

So, if there's not theatre happening, why do you have a rehearsal?

>   EMMA

I'm helping a friend develop her new work. We're rehearsing - in the park - socially distanced - for a play reading next week...on Zoom – of course.

>   JODI

Of course. *(beat)* Is there something wrong with Zoom?

>   EMMA

For theatre - everything is wrong with Zoom. It's like...um...it's like trying to experience a sculpture, by looking at one photograph. Two dimensions.

Theatre is meant to be experienced - with an audience. Did you know that they've done tests, and an audience, watching a play together, begins to breathe together -they're hearts beating in rhythm. It's like magic.

>   JODI

I can't remember the last time I saw a play. Probably high school.

(pause) So - what do you do for a living?

        EMMA

Um...I work in theatre.

        JODI

I know that, but what's your real job?

        EMMA

I work in theatre.

Jodi laughs, then stops abruptly.

        JODI

Oh. You're serious.

        EMMA

Yeah.

Awkward pause.

        JODI

I thought everyone in the arts had real jobs - usually in the service industry.

        EMMA

Often. Not always.

        JODI

So, if the arts were the first to shut down, and you don't have a job at Starbucks, how are you surviving?

        EMMA

Economic Response. *(beat)* That government thing.

        JODI

Oh - oh, I'm so sorry.

                    EMMA
Oh, I'm not. Not at all. It's actually more than I'm used to living on.

                    JODI
And yet you're excited to get back to work?

                    EMMA
I love what I do. Creating something from nothing, rehearsing, developing a new play, getting into the character's head. The first time you read it, you don't know her. You haven't met yet.

The more you rehearse and delve into her character, the more real she becomes. Acting isn't really about pretending to be someone else, it's more about becoming someone else. And the people are funny, kind, smart - so smart. The only people I've met smarter than the artists are physicists.

Jodi laughs. Stops abruptly.

                    JODI
Ah. Serious again?

                    EMMA
Yep.

                    JODI
And all you've been doing is rehearsing this one play?

                    EMMA
Actually, I've written my own short play about robotics, taken online courses - stage lighting, advanced Shakespeare, learning accents, 2 courses on screenwriting and life drawing classes - with a nude model - on Zoom.., oh, right, and how to change your spark plugs.

                    JODI
Wow. I joined TikTok...but I only have 67 followers...Silly me...thought I could be an Influencer - you know?

                    EMMA
Yeah. I know.

                    JODI
I don't get it. All those hours you put in, for crazy low pay. And the people in the arts...kind of weird, aren't they? I was told an actor used to be considered just one step up from a prostitute.

                    EMMA
Actually, prostitutes make way more money. *(Beat)* Just who are you getting your information from?

                    JODI
Oh...well...my grandfather, Jerome. He had this crazy...

The elevator begins moving. Emma looks at her watch.

                    JODI & EMMA
Oh, thank God!

                    EMMA
So - your grandfather...
                    CUT TO:

INT. CONDO LOBBY. MOMENTS LATER.

AS The elevator doors open...

                    JODI
...after that, he was excommunicated. Huge scandal! Gotta run!
Jodi shoots out of the elevator. Emma comes out slowly. Jodi rushes to where packages piled below a row of mailboxes near

the door. She rifles through, raising one in triumph.

>JODI

Woohoo! Unicorn head squirrel feeder!

She rifles through more, raising another.

>JODI

And... my Sushi Bazooka! Woohoo!

>EMMA

Very nice to meet you, Jodi.

>JODI

How did you know my...

>EMMA

When you were giving yourself the pep talk.

>JODI

Ah. very nice to meet you...?

>EMMA

Emma.

Jodi goes to shake Emma's hand. Emma puts her hand behind her back, shaking her head.

>EMMA

Sorry - Can't.

>JODI

Almost forgot.

Now Jodi indicates she wants to bump elbows.

                EMMA

You know what's wrong with the elbow bumping thing? They tell you to cough all your germs into your elbow. So they land there, hanging around, waiting for an elbow bump so they can jump ship. I try avoid them. But very nice to meet you too.

                JODI

You're pretty uptight for an artsy fartsy type.

Emma heads for the door.

CLOSE UP:
EMMA'S FACE.

                EMMA

What the hell is a sushi bazooka?

CUT TO:

INT. CONDO ELEVATOR. MOMENTS LATER.
The doors are beginning to close on Jodi in the elevator.

                JODI

What a loser!

The doors continue to close.

CLOSE UP:
THE LIT BUTTONS INDICATING THE ELEVATORS' LOCATION.

The light stops at six and goes back and forth from floor five to floor six.

                JODI
(off screen)
NOOOOOOOOOOOOOOOOOOOOOOOOO!

BLACKOUT

Paddy created a screenplay that depicted two people in an elevator. What emotions and feelings does that image evoke now compared to how it might have done pre-COVID-19?

GOKHALE, NUPI

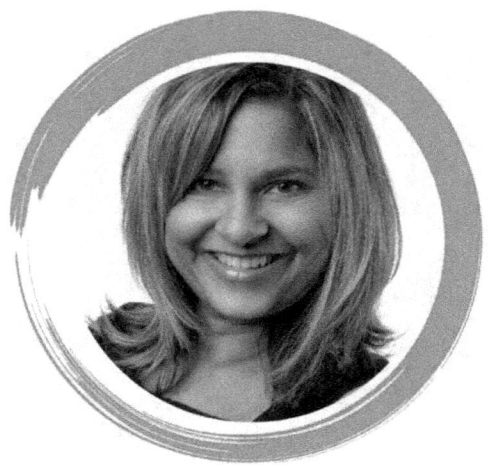

Nupi Gokhale, M.Ed is a self-employed, education consultant who currently serves as President of Theatre Ancaster. A life-long performer, dancer, and director, Nupi has devoted her life to enhancing community theatre and providing opportunities for youth in the community.

Be-Ing

I write this as a letter to my future self,

My relationship with the arts involves dynamic intersections of family, interest, 'right place, right time', hard work, education, mothering, and relationships. When asked to write a piece for this collection of experiences during COVID-19, it was difficult for me to find my voice. Added to that was the very recent passing of my father which has made collecting my thoughts and writing all the more challenging. In the end, it was a dear theatre friend who gave me the little push I needed to write down my thoughts. I live my life through multiple lenses with the common thread being one of artistry. Growing up in an upper middle-class small town, we were one of a handful of families of colour. I was always aware of my 'otherness'. My parent's immigration story to Canada was one of sacrifice, struggle, encounters with racism and of seeking out community, like many others. As an East Indian child, I knew that my 'duty' was to become educated, to focus my attention on schooling and to make something of myself. This was understood.

Growing up in Ontario meant that I wanted to do all the things that little girls my age did. Apart from learning to swim (which against my wishes was mandatory) I had the good fortune to have parents who wanted me to experience everything that Canada had to offer. Every week we went off to lessons in skating, gymnastics and at age 9, modern dance. My first bodysuit was bright red, and I went to a small modern dance studio in Hamilton with family friends. I fell in love with dancing....

Over the next few years, I experimented with different forms of dance, different studios, never fully understanding what was 'needed' to become a real dancer. Unfortunately for me that meant that ballet was not something I knew I needed until later. Once in high school, a tiny, brown, grade 9 student, I decided to spread my wings and I auditioned for a high school production of Jesus Christ Superstar AND I tried out for the gymnastics team. Both activities were demanding, both required my full attention, and while I enjoyed floor work, there was something about dancing in a musical that drew me in. I had to 'choose', and I have never regretted my decision. That singular decision has shaped my identity as an artist.

That grade 9 musical experience opened my world to artistic possibility. I found like- minded friends, I became committed to a discipline in a way I had never experienced before, and I was introduced to musical theatre as an art form.

Throughout high school, I was the girl that danced in musicals. Remembering my East Indian heritage, I was allowed to participate in musicals, but I knew that came at the cost of maintaining my grades. I could take drama, but I also had to do well in math, English, and science. Until it just did not work for me. I tried every which way to keep my grades up in academics and yet everywhere I turned I found more opportunities to commit and focus my energies on artistic projects, both at school and in the community, as a choreographer and dancer. The single greatest gift my parents ever gave me was the freedom in grade 12 to chart my own path. Recognizing my strengths, seeing me for who I really was and not only being proud of me, but supporting me and bragging about me to their friends was something that I did not fully appreciate until I was a parent myself. It is all the more difficult to write this knowing that I have just lost my father and I can never tell him the impact that his decisions to let me find my own way meant to me. The confidence it gave me and continues to give me is indescribable.

And so, now, at age 50, at the urging of my theatre friends who are producing this inspiring collection of experiences, I am collecting my thoughts and telling my story. As a result of my childhood experiences, I have spent my life-giving back to my community. That sounds self-serving to write it down, but the truth is, I entered education as a career because I wanted to provide kids with experiences like the ones I had. I wanted to open doors for kids who didn't know where the doors were. I wanted to offer up alternatives to sports that could give kids the confidence to face whatever life brought them. So, I went to Queen's University, got an honours degree in drama and history, (supported emotionally and financially by my parents), continued straight to the Faculty of Education at the University of Toronto, became a qualified history and drama secondary teacher and landed my first teaching job by the age of 24.

Working in a dynamic, diverse school in Brantford, Ontario I began to realize that my passion for helping kids be 'seen', as a result of my 'visible minority' status (what we called it back in 1994) was another way in which I could make a difference. Teaching history and opening the eyes of students to other ways of remembering stories, telling the stories of those who are often forgotten about, became a passion for me. In my career, I focused on developing kids' confidence to be themselves, serving as Department Head of History at one school and then transferring to become Head of a large Arts Department at a second school. Here I spent ten years building a program I am still so very proud to be associated with. Specialist High Skills Major Programs were 'new' and along with a few other very passionate teachers, we were able to create a musical theatre program that students across Grand Erie could apply to. Performing musicals, taking musical theatre credits in performance and production and dance and vocal music was such a privilege. Directing these talented students was the highlight of my educational career. I got to do what I loved to do every day. I got to be the one who opened those doors for students to find themselves.

At the same time as I was building my career, I was committed to giving back to my community. That high school musical I spoke of earlier grew organically into a grassroots community musical theatre company that I have been involved with since its inception. The three founding directors were the same three teachers who had given me the opportunity to perform in JCS as a dancer all those years ago. During my time with the company, I have participated in its growth from a one show a year company to the multi-faced theatre business that it is today, employing part-time staffers and hundreds of volunteers. Theatre Ancaster has grown into a nine show a year season, performing to audiences of over 4000, offering full year programming to kids ages 3-18, with recent additions of a Seniors program and coming soon, a post high school program for 20 somethings. As a producer, choreographer, front of house manager, stage manager and (my favorite) director I learned everything I know about the theatre world through the art of 'doing'. As a Board Member, alongside many other talented and committed volunteers I served as Director of Youth Programming for ten years, Vice-President for three and now serve proudly as the company's President since 2015. The experiences I have gained, in directing/producing, business, community networking, policy making, non-profit governance and human resources, simultaneously helped the company grow and increased my skill set in arts administration. Somewhere along the way I was also a wife and mother to three amazingly creative, artistic children. As they developed different skill sets, my theatre friends and I created programs to meet their milestones. Nothing available in musical theatre for 3-year-old's... ok, solve that problem, Jitterbugs is created, and our kids are the first ones enrolled. Can't find a babysitter because mom and dad have rehearsal, that's ok, they can come and hang out at the theatre. When my kids were 6, 5 and 2 they asked me once why we always went to the stage. I remember replying to them, "you know how some kids go to church for community, we go to the theatre." I didn't realize at the time how true those words were. My theatre friends are my community. They have watched my kids grow up. The theatre has provided my children with the confidence and skills to face whatever comes their way. And it didn't hurt that they also happen to be quite talented at singing, dancing, playing instruments and production leadership roles. Today, because of the lessons learned along the way, my daughter, who has taken ballet since she was 3 years old, continues to dance her way through a costume studies degree program at Dalhousie. My eldest son, while I tried very hard to enroll him in dance, found his passion in guitar (like his father) and after a brief stint as a child performer, decided that 'we rehearsed too much' and didn't return to the stage until high school. Instead, he spent hours rehearsing with his band and performing at local events like Festival of Friends. Recently he spent the last four years at MacMaster, completing a degree in English, but performing in, writing and assistant directing MacSci Musical Theatre. And my youngest son, off to Western Business (in just a few days time), spent his entire childhood performing and as a teenager, performed lead roles in so many shows I have lost count. I watch him with his theatre friends, and it reminds me so much of myself in high school. He seems to truly enjoy the directing end of things as well and I assume his passion for theatre will somehow inform his career in business.

While I was unable to continue working in Grand Erie due to an autoimmune diagnosis at age 39, I never left the theatre. To this day, I am not sure how I managed it, but during a very dark time in my personal life, my connection to Theatre Ancaster continued to define me. Against repeated pleas to 'scale it back' I knew that I had to have a focus, a goal, to keep my mind active with creative thoughts, otherwise, my health crisis would defeat me. Writing that and reading it back sounds a bit dramatic, and if you know me, you may agree that I am dramatic, but both things can be true. Truly dramatic!

Once I knew how to manage my health situation, I returned part-time to education, having spent the last four years in administration and completing my Masters in Education at O.I.S.E (only took me 12 years). Part of my time was devoted to opening an arts high school in Halton and the last while I have focused on obtaining my administrators papers. Currently I have been enjoying my position as an Educational Consultant, focusing on curriculum development at the secondary school level as I await placement as a public-school Vice-Principal in the community where I live. My hope is that post-COVID-19, I can impact the culture of a school through a leadership lens that is inclusive, equitable and open to inviting in the lived experiences of students from marginalized communities.

All of that was my introduction. I am nothing if not thorough. Did I need to write all that? Maybe not... But my background informs my experiences during COVID-19 and the grief I am currently experiencing with the loss of a beloved parent.

What has this past year and a half been like for me?
It has definitely been a year to appreciate the things that we have. It sounds cliché, but when you are told you cannot hug your mother or father for over a year, all you want to do is hug your mother and father. When you watch on television, the alarming daily death toll in Canada and the world, it makes you take stock. When you live with a life threatening auto immune disease that leaves you immune-suppressed, you are scared to go outside, to pick up a parcel left at the door, unable to go to the grocery store, watch videos on how to clean your groceries... While I am no longer married to the father of my children, we had to share them during COVID-19. Being nervous to kiss your kids when they return from their other house is a scary thing. When you must cancel the remainder of your theatre season with no end in sight, it breaks your heart. When your young nieces ask you repeatedly "when can I go back to performing in theatre shows" and you can't tell them, life feels unfair. When board meetings on Zoom become a regular thing and each month's action items include 'What are we cancelling this month' it seems like I'm in a recurring nightmare.

And yet, COVID-19 has given me one gift- time. I say that with sober pause, as I know that for many, many people who have lost loved ones, they cannot attempt to fathom the gifts of COVID-19. I do have a small sense of that pain. My father's health has been challenging for some time now and his biggest fear in the last year has been contracting COVID-19. So, our entire family has been especially careful around all of the grandparents for that reason. And yet, I still say COVID-19 has given me – time.

When we realized the borders 'might' close, my common law spouse and I were in England, trapped with good friends from my university days. Upon landing at Heathrow, our entire trip of London to Barcelona, to Madrid to Lisbon to London was irrevocably altered. Our trip was now London... more accurately, Oxford, in a lovely shire called Haddenham. We spent the next seven days trying to get home. But those seven days were spent with a dear, old friend, pretending we were back in university, getting to know her two amazing girls in ways you don't get to when you pop in for a visit while sightseeing. We were so grateful to be stuck with them and to reconnect so completely. Upon return, we had to quarantine, alone. Quarantining with a spouse can be tricky and dangerous for a relationship. Yet for us, it made us stronger. Friends dropped groceries on our doorstep. My closest girlfriend and I snuck precious moments standing on the driveway in the bitter March cold just to see each other's faces and talk loudly to each other. It seemed as though the world had stopped moving. My parents as you know were born in India. Their siblings, and my cousins live in many different countries around the world. What was shared by many of my friends, was a reconnecting with family through technology. Programs like Zoom allowed us to talk, really talk to each other for the first time in years. We began to look forward to our weekly Friday evening family calls. We played games online, I designed a trivia game that we played based on the history of our family (I did not win!). And we found creative and innovative ways to connect with our students online. I tried to imagine what COVID-19 would have been like, had we not had the technological communication opportunities we have today. And most importantly, greater than any other gift- my grown children were STUCK at home with me. My dreams of everlasting Games Nights came true. We each took turns making dinner which was a huge treat, and we watched more t.v. together than I would care to admit.

Looking back, I would have never imagined that Theatre Ancaster's production of Mamma Mia in November of 2019 would be the last show that we would produce until the writing of this piece. We knew at the time that the show was special. The cast was just the right blend of personalities, energy, support, understanding, compassion, and talent. The entire creative team was female driven which added a special spark to our textual interpretations - 'living out loud' the choices that we make as women to define our own destinies. And now, it feels like so long ago since we were in rehearsal, making last minute fixes, supporting each other through tech week, socializing through 'Disco-themed' dance parties and then bonding in the way that performers do during the run of a show. And perhaps now, upon reflection, the nostalgia of directing creates something of a fantasy of that experience, I can't be sure. The fast pace of a rehearsal, the constant 'other child' in my brain, the running of show songs as I lay my head on the pillow at night, the bursts of energy when a creative idea came to me, the sheer weight of responsibility one feels when directing- all of it feels so far away now. It feels like that was a different version of me. It was the me that never stopped.

While I have missed the stalling of my creativity that was always thinking 'what's next', the loss of our theatre season as a company, the loss of in person touch and education and being laid off from a job I loved, I am not sure I will ever come to regret the time I got to stop moving and just 'be'.

I will never again take a hug for granted.

For many, COVID-19 has been isolating and difficult. My social calendar has suffered greatly. The extrovert in me struggled when I, couldn't celebrate turning 50, missed weddings and anniversaries. And of course, with the loss of loved ones around us, not being able to grieve together and physically support those in need has been heartbreaking. We will not know the impact that COVID-19 has had on the development of our young people right away. For certain, well-being and mental health must be our collective focus as we emerge from the abyss. Many experiences have been lost. And yet, somewhere in there, in my experience, connection has been gained and appreciated.

When forced to stay still I had to spend time with myself, inside my head, analyzing my life choices, my path forward, my relationships and my identity. When does life afford us that luxury? The universe works in mysterious ways. As the world watched in horror at the murder of George Floyd by a police officer, I was emboldened and grew courage from the outpouring of emotion and support. Understanding the nuances of subtle racism and implicit bias is a very dangerous beast. COVID-19 provided us with opportunities to reflect on our own behaviours. For the first time in my life, I am having those important conversations about race and otherness and difference, conversations that until now, only existed in my academic world. The atmosphere has shifted, people are finally listening, taking stock, and owning their thoughts. While by no means have we resolved the divide between the haves and the have nots, the insider and the outsider, coloniality and indigeneity, but important conversations are starting to happen. The black and white binaries are not so binary anymore as we share our stories and find commonalities in 'being'. We can live in the 'grey', live in discomfort with not-knowing. It is an exhilarating, scary and brave place to be. And because of COVID-19, I have time to just 'be'.

I wrote this journal to myself during COVID-19. I provide it here as an 'in the moment' sample of my experience with COVID-19 and how I was feeling last April 2020.

COVID-19– A Day in the Life
Apr 11, 2020

What is this like?
I've spent the better part of my life reading about WW 1 and 2, slavery in the US, Civil Rights, and equality for all as we work to better our society. As a history major at Queen's, I was bound and determined to understand the 'why' of what we did to each other, as if 'I in my wisdom of 19-24 years could somehow make sense

and pass judgement along with my peers on past experiences of other people.

And yet, at 49 years of age, on the cusp of 50... I have been dealt COVID-19. The world has been dealt COVID-19. Not only do I have to deal with it, but I must navigate and lead my family in this battle. Is it a War? No, not in the traditional sense of what we understand War to be. But YES in that we are battling something greater than ourselves, stronger than the individual will to overcome, and something that requires our collective effort to combat, as Ontarians, Canadians, and Global Citizens.

Is this so bad in the short term? Not at all. What if our family members were called to war? To serve on a battlefield thousands of miles away from home with no proper training. What if we were forced to endure the departure of every able-bodied man and woman in our family to leave our home to serve our nation. WE have not been asked that. **Instead, we are asked to stay at home.**

While this is difficult and the end is nowhere in sight, is it even close to what our grandparents and great grandparents had to endure to give us what they believed was 'freedom'?
Not even close.

Our rations include not knowing when the next shipment of TP will come in, BUT IT WILL arrive. WE know that now.

We listen daily to the briefing from our PM and Premier. What a model of leadership they provide. Who cares if they are Liberal, Conservative or NPD, I am proud to be a Canadian and to have them on the front-lines, leading the nation. Their calm but determined approach has made us all feel safe. The EI benefits as promised, have made Canadians feel appreciated and supported in this time of global strife.

We are stronger together than apart.

Tonight, I played a 4-hour strategy game with my teenage and adult children. Never would that have happened in normal circumstance.
We have set up a dinner schedule that includes each child cooking a meal during the week.
The world has become Zoom-literate.
We are daily congregating outside at 7:30 pm to make noise for our front-line workers.
The dog is living her best life. Daily.
And our appreciation for extended family and close friends has never been greater.

These are the lessons of COVID-19.

Nupi writes about shared family experiences that would not have happened if not for the pandemic. What experiences did you have solely because we were in a global pandemic?

BRAIN BREAK
~ANDY WARHOL THESE LIGHTBULBS~

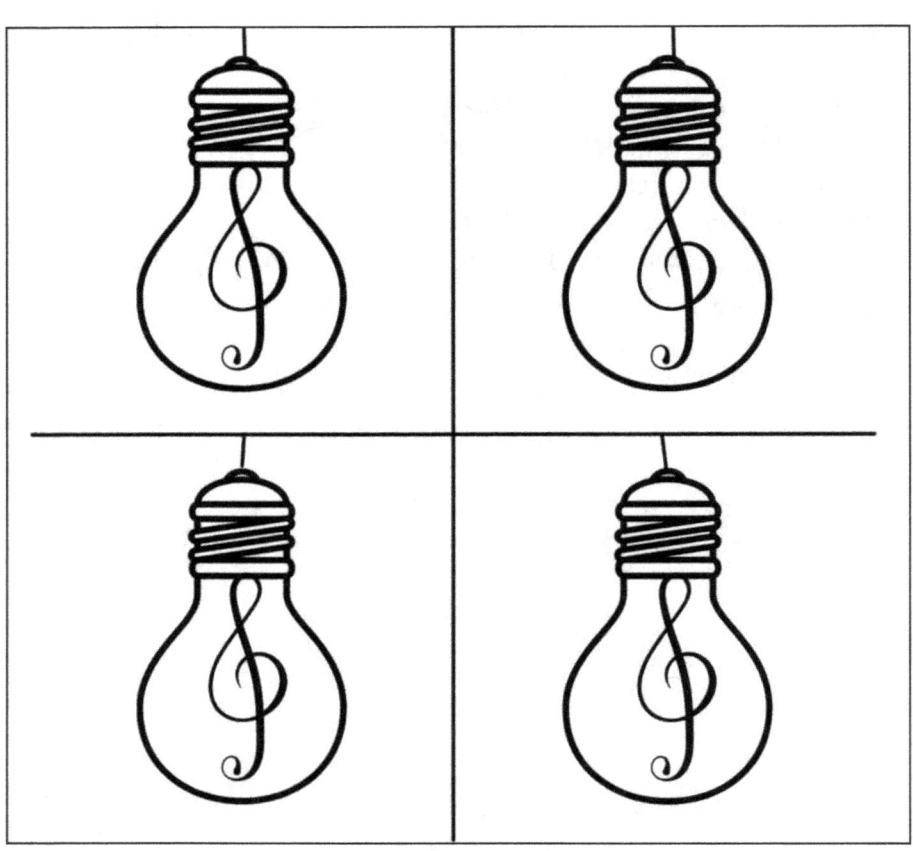

HALL, DANA

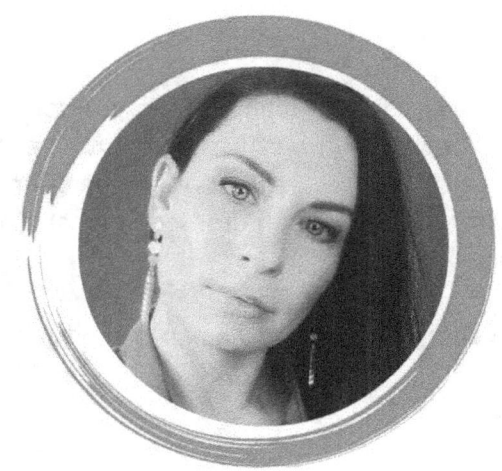

Dana Hall, an American performer, co-founded This Moment Productions, during the pandemic. This Moment Production's mission is to create high-quality virtual theater that unites creatives around the world in a mission to increase diversity, equity, and accessibility in the theatrical arts. Her original comedy The Tenant was accepted to the Rogue Theater Festival NYC (summer 2021) and a show she co-wrote with Kenisha Morgan called No Justice, which is a look at the racial unrest amidst the COVID-19 pandemic was accepted to the prestigious WTFringe21 Festival & Women's Theater Festival. She has gone on to grace the virtual stage in dozens of shows and has become a member of The American Dramatist Guild.

"The power of storytelling will always find a way and I was fortunate to find my voice during a time where I could elevate the platform for others too."

Predictions for My Pre-COVID-19 Self
By Dana Hall

SYNOPSIS: A pre-pandemic version of myself visits a psychic to get some perspective on the year to come.

AT RISE: It's February 2020 at night in Chicago. Dana sees a large sign in a window of a shop. It has 'Psychic' written across it. There is an 'open' sign displayed in the window. Dana opens the door. We hear windchimes as a woman dressed in loose flowing clothing appears.

DANA: Hi. Are you open? I was walking past and saw your sign.

PSYCHIC: Yes, come in.

DANA takes off her coat and approaches the psychic behind the register.

DANA: The sign said 'open' so I thought I'd pop in out of the cold. I thought, 'you know what it might be fun to see what's in store for me this year'... but you likely already knew that.

PSYCHIC: Come sit down with me. There's much to discuss.

PSYCHIC leads Dana to a table that has tarot cards and a crystal ball. They sit on opposite sides of the table.

DANA: Thanks. Cold out there, huh?

PSYCHIC: Yes, very. Did you walk far?

DANA: Oh, no not at all. I saw a show at Second City up the street. You've been?

PSYCHIC nods that she has not been there before.

DANA: Such a fun night. I grabbed dinner with some old friends before the show. They wanted to stop for a drink after, but it was packed. I parked kinda far but your place was on way- I thought why not- what could it hurt?

PSYCHIC: Tell me a bit about you.

DANA: Well, everything's been going pretty well for me lately. Uhh... let's see...I'm finally getting my therapy private practice up and running and business is great. Two out of the three kids are in school. I finally have more time to focus on my goals.

PSYCHIC: Like what?

DANA: Oh, I don't know- I wanted to try and get back on the stage. I've been looking at some audition postings.

PSYCHIC: You're an actor.

DANA: Was- I really miss theatre and now feels like the right time to find my way back. I actually feel hopeful and optimistic about this year!

PSYCHIC: Comfortable.

DANA: *(Reluctant)* Yes, very thanks. It's cozy in here.

PSYCHIC: No, I meant, you might want to get comfortable-there's going to be a lot to process in this reading.

DANA: How bad could it be? *(remembering)* Wait- Trump's in office- forget I said that- okay, give me a second here I have a few things that relax me.

DANA reaches into a giant bag and pulls out a stress ball. She gives it a few pumps then takes out some lavender spray. She

sprays the area and wafts the scent around. The psychic begins to speak but Dana stops her as she pulls out a weighted blanket, a journal, several more stress balls, a Ruth Bader Gingsberg bobblehead. She displays all the objects around her as if for protection.

DANA: *(Continued)* Ok, ready. Wait. *(She takes out a few crystals.)* Ok. Now-go ahead.

PSYCHIC: You travel with all that?

DANA: You know it! *(pauses)* Sorry, I'll stop the psychic humor. Since the election this stuff has come in handy.

PSYCHIC: *(She makes the bobble head move)* I was a big fan of RBG too.

DANA: She's great. Wait. What do you mean "was?"

PSYCHIC: Well, let's get started, shall we?

DANA and the PSYCHIC are at a small table with a crystal ball and some tarot cards in between them. The Psychic lays her hands down and DANA goes to put her hands on top of the psychic's hands forming a circle.

PSYCHIC: Nah, nah...

PSYCHIC indicates the large sanitizer bottle on a little crate next to the table.

DANA: *(She squirts sanitizer into her hands)* Oh-Ok. That's an awfully big bottle that would last a lifetime.

PSYCHIC: *(Laughs)* Oh. Right. Yes, this must seem silly to you "present people".

DANA: How does this work?

PSYCHIC holds DANA's hands and closes her eyes. Makes a low humming sound.

PSYCHIC: I'm intuitive and can feel the shift in energy and aura.

She pauses and sways as she picks up on Dana's energy. She stays in this trance-like state during the entire reading... She speaks in a non-emotional, monotone-like state as she delivers her premonitions.

I see great separation.

DANA: I was meaning to put up a wall to finish off the home office.

PSYCHIC: Do it now.

DANA: Wow. Ok. I mean I barely use it - a home office just feels like a waste of space.

PSYCHIC: Good with computers?

DANA: Me? Uh, I made a power point once in college. I had a zoomy call last month for work.

PSYCHIC: New laptop.

DANA: But I have my old one it works just fine.

PSYCHIC: Long-haired kid needs it.

DANA: My son? He's 7 so I'm pretty sure we won't need a new computer.

PSYCHIC: He will use it daily.

DANA: Uhhh ok...he's in school most of the day.

PSYCHIC: No.

DANA: No, what?

PSYCHIC: No school.

DANA: What? Look in there again- What about his brother?

PSYCHIC: No. Both home- full time.

DANA: What did they do? It was the little one wasn't it!

PSYCHIC: Kids everywhere -learning from home.

DANA: No- no-no! If that happens, I can't go into the office, I can't go anywhere...

PSYCHIC: *(She is ominous as she opens eyes for a moment)* Let's not worry about going places.

DANA: So, lots of quality time at home. Ok. I didn't expect that but that can't be all bad. Some peaceful time at home.

PSYCHIC: Riots.

DANA: Well, they are 7 and 4 so they do fight.

PSYCHIC: No- race riots.

DANA: What! Why? What is happening? Is Trump still in office...was he impeached?

PSYCHIC: Yes, impeached.

DANA: Phew.

PSYCHIC: Twice.

DANA: Ok. Well good. Two times is the...*(charm)*

PSYCHIC: But not removed from office.

DANA: Damn. *(Taking this all in)* So let me get this straight- home with all three kids, civil unrest, no job, Trump is still in office - well, maybe we can travel, we haven't done much of that as a family. We can make the best of a bad...*(situation)*

PSYCHIC: Social distancing.

DANA: Social what?

PSYCHIC: Masks, no contact, travel bans, washing groceries before bringing them into your house.

DANA: How? What! Why would anyone do that?

PSYCHIC: Global pandemic.

DANA: The USA has a pandemic? Are people dying?

PSYCHIC: Yes.

DANA: No! Omg - are you sure?

She shakes the psychic hands and they come out of their trance a bit.
I'm going to need you to be really sure.

PSYCHIC: Energy doesn't lie.

DANA: Listen, one time I went to a psychic, and she said I met the man of my dreams and to marry him.

PSYCHIC: We are very in tune with matters of the heart.

DANA: Maybe you are but not everyone. It turned out he had a double life - he was a male stripper that was ALREADY married with five kids.

PSYCHIC: Sorry to hear that...

DANA: Not your fault. I'm not a psychic but I should've known something was up when he shaved all his body hair...

They both share a nod of agreement.

DANA: *(cont.)* So you see why I need you to look extra hard about this global pandemic stuff...

PSYCHIC goes back to her trance-like state and after several moments continues.

PSYCHIC: Toilet paper.

DANA: Uhhh... I have some tissues in my bag let me see.

PSYCHIC: No- all toilet paper is gone.

DANA: Is this virus like a gastro-type thing? I ate my mom's spoiled potato salad at our last family reunion so I can understand the need for a good two ply.

PSYCHIC: No- respiratory. Your pantry is full of toilet paper.

DANA: Hoarding toilet paper? Future me is so strange.

PSYCHIC: No one leaves their homes.

DANA: How long?

PSYCHIC: Long.

DANA: What about holidays... birthdays... Christmas? What you're telling me impacts so many- so so many and I feel selfish saying this but - how will I live? Will I live?

PSYCHIC: You find a way.

DANA: The life I thought I was going to have is so different from the life I will have- how do I help my kids cope? How do we navigate this new normal- I can't imagine things will ever be the same after all this.

PSYCHIC: Tell stories. Stories that connect people.

DANA: Theatres will be dark- how could I possibly...

PSYCHIC: You're not limited to a stage.

DANA: I'm not sure I know any other way.

PSYCHIC: Creatives always find a way. In the future we will need the power of narratives that connect us to help heal the nation- the world. Step into your...

DANA: Truth. That's what my mom always says to me- Don't shy away from your...

PSYCHIC: Light.

The psychic is now out of her trance and they both share a reaction to the reading. The psychic shakes off the energy and Dana starts caressing the amethyst crystal.

DANA: So that's that. I feel overwhelmed and helpless.

DANA starts packing up her things.

PSYCHIC: Anything else?

DANA: Like I should've stopped for that drink.

PSYCHIC: A look into the future is a gift. What will you do with it?

DANA: I guess we'll find out.

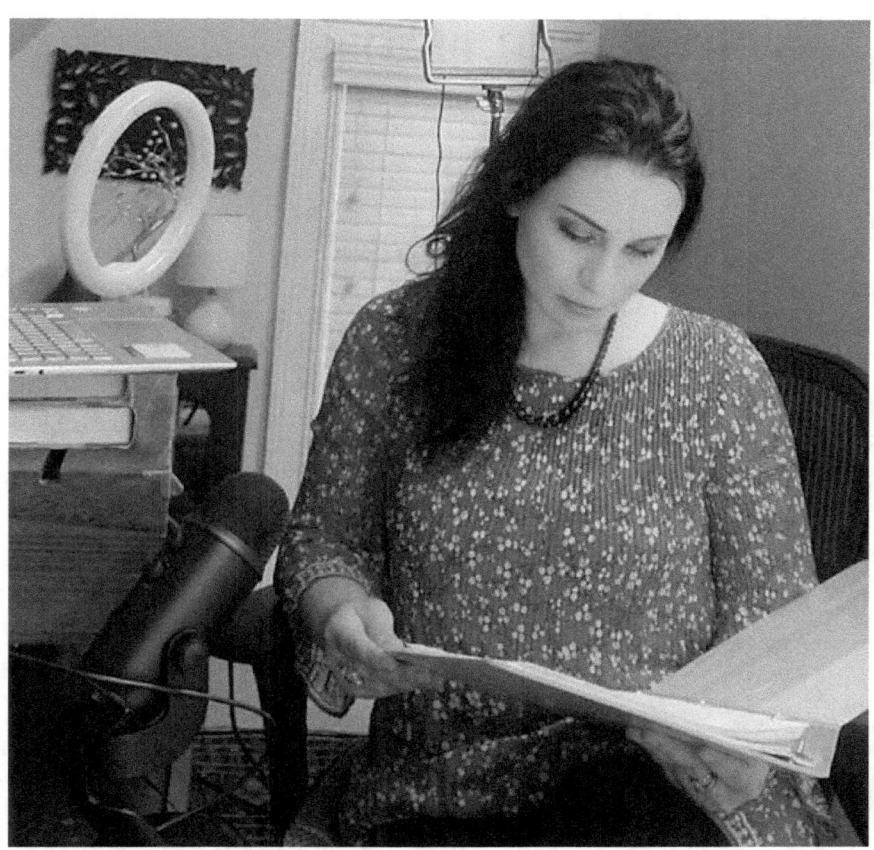

Dana Hall Creating

Dana wrote a play where a psychic reveals glimpses of her post-future. If you could have given your pre-COVID-19 self words of advice, what would they be?

HU, PHEOBE

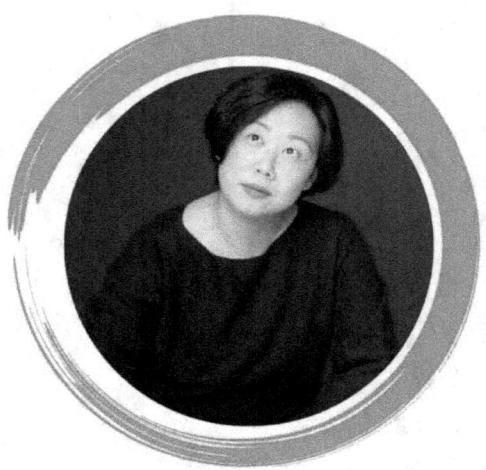

Phoebe Hu 胡馨匀 (She/Her) is a Taiwanese multidisciplinary performing artist. A classically trained musician and street dancer, Phoebe moved to Toronto in 2010 after receiving her bachelor's degree in foreign Languages and literatures from National Taiwan University to further explore and challenge herself as an artist. She then graduated from Sheridan Performing Arts Preparation Program and Randolph College for the Performing Arts, and has since been working in theatre, musical theatre, film/tv and voice as a performer, creator, educator, and consultant.

Recent credits: Alice in Wonderland (Bad Hats Theatre), Mary Poppins and Cabaret (Grand Theatre).

Upcoming: Wedding Season (Netflix) and Orphan Song (Tarragon Theatre).

I picked up my first ever 5-year journal starting 2020 January 1st.

"I think the next couple years are going to be a defining transitional phase in our life."

That was literally what I wrote on the first page.

Well, I wasn't wrong. The statement still stands.
It just unfolded in a completely different fashion from what I had in mind.

2020 was my first year as a full-time self-employed artist. I still have to wear many different hats under the large umbrella term of "performing artist", but no more office job or "shift" job at hand - which means my schedule is in my own hands, but also no more guaranteed supportive income to lean on.

Kris had just resigned from his architect firm to pursue a long-desired path of becoming a freelance furniture/set/prop maker. We saved up the safety net for it and we were ready to go, with nerve-wracking anticipation.

2020 March.
One week before the start of a project I have been looking forward to - the world hit pause.

The initial shock and processing of "this is something bigger."
The period of surreal disorientation, possibly some "hm, this is not so bad?" And eventually, the panic that came and snow-balled fast.

Just like how we become sensually hyper when our eyesight gets blocked, when our physical connections got blocked, we became virtually hyper.

There was a vengeful volume of information, thoughts, and

feelings flooding all over our single person operation centers.

I had to shut down the intake early on, and the daily looming numbers that were precious lives and souls was always a backdrop with weight. But besides that, the initial couple months didn't hit me much at a personal level - sure, all the postponing and possibly cancelling of projects has created emotional void and financial stress, especially with Kris heading into a career change with nothing lining up. But I've been living in the uncertainty called "a career in performing arts" for many years now, so this didn't feel unfamiliar even at a heightened level; and the safety net we built plus the privilege to have options downsizing our living expenses really helped.

Therefore, when CERB first came in, instead of relief, I felt rather guilty about being paid while not working on a project. Especially when I seemed to have all the time in the world. So, I told myself that now is the time to work on all the projects I've been putting off because I "never had the time for them."

I kicked into full gear immediately. I wanted to get my hands on everything - a script, a song, a dance, classes and workshops, instruments, and more instruments...
I have no upcoming projects therefore I get to pick whatever I want to work on.
The world is my oyster.
Until the world turned upside down again.

I think it was June 2020, but it doesn't really matter, because we all know that's not when it all started.

Statements were made. Virtual gatherings were held.
Waves of responses, movements, initiatives, and projects were rolled out.

With my full gear still running high, and residual of old triggers and reminder of responsibilities pounding my heart in my head, I got involved.

It was hard, it was beautiful, it was scary, it was sad, it was exuberating, it was necessary. I was angry, I was grateful, I was ashamed. I was proud, I was powerful, I was powerless, I was reignited, I also crashed and burned.

This was not surprising.

What surprised me was that all the "artistic attempts" during this time - written drafts, potential collaborations, submissions, grant applications, residency possibilities...all of them extremely timely and inspiring, felt extremely off to me come execution time. To the point I had to halt at the edge of meltdowns, and the ones I managed to push through, just left me with big holes full of question marks.

It wasn't the pandemic though, I knew that. It was more like, I've been singing in a room with loud backup tracks with crowds chatting for years and it has been sounding alright, then the pandemic came to shut down the track and took out the crowds, and all of a sudden, I'm hearing nodes all over my vocal cords.

Long existing swollen spots, I never thought to deal with because I was too busy operating under the disguise of justified noise that became paralyzing when exposed.

So, I sat down into a recovery hibernation of just me and my own noise.

What's next? How about what's now?

One day macro another day micro.
One day Zen-like stillness, another day stuck exhaustion.
Avoiding. Staring. Ups. Downs. Numbers. Graphs. My Weight. My Screen.

Does self-care land on the opposite side of social justice?
If it doesn't, why would it feel like it does?
If it does, why? What does that say about me?
Me. Oh right, there's that.

After several attempts to apply the @konmarie and @thehomeedit methods to my stuff, my virtual space, my life, my relationships...I have now also run a pass of both through my identities.

I dug deep and laid out all the titles and terms myself and others have ever identified me with and started with EDITING - I examined them one at the time, asked myself how often I wear them, do they still fit me, are they practical or sentimental, and DOES IT SPARK JOY?!

Surprisingly it wasn't a complete joke of an experiment - I was left with a "maybe" pile to think about, and there were a few "identities" - mostly adjectives I have defaulted to label myself with - have actually gotten my sincere "thank you and goodbye."

The CATEGORIZE and CONTAIN parts I had to modify a bit since it was less about WHERE to store them and more about WHEN I use them; also, less about the HOW and more about the WHY.

Why did I choose to rewrite most of my show bios, or introduce myself differently every time I met a different group of people? Obviously, there are the outside "whys" such as different requests and word limits, but what are MY reasons?

Why did I sometimes feel the need to add "creator" as a title while other times I was afraid of it? Why did I proudly add the word "immigrant" sometimes and other times hesitated? Why did "multidisciplinary" sometimes feel like a sufficient and smart choice for word count, other times it felt like I might as well write "entrepreneur"?

Are these real questions for myself to answer?
Or rhetorical complaints to the void out there called "the system"?

So many rabbit holes led to each other instead of Wonderland. And the clock did stop. So, I sat and wondered about - about the everlasting ones, and about the ones triggered by "the time."

I think about how I need the silence but am suspicious of the silence; how I need to pull back in order to move forward, how I need to disengage to a point in order to truly engage, and care enough about the core to be able to ignore the fluff.

I think about if we all get intellectually more progressive but not fundamentally, if our conversations get too much ahead of the trial-and-error muscle work, will it become harder to realize the changes because talks will get tired before our legs get there?

I think about how I love "The Time Is Now" when it's used like we're all on the same page about the urgency and understanding of how much overdue work there is; but also, how much I am sick of it when it's used like a Black Friday Sale slogan as if change and equity is a discount code we grab while it lasts instead of a long, permanent road that we're already on.

I think about how crucial it is for us (insert identities) to support each other but also how sometimes being brutally honest is the strongest form of support.

How one might need to advance enough in the system before changing the system.
How we might need to utilize our otherness before we can stop feeling our otherness.
How we try to fix language barriers with language barriers.
How we save our physical space with virtual space.
How in order to make things stop we cannot stop.

I think about how as an (insert identities) I am supposed to step up, speak out, take space, and make waves; I also think about how as an (insert identities) I am supposed to respect my own time and space, trust my own pace, and follow my desires.

How every day I feel simultaneously stuck and exactly where I need to be.
How I'm equally full of hope and fear.
How the more I feel like this is home. The more I miss home.
How the more I want to say something the faster I hit delete.
Needing a break in an endless break.
Feeling guilty about feeling content.

This is starting to feel like a never-ending loop, and my mind has turned into a collecting place for all the tangled self-contradicting thoughts and decisions possible.

Restart. Breathe. Everyone has a different way of moving forward.

I picked up my first ever 5-year journal starting 2020 January 1st.

As I'm now into second year I get to compare every day with the "last year today".

Some of them feel like eons ago, some of them feel like yesterday. Some days were exact opposites. Some days were comically identical.

I am the same person but I'm also most definitely not.

I have attended a virtual wedding for the first time and cried despite the lag.

I've rehearsed a musical in masks for a whole month, singing and dancing and all.

I had dinner with a lovely artist I've never met before, welcoming him to the country.

I have met so many other artists that I've never met before; thank you, Zoom.

I've had teaching opportunities I've never dreamed of before.

I've joined a dramaturgy workshop so casually set up yet enriched me for months.

Kris and I have worked on the same set.
We've had dinner at my sister's way more often than before since we're in a bubble.

We took care of our doctor, dental, chiro and vet appointments like never before.

I went from a night owl to a 5am morning person because of Kris' new work schedule, also for our new morning routine together involving French press, and I'm obsessed.

I've cooked for cooking's sake and baked for the first time on a whim.

We had a badminton date and discovered a new dog park on the same day.

I read a book from sunlight to sunset in one sitting, and it wasn't a script.

I wrote for no one but me. I cleaned for no one but me.

I did learn some new instruments, some new fun skills, some new life skills, and lots of new information about the planet, the world, the people, my people, and myself.

And I've learned that I have more time, space, and options than I thought I had.

It shouldn't take a pandemic to teach me this, but it did.

It was scary catching myself rushing through breakfast, lunch, shower, walking my dog, cleaning, exercising and even napping like they're getting in the way of me doing something important, on a day I had absolutely nothing to do.

I was ashamed and I wonder since when/why/how I've developed the ability to on one hand, appreciate all the specific details and the beauty of zooming into the ignored little corners in "arts", but on the other hand, live the complete opposite as a human and not see its irony and pinpoint it as a major dysfunction for so long.

While searching for a certain artist lifestyle and meaning I've ignored life as I live it; and while prioritizing work I've put most things that could inform my work, on hold.

慢慢來，比較快。

It is faster to go slower.

Letting go to take in.
I think I'm less afraid of all the self-contradicting thoughts now. Maybe it's actually my superpower to stop and only see one truth since the day I came from across the ocean and experienced my

first cultural shock.

The projects feeling "off" also doesn't concern me that much anymore.

After holding a cup of fresh coffee at 6 am paying no attention to anything but the coffee and the light in your backyard - after cuddling with your dog face to face for just a tad too long while your cats sleeps in between - after that dance reunion with your body in the dark alone - after self-indulgently discovering your ideal writing temperature - after that late night talk and hand-holding walk that brought you back to summer of 2006 - after the first face to face date where you stare at your BFF's face barely processing...after remembering how our time and senses can shrink or stretch.

To be fully present at least 5-15 minutes a day.
That's 35-105 minutes a week and 17.5 - 52.5 hrs. a month.
Every day, every moment is micro and macro.
I believe that's the magic power we all have, but even more so as artists.

Remembering that, most of my original plans to go about the projects just seem disproportional and doesn't make sense anymore. But that's ok. That's what I'm here for. And I've got time now.

Not because I'm stuck at home having no other options and nowhere else to go.

But because I've had the time to redefine work, life, time, health, richness, and worth all according to my own standard and not anyone else's, just like the other words such as tall, smart and beauty, I forgot how much closer we all already are if you just claim those definitions ourselves.

Because I have allowed myself the time and space to sit in all the blackhole loops and accepted it as a necessity.

Because I did not come all the way to the other side of the world to feel stuck by what I love.

Because if I can become even more of a light myself, I can worry less about how many lights I'm carrying or where I should direct them to.

Because there's much to be done ahead. But, before that, there's also so much to be felt and loved in the moment.

Because this big black hole that COVID-19 is has also shed a light on how dangerously free arts workers can and should be with some sort of UBI...

Because the last and most important step in @thehomeedit system is MAINTAIN. Everyone has a different way of moving forward. And for me, I've learned that instead of telling myself I need to work towards a better future, reminding myself that I am already living my life on a path I want and if I just keep going it will only get better is a more effective way to go.

I have stopped expecting the world or myself to have it all figured out by the time we "come out of this" or become suddenly wiser. But if we just keep going even just 5-15 present minutes at a time...

I think the next couple years are going to be a defining transitional phase in our lives.

Emerson Arts   The Stage Light Flickers   Pandamonium Publishing

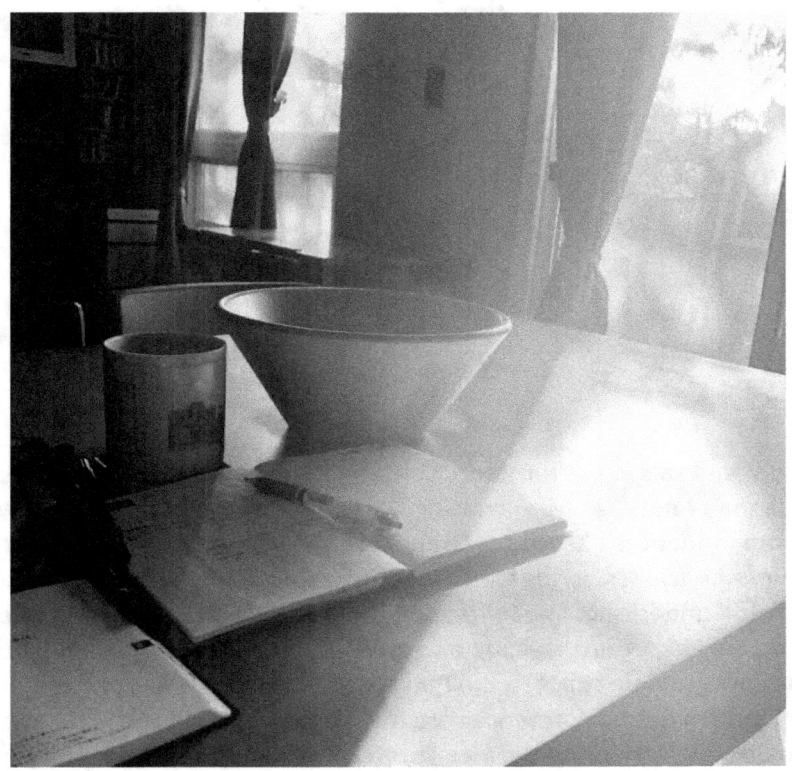

Phoebe began to feel like every day was a never-ending loop. What did you do to keep things fresh and interesting during lockdown?

JONES, JULIANNA

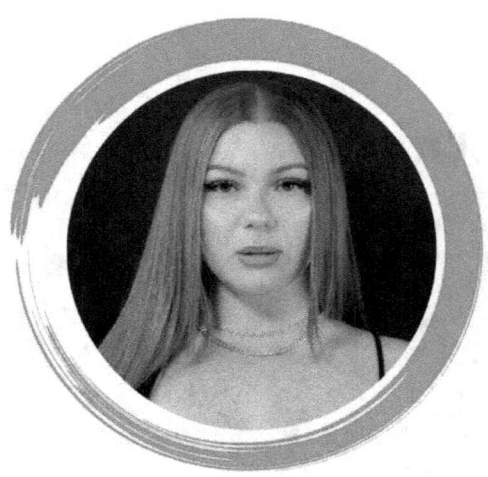

Born and raised in Brampton, Ontario, Canadian singer-songwriter Julianna Jones has been crafting her sound for over 17 years. Drawing from influences like Ariana Grande, Julia Michaels, Larkin Poe & Summer Walker, Jones has developed a Pop/R&B sound with a Rock 'n' Roll undertone. She infuses multiple genres and writes from her personal experiences in life and love, using these tools to carve out her own unique space in the Pop community. Jones has had major success in her performance career with performing in the lineup of major festivals in the Greater Toronto Area and the opportunity to sing in the well-known stadium, the Scotiabank Arena in Toronto, Canada. She continues to prioritize her love for music as a solo recording artist, as well as a vocal coach and businesswoman.

Never in a million years did I ever think that I'd be writing about my experience in the music industry, within a pandemic. Never in a million years did I ever think I would be living in one. It's hard to even fathom the thought of that, even still. The past year and half has been a rollercoaster of ups and downs, but it is truly an experience that has changed my entire life, in every single way. I believe that change is something we can all agree to disagree is a fear of some, and I can agree to a certain extent that within someone's career, change can have a huge impact on one's entire existence. I, Julianna Jones, get the privilege to share my experience and the challenges many of us musicians and recording artists have struggled with in this historic event. I have written yearly letters to myself since 2015 that I get to open and read about how the previous year had been and see how the growth and development had changed my perspective and helped me grow as a person. Writing the year 2020 to 2021, was insane to draft.

Now travel back in time with me. Before all the chaos.

Imagine it's early March 2020. You're getting ready with your friends, grabbing drinks and a bite to eat before heading out to a sold-out show with 25,000 people. As a fan of the artist, it's such an amazing feeling to get the chance to see someone's art being brought to life on stage. Music has such an inexplainable feeling. Now imagine you are the artist; you have prepared your whole life for shows like this. The countless hours of prep in choreography rehearsals, studio time, meetings after meetings and multiple tour dates. But you can never get enough of it because as soon as you hit the stage, all of your problems go away. All the stress and anxiety you had, has been tossed out the window. You are living the dream. This is your career. There seems to be no end in sight for you. Little did you know, everything that you have ever known, would be pulled from right under you. All of your shows you've planned for months get cancelled and live music is prohibited everywhere. No artist can tour, and almost every single country is locked up and encouraging every civilian to stay home. Your entire existence has been shattered like glass. That's the exact feeling I felt when we first entered the worldwide lockdown when COVID-19 was declared a threat to human existence on March 17th of 2020.

My thought process at the time was a little simpler than it is now. "Give it a month or two, and I'll be able to reschedule that one show that I had to cancel right before the pandemic started," I kept saying. The two months had passed, and the lockdowns were stricter than ever. To say I was confused was an understatement. Not to say that I didn't enjoy the time off from the stress of the musician lifestyle, but at that very moment, I had nothing to do or say. Nothing. Just like an empty brain of sorts. This was the time gap that I never knew I needed.

In quarantine, I was able to evaluate a lot of my goals, aspirations and career successes thus far, and see where I saw myself going and what was lacking, so I could improve on it. I finally had the time to start analyzing myself as an artist and what I wanted for my career. When life throws these curveballs at you, you can't always make music a priority if you don't have the funds to support yourself, so this was a blessing in disguise that I finally had the time for myself and my own music. When writing my songs, I always base it off of real-life experiences and through 2020, there was so many ups and downs in my life, within my relationships, friendships and my own mental health. But now I had the time to be creative and check in with myself. I finally had the time to book co-writes and connect with others I wouldn't normally connect with, online or not. This helped me build a stronger and larger catalogue of music that I have today. It also led me to create the business mindset I was curating for the 2 years prior with my "freelance" business education, or so I like to call it. With graduating from Mohawk College's music program for performance in 2019 in Hamilton, Ontario in Canada, it set me up for the years to come as I continued to educate myself in music, even though the pandemic, which was a huge blessing. It's always about setting yourself up for success in these situations, but needless to say, we all never prepared for this kind of event, but every little bit counts. It led me to do more research in quarantine to find Humber College's Music Business program in Toronto, Canada that ran through the summer of 2021. Although I never thought I would go back to school, especially with all online courses, this was a huge opportunity to increase the Plato from the past year and a half. And for that, my life has done a complete 360. If you would've asked me last year what my life would've looked like in a year from now, it would be nothing compared to what it is now, and if it wasn't for COVID-19 affecting everything in my "current past", I would not have this amazing future to look forward to because I had the time to work on everything I've wanted to, to set myself up; to continue and build more successes in my life. I had the opportunity to work with artists that have written with artists from across the world, and get the fortunate opportunity to move to Toronto, Canada on my own for work. My network circle is 3x times the size it was a year ago, and it's ONLY been a year and a half. And it's insane that all this positive came out of a negative worldwide event. The one thing I would love for people to take away from this historic situation and all the readings you read about it, is to never underestimate the time you have on earth and never take it for granted. Never miss an opportunity, even if you don't see the value in it right now! Everything and everyone in life is so precious. You matter, and every second does too.

For Julianna, her network circle grew considerably during the pandemic. As an artist, did you experience increased exposure while in lockdown? What have you learned about social media and self-management?

KANGAS, MIKAEL

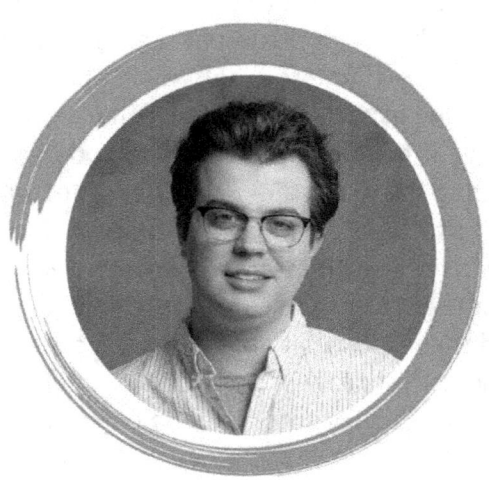

Mikael designs lights for theatre of all types & was previously the production manager for the now closed Lower Ossington Theatre. Mikael is a passionate theatre creator and collaborator with over 300 production credits to date. Mikael's recent work includes; Trouble in the Mind, Glass Menagerie, O'Flarety VC (Shaw Festival), Newsies, Crazy for You (Sheridan Theatre), Dear Evan Hansen (Canadian Asst. Design) Rusalka, Onegin, Cosi Fan Tutti, Elixir of Love, Abduction from the Sergalio (COC, asst. design), Holiday Inn, Brigadoon, Magician's Nephew, Grand Hotel, Dracula, Me & My Girl, Saint Joan, Sweeney Todd, Alice in Wonderland, Woman of No Importance (Shaw Festival, asst. design). Mikael is an assistant & associate lighting designer working for some of Canada's most prominent performing companies including the Shaw Festival, Canadian Opera Company, Mirvish, Toronto Symphony Orchestra, Tarragon Theatre, National Ballet School of Canada, and the Banff Centre. Mikael is a member of the Associated Designers of Canada.

www.mikaelkangaslighting.com

When the world stopped in March 2020, no one knew if we would ever return to work in our theatres again. We didn't know what the next few weeks or months would hold for us and for our families. We endured the heart break of paused, abandoned or never-to-be projects. We figured out how to survive in an isolated world. We thankfully are starting to come back and with that return comes the responsibility, not just to resume, but also to reset. The collective forced hiatus from theatre has offered us an opportunity for both personal and collective reset. Reset how we agree to work, reset what we work on, reset what we work for, and reset who we work with.

This reset needs to start to value the participation of everyone in the theatre in a way that allows them to live gainfully from full time careers in the theatre that don't carry automatically long hours for low wages. The theatre needs to learn from the value placed on people in other comparable sectors and do better. Theatre work is a skilled set of trades and artistic skills that needs to take itself seriously by valuing its workers properly.

In turn the theatre needs to reset its relationship to the public, to create work that brings as many people from every possible part of society into theatre, rather than playing to an elite and effete group of insiders.

We must value ourselves, and see that value reflected in how we work in theatre going forward. This break should provoke all of us to reset this industry, to stop it from harming people, and reset how it interacts with the wider culture.

If we cannot reset now, when will we?

Mikael discusses the state of the arts community and how we are at turning point. What do you think should be done to ensure that communities and artists have reasonable and equitable access to artistic spaces and programs?

KHAN, RAMI

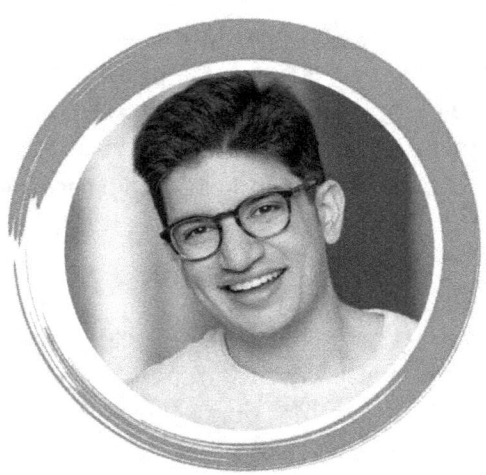

Rami (he/him) is a Pakistani-Canadian, multidisciplinary artist and a recent graduate from Randolph College for the Performing Arts. As an actor, singer, and dancer, Rami has loved performing from a young age and always knew it's something he wanted to pursue. Storytelling is in his bones and writing is just another extension of this. It's something that he is passionate about and has always intrigued him, which is why Rami is beyond excited to be making his writing debut as a part of this project with Emerson Arts. The past year has been tough for all artists and Rami is ready to share his story hoping it's something everyone can relate to in some way shape or form. Whether it's a good laugh, an emotional response, or that it's so poorly written you just cry. Whatever it is, hopefully you get something out of it! Recent Theatre Credits: Blackout (Musical Stage Co.), You Can Do It Put Your Mask Into It (Toronto Fringe), Bend It Like Beckham: The Musical (Starvox Entertainment). Recent Film Credits: 1Up (Buzzfeed/Lionsgate), Ginny & Georgia (Netflix), Private Eyes (GlobalTV).

What a Time to be Alive:
The Trials and Tribulations of a Twenty Something in 2020

It's taken me a long time to get in front of my laptop and write this piece. Not because I was lazy and left writing this to the last minute. But because I had no idea what to write about and was lost for words when asked to share my experiences as an artist throughout the pandemic. I feel like my brain shuts down whenever I must recall anything from the past two years, I mean, this is not what I thought my twenties would be like. Your twenties are supposed to be some of the best times in your life! You're supposed to "find yourself"', make mistakes, travel the world, launch your career, and all that jazz. But I spent it scared, tired, annoyed, and a little hungry if I'm being honest (but when am I not hungry?). I was scared because every day felt like it could be the apocalypse. Tired because the past two years have been some of the most emotionally and mentally exhausting for all of us. Annoyed because people were not following the rules. And hungry...well, I already said it...when am I not? Obviously, the pandemic has not been kind. On top of all our own personal feelings the world has been in uproar. People don't have easy access to health care, people are homeless, people have died, and the world is literally on fire. How can my personal experiences as an artist during this time be beneficial in the grand scheme of things? Like is it even worth sharing when the world is in flames? Or could it bring joy and maybe some hope to people? Or even myself? It's a lot to think about. One thing I do love about being an artist is that by sharing a story I can allow people to escape, feel seen, or even discover a new point of view. So why not? Let's see if I can take all the emotions I'm feeling and share them with you by telling my story. Let's put them to good use, or at least try to.

At the beginning of 2020, I was an emerging artist in Toronto, I had just graduated college with a Musical Theatre degree and high hopes of being a successful actor. On top of that, I finished my first professional theatre contract and had started to work in tv/film. Things were looking up. But, of course, COVID-19 showed up and decided to make some tomfoolery out of everything. The entire entertainment industry shut down in a split second. I felt hopeless and useless to the world. So, like any JLO rom com when she is at her lowest, I decided to move back home to London, Ontario. I wanted to get some space and maybe find some will to do anything else besides binging JLO rom coms all day.

Being back home for the first time since graduating school was a whirlwind of emotions. There were a lot of existential questions ranging from "is this the end of the world?" to "what if I shaved off all of my hair?" Fortunately, I didn't shave off all my hair, but it did feel like the world was ending almost every day. Not knowing when my next job would be was probably the scariest part. As actors we are used to living in the "not knowing when our next contract will be" feeling, but because of the uncertainty of the pandemic, this was that feeling times a thousand. Our industry had completely shut down and was deemed unessential. So, of course, I felt unessential. Like I had to completely change my career path to have any sense of self-worth in this new "COVID-19 World". It got me questioning why I even wanted to be an actor in the first place. It's tricky to describe what kept me on the path of being an artist. It was almost an out of body feeling. Someone once told me that, "We, as humans, don't only need to survive in this world. We need to thrive. We need ambition and goals and joys and love and heartache to truly feel alive." Storytelling and performing is where I thrive and feel the most alive. Of course, it has its ups and downs (sometimes a lot more downs than ups), but it's where I feel like I'm meant to be. It was an instinctual and guttural feeling. It's something I realized I couldn't give up. So, I learned to let go of any feelings of doubt and trusted that our industry would open up once again.

All of this allowed me to realize that the real blessing of being home was that I got to spend a lot of time with myself, my family, and friends. This much needed time away from constantly worrying about my career made me get in touch with what else I needed from my life to thrive. I found myself being less caught up in what the next big career move was going to be and let myself spend time with people who I wanted to keep in my life, socially distant of course. I was able to let go of things that were out of my control and focus on the things in my life that were in my control, like my relationships with friends and family. I got to explore boundaries in these relationships, find out what I needed from them, reassess my positions in the relationships, and make more honest connections. Let's just say that I'm grateful that the pandemic gave me time and space to do something I never had the mental capacity to do before.

I know it's the most cliché thing to say that over the course of the pandemic I had a lot of time to be introspective, but the weird thing is that it WORKED. Don't get me wrong there were days where I was a depressed, anxious, total mess, and couldn't see the light at the end of the tunnel. But, by taking it a day at a time I found that going through all the motions, the peaks, and the valleys, helped clear my mind about many struggles I was going through: career based, personal, familial, and in my relationships. It was an ongoing battle, but by letting go of what was out of my control and focusing on what was in my control I felt like I was on the track to becoming a better person and, therefore, a better artist.

As the year went on, restrictions were slowly lifting, and I was starting to feel safer going out. I thought why not get a job that's essential to help out with pandemic aid in any way I could. I also wanted to keep busy, and maybe make some money. Let me tell you, trying to find an "essential" job with a Musical Theatre degree was pretty hard. But eventually I got a job as a COVID-19 screener at the hospital in London. The job description seemed manageable. Basically, all I had to do was sit at the entrance and ask patients and visitors entering the hospital if they had any COVID-19 related symptoms or exposure. All patients had to have an appointment and visitors had to be approved by the unit they were going to. So, there was a lot of searching through a database and relaying information to people, but nothing too intense. Oh, and if you got scheduled to work at a staff only entrance it was easy peasy. All you had to do was make sure that staff members completed an online screening form and check their hospital I.D. badge. Once I started to get going, the job was kind of enjoyable. It was really good for my mental health to have a routine again. Plus, since we were doing 12-hour shifts, we had a lot of down time. Whenever I got bored, I had books, my phone, and binging the Real Housewives franchise to turn to.

One thing I didn't expect from this job was how it would affect my artistry and point of view as an actor. I know what you're thinking, "Rami you're sitting down and watching The Real Housewives all day. How in the hell can this help you as an actor?" Well, funnily enough, it wasn't the actual job itself. It was all of the other factors that surrounded it. The building, the atmosphere, the staff, the doctors, the physicians, my co-workers, the patients, visitors, and of course the pandemic itself.

See, this was my first time back in London after living in Toronto for the past three years. In Toronto I had completely different surroundings, both physical and metaphorical. Obviously, there were the buildings and general hustle and bustle of the city. But I was also surrounded by other creatives, performers, my peers at school, people of all different shades, sexual orientation, gender, and so many other types of wonderful people. I was in my element and felt so comfortable in Toronto. I learned so much about the world and how it works just from being there for three years. Back in London, it felt like a huge step back. People's mindsets were in total contrast to the one I had spent the past three years trying to build. Working in my hometown felt like I was back in high school. I was instantly pegged the "weird different artsy kid". On top of that, I was one of the only people of colour in my workplace. I was one of the only queer people and the only queer man in the space. It was a huge adjustment for me to "fit in" with this crowd since I already stood out by just existing in space. Also, all my co-workers were either in school for Respiratory Health or were on their way to becoming a police officer. These were polar opposites of what I went to school for. The job was first offered to Respiratory Health students because we were working under the COVID-19 Department, and it was to help them get a foot in the door at the hospital. Then it was offered to people who completed a Police Foundations course because it was considered a Security position. And then they started to get desperate and needed people to fill positions so there I was tap dancing in a corner waving my Musical Theatre degree around. To say that I was very much out of my element was an understatement.

It was an eye-opening experience for me. Of course, there were people who I got along with, and I can honestly say I made some pretty great friends from the experience. But of course, with having many people who were such opposites from me, there were bound to be some clashes of opinion or personalities. Like while my co-workers were talking about golf I would try to join in, but would rather sit at my desk and watch the latest episode of Rupaul's Drag Race. Or while everyone was talking about their relationships, they would turn to me and ask, "Don't your people do arranged marriages?" followed by "That must suck, are you gonna get an arranged marriage?" (I'm South Asian so yes, it is common, but no I don't really want to talk about this at 6:00am, Carl). Or the men specifically would talk about their newly purchased, used Honda Civics and how they were a total "babe magnets" ...verbatim that's what they said, "babe magnets". What is this, 2003?

But this was just the icing on the cake, because on top of this came much more cringeworthy and uncomfortable interactions…

One thing I am truly grateful for in 2020 is how much attention the Black Lives Matter movement got. It sparked global conversations about systemic racism, police violence, religious discrimination, as well as many other problems with our political systems and how they are all intersectional. In my "outside of work" life these conversations were vital to me. Talking to my white friends/colleagues as well as marginalized folks in the Toronto Entertainment Industry was truly eye opening. I finally felt like I had a voice. I could have open, honest conversations with people about my experiences. I could hold people accountable for their actions and they would make the effort to listen. People in my community were educating themselves and it allowed me to feel safer sharing parts of my experience as a person of colour with them, that I felt like I couldn't share before.

But when I went to work at the hospital it was the total opposite. I was so aware of the fact that I was one of the only ethnic minorities and that my current socio-political views were extremely different than those of most of my co-workers. Since it was in the mainstream news cycle, there were many conversations had about the death of George Floyd, Breonna Taylor, and countless others who lost their lives due to police brutality or hate crimes. A lot of my co-workers were opinionated on the topic because many were on their way to becoming police officers. But the conversations were extremely one-sided and defensive. Yes, the world needs law enforcement to make sure no one breaks the law, to have first responders, and to provide other services that help our social systems succeed. But, when there is cognitive bias in the making of said laws and systems, it leaves so much room for error. It makes all of our systems one sided and disregards the needs of all people. This is one of many reasons why we have protests from marginalized and silenced voices. We were completely left out of the system and don't have equal rights compared to the people who the bias leans towards, A.K.A white people, even though marginalized people were a part of this country when said systems were created. This is also why racism is such a systemic problem. If the system itself is racist, it's going to breed racism amongst the people who are brought out to protect it. In my opinion, they are essentially protecting their whiteness. This isn't only a problem with Law Enforcement. It happens in all systems of our society, like Politics, Medicine, Trades, Entertainment...everywhere. My co-workers didn't want to talk about any of these systemic issues that movements like Black Lives Matter or Stop Asian Hate were trying to bring awareness to. Instead, most of them thought that the sole purpose of the movements were to "tarnish the name of law enforcement"; It felt like I was stuck in a room with people who don't see me, or people like me, as human, for 12 hours a day. That I am not worthy enough to be a full human like them because of something I have no control over, the colour of my skin.

One time I was having a conversation with one of my co-workers, let's call him Craig. Craig came over to cover breaks for my other co-worker, let's call her Kelly, and I. So, when Kelly went on her break, I was stuck with Craig for what was the longest half hour of my life. Craig was one of those co-workers who just graduated school in Police Foundations and wanting to be a cop was his LIFE. I kid you not, it is all he ever talked about. I mean it's great to be passionate about something, but he did not know how to have a conversation about anything else. You'd ask him about the weather and he'd somehow make it about his application status to the London Police Force. So, Craig and I are sitting in silence, because I knew that if I said anything he'd start talking, and I just didn't want to deal with it. But this time he decided to start the conversation, which never happened, so I was in for a treat. He started talking about how social media is ruining the planet. I looked up from scrolling through Instagram on my phone and said nothing. I guess looking up was enough of a response because he kept going. He went on and on about how it's ruining people's privacy and that people are using it to get attention, views, and to be "seen". Um...YES, CRAIG! That's what people do! Where have you been since the birth of the internet and why are you mansplaining social media to me? Can't you see I'm busy stalking Timothee Chalamet's Instagram profile! But I said nothing and went back to staring at my boy Chalamet. He then went on to say, and I quote, "if you see a video on YouTube that says 'White Cop Shoots Black Guy' it's gonna get a ton of views because that's what's popular right now and people won't realize that the cop was just trying to do his job." See what I mean, it took him no less than fifteen minutes to make the conversation about policing. I was feeling a little feisty that day, so I decided to dig in a little and said, "I mean, that's not someone trying to get views, it's someone trying to show that racism is real." He went on to say, "yeah, but is it?" I really didn't want to get into the history of racism with this guy, so I just said, "you're here for nine more minutes so if you wanna get into it, we can get into it, or you could just Google it." And it SHUT HIM UP! BAM! After that, he started to ramble to himself about All Lives Matter and I was gonna throw some facts his way, but then Kelly came back, and he ran for the hills. Kelly asked why he ran away so quickly, and I told her what happened. Then, Kelly went on to tell me that this wasn't the first time he brought up racism and police brutality to a co-worker of colour. Apparently, he tries to have conversations with all of the marginalized folks that we worked with to make them see these social issues from "his" point of view, the view of a CIS gendered straight white man. And he got so uncomfortable when I hinted for him to see it from the view of the people who are affected by racism. You can't end racism by making everyone white, you must educate yourself and empathize with your fellow people of colour. You must understand that the bias is in your favour. The audacity, the 'caucacity', was too real.

But in that moment, I realized this was the first conversation I had with an overtly racist, white person. I was proud of myself for holding my own, even if it was for a short time. I felt like because I spent so much time educating myself outside of work and learning how racism affects my everyday life, I was well equipped to have this conversation (and is probably why I was feeling feisty that day). I was more in touch with how I view myself and how the world views me. Knowledge and a sense of self are truly some of the greatest weapons you can own.

So, when I say that this job helped me as an artist, I meant moments of realization like these. Moments where I arrived as my full Brown, Queer self. As well as, knowing that me arriving in a predominantly white space is a disruption because people are just not used to seeing someone of a marginalized community completely own themselves.

It's funny to me how in the strangest and scariest of circumstances, like this pandemic or a job at the hospital, you can always find beauty. Something to learn, something to help you grow, human connection, and even reconnecting with yourself.

If there's anything I can take away from this past year, it's that owning and knowing who I am in the present is so much more fulfilling than worrying about what's next or what's yet to come. I'm not saying that this pandemic has been my "Eat, Pray, Love" journey and that I am a perfect, whole person, but it's been a step in the right direction.

I guess the start to my twenties had a lot more peaks than I thought. It wasn't just filled with being scared, tired, annoyed, and hungry (but I did eat a LOT along the way... that's a story for another time). Through all the unfairness, the hardships, the mental strife, and the losses, there were lessons to be gained. I feel like I'm more equipped to becoming that person who "finds themselves", makes mistakes, travels the world, and launches their career...just like every other twenty something. I hope that maybe you took something away from this. Whether it's a story about reconnecting, a lesson on anti-racism, hope, or that Timothee Chalamet has an Instagram. Literally anything works for me. I'm just happy that through all the wild, crazy things this pandemic has thrown at us, I got the opportunity to share a little bit about myself with you.

Stay safe and never stop learning.

At a time when the world relied on artists for entertainment, our artists were told they were unessential. What changes can be made immediately to ensure art thrives and artists can sustain themselves through their craft?

KWEEN

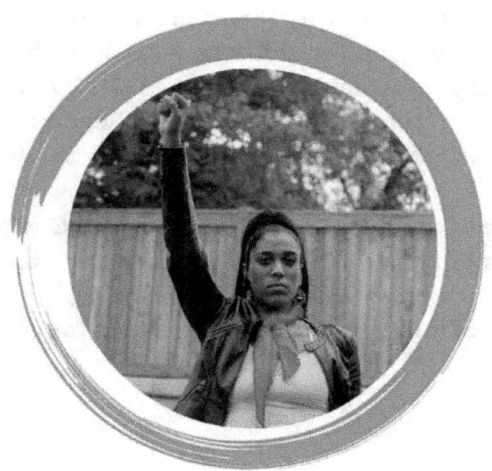

Thadinadonnih (Guelph) born and raised, University of Guelph Alumni, Valedictorian Graduate from the Randolph Academy for Performing Arts, Kween is a Black settler living out her passions. She is a dancer, teacher, actor, singer, choreographer, director, producer, advocate, marketing/social media guru and TedX International Speaker.

Kween is the CEO and owner of The Kween Company which is a multimedia arts and marketing company, Co-owns The Heels Academy with her partners Michelle and Vanessa and runs Soca/Dancehall/Afro dance classes. Kween is the team coordinator and choreographer for The Guelph Nighthawks Basketball Flight Crew. She also gives back to her arts community as a Guelph Fringe Board Member.

Within advocacy, Kween uses her platform of activism and mentorship for her Black community through Carnival, Black Heritage Month, BIPOC Social justice, social enterprise projects and through cannabis advocacy. She works closely with schools, local organizations and businesses, Indigenious communities, The Grove Youth Hub, grant funders, Ontario Health Teams, festivals, the City of Guelph, dignitaries and officials to make representation for the global majority. In addition she is a long time cannabis educator and Cannabis Curation Committee member for AHLOT.

Kween is the leader of Solidarity March in Support of BLM in 2020 and the Executive Director and Social Justice Initiatives Coordinator for Guelph Black Heritage Society. Through the GBHS, you can catch her monthly as host and community producer on Rogers Channel 20 with her show "Diverse and Converse", a BIPOC panel discussion.

Kween held one of three Artistic Residencies with Guelph Dance 2020/2021 promoting her BIPOC art through movement and dance. Kween currently is a title holder for Woman of the Year 2020, nominee for RBC Women of Influence 2021, and nominee for Women of Inspiration 2021.

A spoken word/ poem
Title: My People Our People

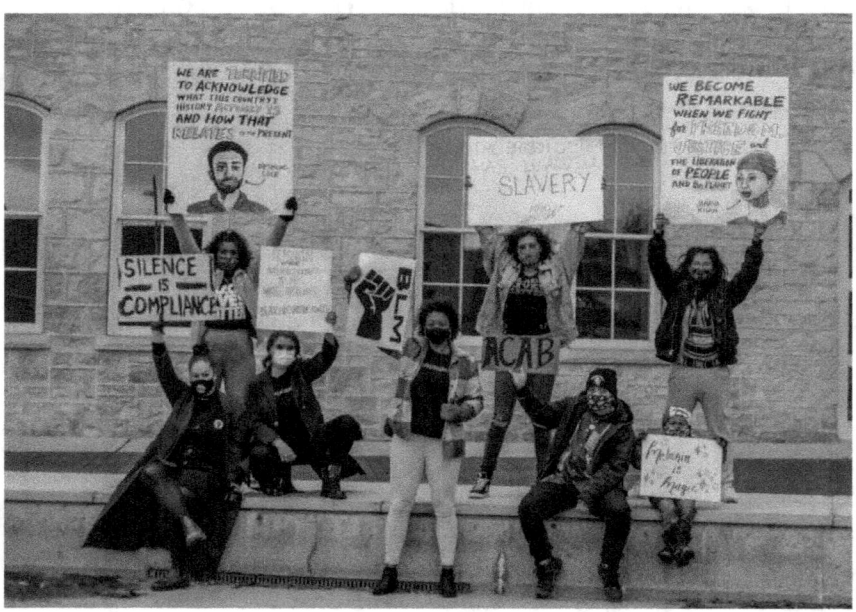

Photo By: D3VI Photography   The Rise of the Global Majority

I am just so angry, I want to scream out loud
I was watching from the outside and just part of the crowd.
I couldn't run away - I couldn't turn a cheek
Drowning underwater - can't even speak

Words from my brain, coming from my heart
Soul and the spirit, I know I am smart
Trying to decipher, trying to see
What's happening to my brothers, what's happening to me.

Able to determine what is really going on
Using my skin as armour to try and stay strong
Black Lives Matter, but why don't you see
The world ain't for all of us, until we are free

We are splitting apart, because racism lives on?
Why can't people see that hatred is wrong?
Let's get real - slavery started this all
Because before we ruled empires, we stood tall

Our history, this narrative - **we won't take it NO MORE!**
We want to work together to stop this racial war.
Call KKK the terror, abolish the systems that be
Get rid of the garbage we call white supremacy

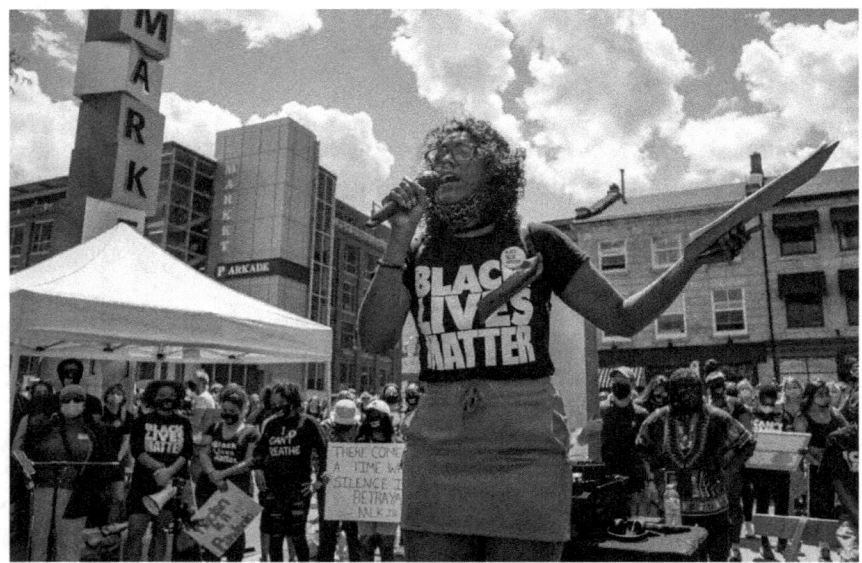

Photo By: Andrew Nosbic   Protest in Solidarity with BLM 2020

Because I am not sure how long I can go on
Feeling tireless, defeated and not at all strong
But if I keep up, and follow God's plan
Do it for the youth, our ancestors and this Land.

But this is what people really don't understand
You must also work internally to work on the mend
It's is truly a race thing - you're racist, okay
Now work on yourself, so Black people don't cry everyday

Call it our opinion, say it is make believe
But we keep getting killed, and just have to deal and grieve?
"I can't Breathe" isn't just an expression
These killings are in daylight, this is systemic oppression

Honestly, I am really sick of it and things needs to be changed
Because my brothers and sister need it explained.
We need to know why we keep saying goodbye
To innocent Black bodies to heaven in the sky.

So, keep fighting, keep pushing, and do not give in
Because we cannot keep living in this racist sin.
What we got to do is pray and we got to commit
If we abolish some systems, we will be more legit

Black men matter, Black women, Black Trans and Black Queer
No Black lives should be have to live through this fear
I will keep on this journey, until I can no longer embark
Leaving an impact and leaving my mark.

Kween turned her art into activism to create positive change in her community. In what ways have you seen artists use their craft to work towards equality and equal representation since the beginning of COVID-19?

LACAS, MATT

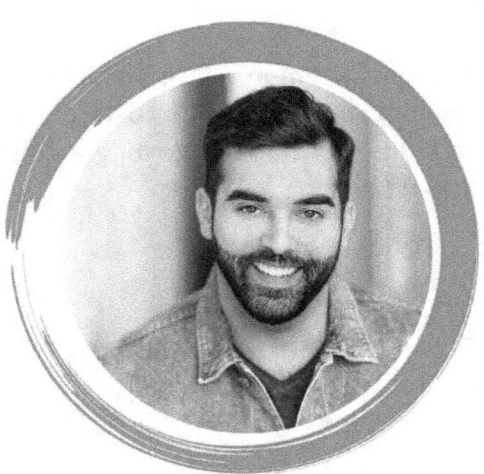

Matt is a Montreal native working and living out of Toronto. Matt has had the privilege of performing on stages across Canada, US, Europe and Asia. Selected Credits: A Brimful of Asha, Ben Hur (FAST), Fabulous Lipitones (Miracle Theatre, BC), Les Moutons (Japan Tour) and most recently Baloo in the US National Tour of Jungle Book directed Rick Miller and Craig Francis. Matt is also the founder of We Are Here Productions, A non-profit theatre company that aims to turn art into tangible aid for those in need worldwide. During the pandemic, Matt and his partner Rosie pivoted into teaching cocktail classes online to folks across the world with their new company Isolation Cocktails. Matt would like to thank his family, friends and his Mo for keeping him grounded.
@is_that_mattlacas
@weahereproductions
@isolation.cocktails

The Isolation Cocktails Flight

Old Fashioned
- 2oz Whisky
- 1 Sugar Brown Sugar Cube
- 3 Dashes Angostura Bitters
- Stir in Mixing Glass with Ice
- Strain & Garnish with Orange Peel over Fresh Ice in Rocks Glass

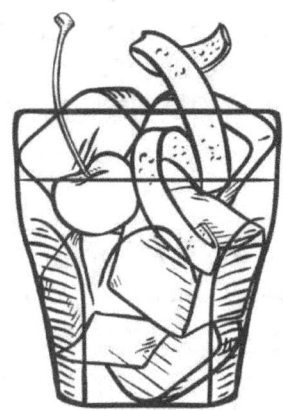

Before the world was locked away behind COVID-19 protocols, masks, and the fear of gathering, I was lucky enough to be performing on stages all across the world. I was living my dream; being paid to perform and explore everything this little blue marble had to offer. A dream that I didn't appreciate properly while I was living it. My favorite part of my job as a performer is sharing stories with others. The theatre is a place where people come together to laugh, cry, celebrate, mourn, and experience the full spectrum of human emotion. As the pandemic hit and I was quickly sidelined in Toronto, I started to look elsewhere for that similar excitement. Storytelling, a sense of connection, and a wide range of sensations. It led me to further pursue my second passion in life: **Spirits & Mixology.** With the help of my partner, Rosie Callaghan, we set out to put our attention and love into something new that felt helped us cope with what had been wrenched from us.

An **Old Fashioned** was, for as long as I can remember, *My Cocktail*. I've had it after every opening and closing of a show, every time I was rejected for a big role, celebrating birthdays, or mourning a family member, it's what I knew. Having shared this tipple with countless people over the years, it is what I, and most people, think of first when talking about cocktails. The O.G cocktail, created sometime during the 1800's, The Old Fashioned has gone mostly unchanged since its creation. There are few things in this world that are timeless, but the Old Fashioned is certainly one of them.

Flor De Don Juan
- 1.5oz Reposado Tequila
- .75oz Elderflower Liqueur
- .5oz Simple Syrup
- .75oz Lime Juice
- 5 Basil Leaves
- In a Cocktail Shaker, Muddle Basil and Simple Syrup. Add

All Other Ingredients and Ice to Shaker. Shake Vigorously for 30 seconds

- Double Strain Over Fresh Ice into Stemless Wine Glass
- Garnish with Basil & Thyme

I am easily excited. I am someone who often doesn't think things through. The spark of an opportunity is usually all it takes for me to run full speed ahead with reckless abandon. This, for the most part, whether by dumb luck or through my own perseverance, has rarely bit me in the ass.

During March of 2020, with all current and prospects now circling the drain, I was desperate for that spark. Watching my friends start to pivot into new careers, find new hobbies (anyone remember when everyone was learning to bake bread and make whipped coffee?) or taking their talents to an online platform, I found myself asking,"*What do I have to offer?*" I felt like the answer to that question was *"not much"*. The only skills I ever truly had were that of an actor, working gig to gig, production to production, and of course the time I spent behind the bar between those gigs. What could an out of work performer/bartender give to those who had lost everything? That question sent me into a downward spiral. Not knowing how to deal with this new heaviness, I did the one thing I knew how to do; **connect**.

Usually what that meant was calling up some friends and heading out for a pint or a bite to eat. Sharing a drink with someone always allowed me to vent what I needed to and simultaneously allowed me to listen to anything my friends were going through. With bars and restaurants closed across the country, this was an impossibility. With everyone being forced to move onto online platforms to connect, why couldn't drinking do the same? Without more than a nudge, Rosie helped me set up the lights, sound and a camera and together we streamed our first virtual cocktail class/get-together over Instagram LIVE. All we wanted to do was share a drink with our friends the only way the world would allow us to. To bitch, to cheers, to laugh, to mourn our industry and everything in between. What started as a one-night affair turned into a consistent 30 "episode" commitment to our friends and each other. It gave us structure and something to look forward to night in and night out when things in the world were filled with countless uncertainties. After our 30th, and what we thought would be our last, Instagram Live cocktail class, a notification hit our inbox. A company out of the US was curious if we offered our services to other platforms and what our rates were. Suddenly, Rosie and I saw it, **The Spark**.

At the start of the pandemic, Rosie and I were at odds over one specific spirit: Tequila. Rosie loved it and I hated it. Everyone has one spirit or alcohol that is their "no, no thank you" drink. For me that was tequila. The first spirit that sent me overboard, the first spirit to have me puking on the streets of Montreal, the first spirit that gave me a debilitating hangover. With a little coercion and combined with my passion for learning, Rosie slowly introduced me to tequilas that wouldn't make me nauseous just by smelling it. Slowly but surely, I started to play around with the agave-based spirit and discovered quite a few cocktails that I enjoyed it in. The **Flor De Don Juan** was the cocktail that officially turned my biased against tequila into an admiration. The lovely mix of agave, elderflower, citrus, and fresh basil create a purely unique drinking experience. To say this cocktail helped my knowledge of tequila blossom is an understatement.

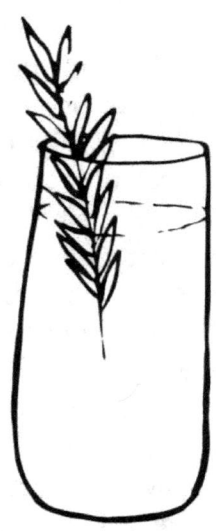

Blue Bullet
- 2oz Kentucky Bourbon
- .5oz Maple Syrup
- .5oz Blueberry-Basil Syrup
- .5oz Fresh Lemon Juice
- Handful of Blueberries and Basil
- In a Cocktail Shaker, Muddle Blueberries, Basil, Maple Syrup and Blueberry-Basil Syrup.
- Add Bourbon, Lemon Juice and Ice To Cocktail Shaker. Shake Vigorously for 30 Seconds.
- Double Strain into an Old Fashioned Glass Over Fresh Ice
- Garnish with Basil wnd Blueberries

It hit us like a bullet. We had stumbled our way into a business without meaning to. We didn't know at the beginning of all of this that we would soon be having drinks with folks all across Canada, US, Europe, Asia and with executives in companies like RBC, Amazon, Sunlife Financial and many others. Interviews on CBC Radio, articles written about us in the Montreal Gazette and the creation of our very own community we would lovingly dub the #CocktailFam. **Isolation Cocktails** was born out of the desire to connect with our loved ones during a time of unprecedented separation. Thing is, we had no idea how to run a company. Not a damn clue. So let me tell you that we made **TONS OF MISTAKES** and were constantly tweaking and changing our formula of what Isolation Cocktails was. We still are. When you don't know how something should run, you get the lovely yet often frustrating opportunity to learn as you go. To improvise. Weirdly enough, being two performing arts graduates handed us one of the most often overlooked tools in successful entrepreneurs; the ability to ebb and flow with victory and defeat. Now, am I saying we are a perfectly optimized company that can do no wrong, hell no. I'm sure there are business graduates out there who would laugh us out of a room if they saw how we operate from day to day. The thing is, when something is a passion project, it doesn't have to make tons of money to be deemed successful. Isolation Cocktails has been able to connect thousands of people over the past year and in our eyes, that's what we set out to do in the first place.

The Blue Bullet is one of our most requested cocktails at Isolation Cocktails. After a full year of teaching, we have taught over 300 unique cocktails, and this is the one that is continuously requested. Not only is it a favorite of both our community and one very well-known pirate, Johnny Depp, we can guarantee that after just one sip, it'll end up on your list of favorite cocktails as well. The Blue Bullet, in a lot of ways, sums up what we do at Isolation Cocktails. Its ingredients and beginnings are as simple as some berries, herbs, and alcohol, but the result is something no one would ever dream of.

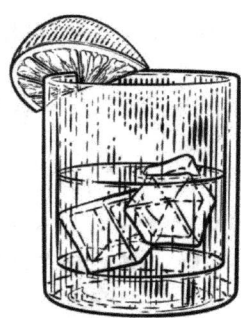

We hope that you enjoyed this flight of cocktails and Rosie and I's pandemic story. We don't know what will happen to this little pandemic business once the world opens. What we do know, is that when is does, we'll be ready to share a drink with you all.

Cheers!

Matt found success through a new artistic venture, combining practical experience and the desire to help others. Society has been instructed to 'pivot' and adapt. Have you created a new opportunity for yourself during the pandemic?

Brain Break
~Time to record a music collaboration video~
~help the singer find her headphones~

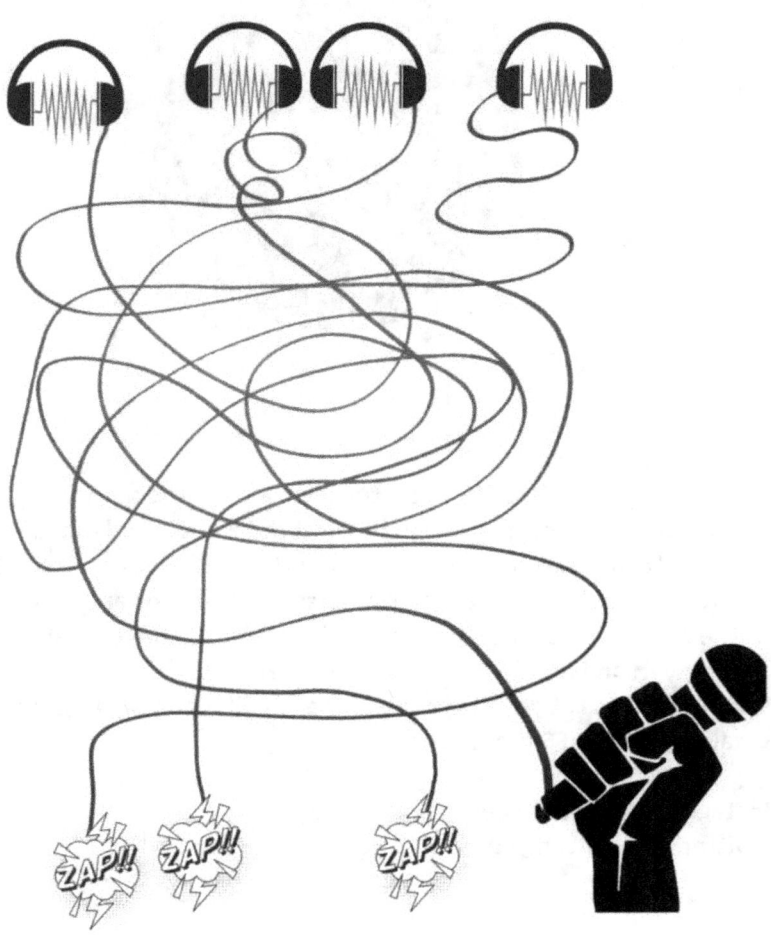

LANGE, HEIDI

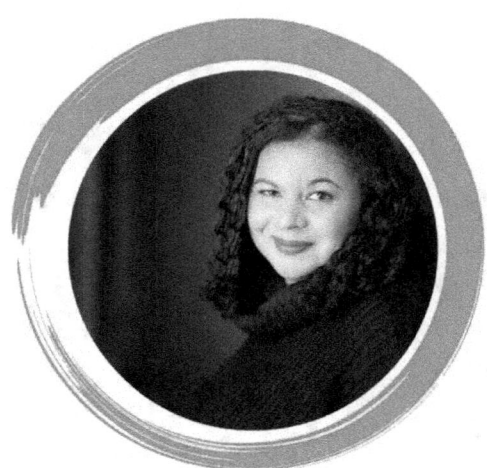

Heidi is a Toronto-based singer, teacher, writer and actor. She has been teaching voice, piano and musical theatre to students of all ages for over 16 years. Born and raised in Burlington, Ontario, Heidi has studied musical theatre at the University of Windsor and is a graduate of the Mohawk College Applied Music program. She has performed regularly in and around the GTA. In January 2020, she released her second album, Let Your Honesty Shine, a collection of songs from the catalogue of Paul Simon.

Instagram: @heidilange
Twitter: @HeidiLange1

Dear Mason,

Although I am a champion procrastinator by nature, this assignment has been particularly insidious, especially because I haven't procrastinated thinking about it. I've had several ideas and approaches over the last couple of months, and yet, I've been scared to really sit down and follow through. So, finally, I want to get to the root of that, because it's definitely connected to what the Pandemic Experience™ has been like for me. Please feel free to use as much or as little of this as you'd like. It honestly reflects my disjointedness, but as I explain later on, I'm learning to accept it all. It's the truth, and these days, that's often all there is to hold on to.

Heidi

PART ONE:

Like so many, I have had a chronic case of impostor syndrome throughout my artistic life (and of course, only my artistic life!) Did the pandemic wash my impostor syndrome away? Ha, I wish. It didn't take long after the initial lockdown in March 2020 before people started sharing videos and I began to think, I'm such a fraud, sitting terrified on my couch, binging *Parks and Recreation*. I wanted to share, I wanted to write, but what did I have to contribute? Was there any way I could share anything that would make anyone feel better; and since, of course, I could not, what would be the point of doing anything? Who was I to think my single little voice was worth being heard, when, hello, the world had stopped? Besides, so many of the people I saw sharing could play their instruments much more competently than me, had more profound things to say, and, as had so often happened before, I thought, I'm just not good enough. (Spoiler alert: these feelings and thoughts continue to recur even today, so this is not exactly the story of how I really "conquered" anything.)

Two things pushed me forward: the first, practical. (A girl's gotta eat.) It wasn't long before my jobs (all 3 of them) started figuring out ways to keep classes going for our students. (After all, an employer's also gotta eat.) What began with posting short videos eventually led to the now ubiquitous Zoom (Sidebar: Where was Skype during all this? Was it not an online conferencing platform? How did Zoom literally "zoom" in and clean up?) Before long, I was (very skeptically, it must be confessed) figuring out how to adapt both group classes and private lessons. Music lessons. Singing. On a platform which has a delay that makes it impossible for group singing. Or accompaniment. I started to get used to doing warm-ups and practices where all the students were muted, and my lonely single voice rang out in my apartment. So weird. It's funny to think of that early transition period now and how certain I was that this new thing would never work. However, in spite of my early resistance, of course I eventually adjusted. Most of all, I looked forward to seeing my students, and felt the importance of my responsibility to them. As it always has, the necessity and sheer obligation of my work sustained me because I had no choice but to figure it out. So, I did.

Second: I started singing and playing and sharing, in spite of my aforementioned fears and insecurities. I tended to add lots of disclaimers, at first (mainly about my limitations as a pianist), but it felt freeing to just make music and not concern myself with what I thought others would think. I was doing it more for myself than anyone else. I started asking for requests, and this eventually snowballed into a weekly Facebook Live show where I sang and talked about musicals. The show lasted through the summer, during which time I surprised myself with how much I began to look forward to this one time a week when I put on some makeup, gabbed away on a subject that mattered to me, and sang wonderful songs. I had my small group of friends/loyal viewers who joined me each week and brightened up my life.

The fall brought with it some family responsibilities, as well as a different work schedule, and I had to stop my show. My postings dried up as well. I still taught and took a risk by auditioning and getting a gig recording an audiobook. And just like that, I have a new area in my career, one which I've always wanted.

PART TWO:

2021 has, to be honest, been a difficult one in which to feel creative and as free as I apparently felt in 2020. (Strange and surprising to me!) I've been fortunate to keep working and continue to be moved by my students and finding my creative fulfillment in new ways. (Stumbling into amateur music production, for example.) I think the lessons I am gaining the most from the Pandemic Experience™, while not necessarily new, are still important:

1) There are no "rules". Yes, you want to try and develop a practice and a discipline to improve, but there are so many forms that can take. Believing there is a way you "should" be doing things is, at least in my experience, utterly paralyzing. I am endeavouring to remove the word "should" from my artistic vocabulary entirely.

2) Comparison is not only the thief of joy (said the wise Thedore Roosevelt), I believe it's the thief of creativity and productivity as well. When it comes to what others are doing, certainly enjoy and be inspired, but don't hold yourself up against them. You are not me and I am not you and that's kind of an incredible thing. Think of it as an advantage and an asset.

3) I am an artist. The other people who have contributed to this collection are artists. (And there's a very strong chance that you, reading this, are an artist as well.) We're not defined by how we measure up against each other, nor even how we measure up against our own conceptions of what artists are. It's not about how busy we are, how prolific and certainly not how successful.

4) What I've come to understand, in a way I couldn't see

before, is that, in spite of this awful, sad, often despairing time: as an artist, I have drive. What is it, other than drive, that fuels all of the ideas I have (fleeting though many of them may be)? What is it, if not drive, that keeps me excited about teaching? What is it, other than drive, that fuels my oh-so-passionate opinions on the art that I consume? I care. I get stuck, I judge myself too much, but I am not indifferent. And I persist. (As I bet you do, too, fellow artists.) Which puts us in good company. There's so much worry about what the future holds for artists, and I share it. But history is on our side. The artists and the art they make somehow come through the darkest times. They reflect, they document, they preserve, they inspire, they push us forward.

Heidi acknowledged that she has drive. It has taken her far during this time. Can an artist be successful without drive?

MAGRATH, MELLY

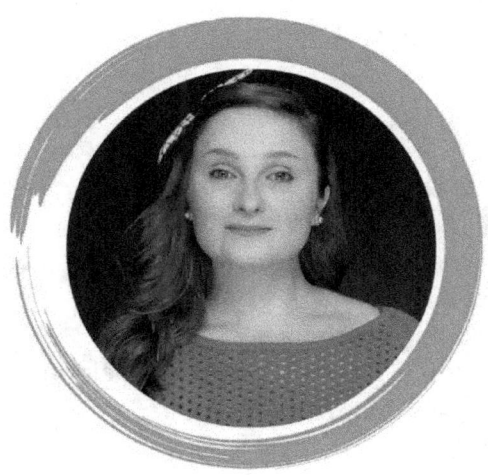

Melly is a multidisciplinary artist from Toronto. She is thankful for this opportunity and cannot wait to read the other passages included in this book. Past writing credits include: Till Death do us Part the Musical (SBM Productions), The Grid (Tree of Life Productions),Villians: An 80's Musical Cabaret (SBM productions), Plays in Cafés (Writer/Shadowpath Theatre), Love You to Death (SBM Productions), Motherlouges (Camden Fringe), Stuck in the Sky (Daisy Productions)

I didn't really understand the word **abundance** until 2020.

Obviously, I knew the word.
I would throw it into the ring while writing to seem more-intellectual.

I used the word in jokes or exaggerations while telling stories.

But.
That didn't capture the true meaning of abundance.

Time was the last thing I ever had an abundance of.
Going from one thing to the next.
Project after project.
Flight after flight.
Class after class.
And, of course, burnout after burnout.

I hate to admit this, but I was just screaming for a break before our first lockdown.
I didn't feel like doing anything anymore.
I felt pressure from loved ones, throwing their unwarranted opinions my way any chance they got.
"It's because they care."
"They want you to stay here."
Stay here and do what? Stay here and look for a job and feel miserable because I'm living at home and still trying to pay my student loans down?
Stay here and become the baby of the house again?
Or go a million miles away for some independence, but have them constantly worried for my safety.

So, I froze.
I couldn't make up my mind. I stopped using the words- I want.
I kept asking the world to make a decision for me.

Stay or go.

Procrastination.
Another word that would become something I understood more in this past year than I ever did before.

Then it happened.
The loudening static that I could barely hear myself think any

more was turned off.

Silence.

Stillness.

And an abundance of wide-open space.

At first, this abundance of time was exciting. I hit the ground running and could focus on writing.
I had time to work and age my words like fine wine.
I would set goals for myself when writing. Do a little every day.
There were people to hold me accountable.
Regular Zoom meeting to discuss goals, changes, feedback.
Flip-flopping between different projects and achieving deadlines.
It was wonderful. Feeling this abundance of energy to devote to art.
Perhaps this is what it was like during the Renaissance.
Artists working slowly, carving away their masterpieces. A feast of inspiration at their fingertips.
Curating their masterpieces.
The abundance for artists to take time to think, reflect, and enhance.

But that's a very flowery way of explaining it all, with rose tinted glasses.

For a month or two, my mind was going a mile a minute with ideas. I was manically typing away.

Highlight
Spell check
Edit
Cut
<u>Add</u>
Delete
Add
Add
Add
Delete it all.
Start again.
Leave a note

It felt like I was on top of my game. The motivation I wanted. The encouragement from people I respect.
The passion for my craft that had dwindled was now back in full force.
I am a writer.
I am a creative.
The signs from the universe that I so dearly wished for all happened for a reason.
The me from a month earlier was unrecognizable.
The me who was unsure and frustrated. Who came back to Canada in more pieces than I had left in, suddenly felt motivated to rebuild.
Small things mattered again.
The smell of coffee in the morning filled the room while I worked.
A light-hearted text from a soon to be the main character in my life to help fuel inspiration.
It all felt like I was meant to be where I was.

I would chuckle back, reading the words I wrote.
My personality was all there. The zany characters would come to

life before me, and we would work out a million and one scenarios.
They were as alive as I was.
It was hard to leave them each night. I was buzzing with ideas and slept only to wake up.
The characters would greet me as soon as my eyes opened. Just buzzing with an abundance of ideas.

A friend reached out to me during this time.
To help her with a one woman show.
More buzzing.
More characters.

 New ideas.

More and more hands reach out for my help.
Yes.
 Ideas.
Buzzing.
Downing coffee.
 .
 .
 .

Spilling on myself and my computer.
Wiping it away.
Typing
Typing becomes more sticky.
Thoughts are becoming more sticky
Add note.
Delete.
Delete
Reading it back.
Going on to another task-
Just push myself through it.

Spreading.

Myself.

Thin.

Saying yes and wanting to appease everyone.
An abundance of opportunities
Why do you do this to yourself?

                                                                              Take a break!
                                                                                 Just take it!
                                                              Seeeeeeelfffcare!
                                                                  You deserve it.

                                                                                      .
                                                                                      .
                                                                                      ,

                          No I DON'T.
              Leave it for a couple days.
                              Weeks.
                             It's fine.

                                 .
                                 .
                                 .
                                  .
                                  .

                             Procrastination.

Remember that scene from The Queen's Gambit?
The one with the girl with red hair?
She would see pieces on the ceiling and mapped everything out.

Hyperfocus.

Then- the pieces disappeared.
Things started to feel like that.

With high came the inevitable crash.
There was a shift.
Things went from we should be worried, to feeling trapped in your home for safety.
Fear became a constant state for everyone.

What if?
Images filled the screen with loss and our utter lack of control.
Updates on my phone and apps to download just to maybe stay safe.

This was all supposed to be temporary.
My extended visit home with my family had long outlasted its novelty.
I couldn't keep all the plates spinning.

I spiralled.
My sleep cycle went awry. Shutting my brain off became almost impossible.
I started to binge.
Watching. Just transferring from screen to screen.
Eating. As much I could shovel into my mouth.
Drinking. Always having an excuse as to why it was warranted.
I stopped going outside altogether.
Not that I purposely meant to. It just kinda fell to the wayside.
And you would think that my blood test results showing deficient vitamin D and my doctors' plea to "get some sunshine" would snap me out of it.
But it didn't. I just started to take daily vitamins instead.

One night I cracked.

I had to knock on my mother's door at a late hour and present my state to her. Like I did as a child when I was sick. It felt like my heart almost burst out of my chest. I couldn't stop shaking or hold myself up.
I have no memory of getting to the hospital. Just blurs of blue rushing around me- testing me, hooking things up to my body. Words and questions sounded like muffled yelling I couldn't quite make out.
What were they going to do with me? How could I get out of here? I was stuck in a fragile shell.

What if I was stuck like this forever? I have things I need to get done. I thought of all things I would miss out on in life. Guilt. That my family would have to take care of me because I couldn't handle stress.
I was a burden.

For almost a week, I was easily set off. Doing the most minor thing took excruciating effort. The only thing that was allowed to be on the TV was animal documentaries.
And even then, one of them about a mother deer, antelope, something- losing its baby during the night triggered another attack.

Be careful what you wish for!

Writing stopped.
I tried desperately to make it work, but the words felt flat and forced. I started to hate everything I created.
Procrastination.
With deadlines removed, I had nothing but an abundance of time to make excuses for why I wasn't doing what I should.
Some of them were real.

I stopped taking the subway.
I never thought I would miss riding the silver rocket. Or hearing

those screeching sounds, but I did.
There's something so calming about being in a crowd where everyone is actively ignoring each other.
People watching. Thinking about their lives, where are they going?
What do they worry about?
Eavesdropping on conversations like they are little scenes happening in real-time.
I can't count how many times I've missed my stop because I furiously typing away.

Some of my favourite plays have been entirely going back and forth to work.

But not all excuses I made were the truth.
Some of them were just to close a conversation.
If I knew they wouldn't check in on me, I would just leave the conversation bare.
Little pop-ins. Just enough to have them not worry.

It's not that I didn't want to work and make art.
I did.
More than anything, but I just couldn't.
There was no fuel to my fire, and the harder I tried, the more disappointed I was with the outcome.

I started classes during the lockdown. Something practical but still in the arts field. Something to look good on my resume and at least makes me feel like I was doing something with my time.
It helped.
But it wasn't the same.
There was a creative writing aspect of the course, and even though I was always marked high- I would read it back and question the teachers' standards.
It was clear I wrote this the night before it was due.

There were so many small mistakes and unedited paragraphs.
   I didn't even try.

Procrastination.

It went on like this for a while. More extended than I would want to admit.
I started to feel spiteful to people around me creating art.
Not that I wanted their work to flop or be ill-received.
Just wishing it was me. I was mad they were having that feeling of euphoria when you put inspiration to ink. Reading things back to yourself and the rush of ideas spilling out of you.
What were they doing to stay inspired?
What did I have to do to be like them?
How do I get abundance back?

By the winter, very little has changed. I started helping a few friends with their projects behind the scenes. Just something small to dip my toes back in.
What usually came naturally to me felt like relearning the whole wheel.
This anxiety of "doing it right".
Was I always this slow and bad at this? They will never ask me to help out again.
Burning bridges here and there.
Give up.
I started to imagine those thoughts as people. A faceless group in dark clothing.
They kept telling me things I didn't want to hear.
I kept listening.
And when I tried to let go and tune them out, the small crowd gathered around me to breathe at the back of my neck.

I tried to keep the small crowd at bay, I really did.
Just breathe.
but it became increasingly tricky after a series of doctors'

appointments.

> Breathe for me.
> This might hurt a bit.
> Take it easy for the rest of the day.
> We only have 8:15 available - is that alright?
> Go in that room and put on the gown please.
> I'm going to refer you to-

An abundance of tests.
That small crowd became a stadium of people yelling things at me. Knocking me down to nothing.
The waiting game for results.
I would try and sleep, but I would circle thoughts in my head.
Every scary thought. Every option.
If I wasn't dying- indeed, the lack of sleep would do me in.
Or the intruders in my mind yelling abusive thoughts.

Maybe I can write one last play before I kick the bucket. Maybe it would have the sentimental value I've not been able to achieve in my writing thus far.
Bet it wouldn't be good anyway. You'd be laughed at even after death.
Maybe I deserve all this.

Then I got the news.
I wasn't in immediate danger. Just high risk.

> "A high risk we can deal with", said my doctor.
> "High risk is for another day."

Sitting there in the office. Taking everything in that was just said to me.
The sound of clicking on the keyboard soothed me.

Click.

Click.
A shuffle of the mouse.
A printer that actually prints when you ask it to.
Breathe.
The signing and filling of prescriptions.
A thick stack just for me.
And sleeping beauty pills.

An abundance of sleep.
Finally.

The great hibernation of 2020.
The stadium dispersed after 9 innings, and I was left with my crowd again.
Which before was overwhelming, but now, they just watched me in silent judgment.

More meetings about projects I haven't started.
Check-in hellos! How is everyone doinggggg?!
Excuses.
Procrastination.

I have to show them I can do it.

But instead of working on those projects- I decided to take a sharp right turn.
Work on something else entirely.
Create more work for me.
That makes sense.

And take it all on and produce this idea I have.
At least I have an idea- It's been a while.
Work with a big group.
An abundance of talent.

And I barely did the outreach, they all came to me, wanting to be part of it, and it was such an honour.
An abundance of yes.

It was great to love and nurture something again.
I even found the motivation to write something for it.
I think the anonymity helped.
A little secret I could have for myself.
But-
Completing it became more challenging than expected.
I had all the pieces but putting it all together felt so much harder.
Granted, I was recovering from surgery.
But I should have prepared more! I knew it was happening.
I wanted to take on the world and not ask for help.

Procrastination.

I did get it done. And although I could make a thousand notes on how to make it better.
Tearing down everything and every choice.
I stopped myself.
I let go and put it into the universe to hold.
It's not perfect- it doesn't need to be perfect.

I still struggle with starting up again. It's not been linear. I lack a lot of motivation I once had.
But-
I'm trying to be patient with myself.
Forgiving when I have no more spoons to hand out for the day.
It's okay to need more time.
It's okay.

I've been peeling back the layers of defense my body has put up for this last year; my heart singed from burns and self hatred. So delicate, it might crumble if the layers peel away too fast.
Trying to find the being within.

You're safe now. You don't have to hide.
I am in there- I know I am.
But this takes time.

I've been taking the subway again. Not daily. But enough to get ideas happening again. It's been good.
I mean, not riding the subway itself, that's a damn mess down there.
But-
My designated writing time is back.
It's how I was able to write this, actually.

I can do it.

I started to think about all the people who believed in me.
Their understanding.
Their waiting when I'm ready
Reaching out.
Their trust in my work.
I am so thankful and appreciative of them.
I can feel their warm hugs reach out to me through the Zoom calls.
They have been gentle, even when I'm not.
Their abundance of positivity outweighs my crowd of intrusive thoughts.

Gratitude.
Now that's the word I've started to learn the meaning of in 2021.

Melly's piece depicted chaos among monotony. Was there a time during the pandemic when you felt totally in control or totally out of control? Describe your chaos and your monotony during COVID-19.

MCGINNIS, CAITLYN

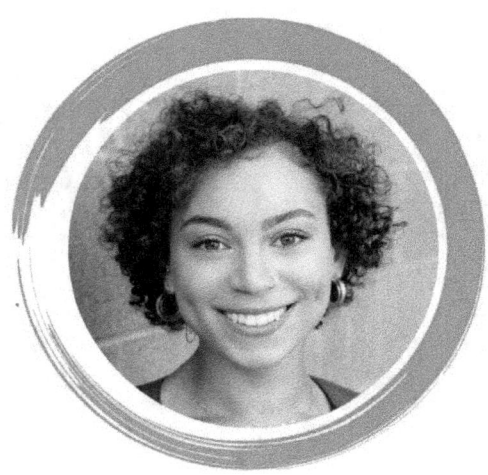

Caitlyn MacInnis (they/she) is a queer, non-binary, biracial (Afro-Carribbean and Celtic Settler) multi-disciplinary artist. Their practices range from, but are not limited to: singer, songwriter, dancer, actor and choreographer. They are based in the traditional territory of the Huron-Wendat, the Haudenosaunee, the Anishinaabeg, and the Mississaugas of the Credit; colonially referred to as Oakville, Ontario. They are entering their final year in the Musical Theatre Performance Program at Sheridan College, and are ecstatic to enter the professional industry.

Caitlyn strives to challenge the binary. They are passionate about creating, producing, amplifying, and collaborating with artists and companies who prioritize diversity, equity, inclusion, and accessibility. Caitlyn is committed to amplifying historically marginalized voices, such as: LGBTQIA+, women/femmes, IBPOC, and disabled individuals. They implement these practices within their activism, coaching, and facilitated spaces.

If you are an artist, art lover, or creator they would love to connect with you! Slide into their inbox anytime.

@caitlynmacinnis

Self-talk

It's going to suck.
But it's for my safety and the safety of others.

It felt like chest pains,
and binging reality TV.
Like going to the gym.
Scratch that.
~~Like going to the gym.~~

It's all blurry.
It's really blurry.
Time is obsolete,
Weeks pass,
It worsens.

Routines change.
Routine, routine, routine.
Try your best,
Do what you can.

Stop - breathe -
Ok... That's better.

This was a wild ride, huh?
It still seems weird the more I think about it,
the more I forget it's still happening.
It's not a long gone, distant memory.
It's here.
Where we are *right now*.

And now, to think that there might be a 4th wave after finally getting a taste of what we used to call "normal".
It's going to suck.
But it's for my safety and the safety of others.

'No. No. Please! I can't go back!'
I get it.
Not back to the way it was.
But I will
If I have to for my safety and the safety of others.

Safe at home, Stuck at home...
Depends on if you've got a home.
If the place you call home is even safe for you.
Lucky to have a home,
Wish I painted my room a different colour.
I'll do it tomorrow...
I've said that for a week...

The Present.
I'm in the present;
The now.
But I don't feel present.

Finding ways to cope
We adapt,
It's what we do.
I've got the strength.
The power.
The grit.
We all do.

The best parts are when you forget that we're in a straight up pandemic, panorama, Pandora box. You're so present that you get lost in the moment with a friend. Seeing a family member you haven't seen in a year. Maybe it's being with nature? Or walking your dog?

It's a short break,
a nice break,
when you disappear.
When you can drop your shoulders,
relax your jaw and exhale.

But then you realize you forgot to put on your mask.
Shit!
You get embarrassed that you put others at risk by accident. It's a mixture of embarrassment and annoyance.
It's on. I'm covered. We're good.

Life is so beautiful.
Even in all it's misery and darkness.
There's no time to hang on to things that will only steal your energy.
Give to what feeds you.
Give to what truly makes you happy.
Give to what replenishes you.
Don't give to what only takes, and takes, and takes.
Or do...
It's your choice.
That's another part of what makes this life beautiful.
We are so privileged.
We have free will.

Some have their skin colour,
or income,
or family,
or health,
and that's their privilege(s.)

Some fight for those who are less privileged.
Some use their privilege to push for change.

Some use the blinders of their circumstances to ignore the reality that other lives around them differ from theirs.

I fight for those who had to see innocent people that look like them -
their mother, father,
sister,
cousin,
brother,
daughter or son -
get brutally murdered,
lynched,
gunned down,
pushed off of balconies
in broad daylight
by bigots, white supremacists, transphobes,
or by the ones who are supposed to serve and protect.
Many times, these individuals are synonymous to one another.

I fight for those who had to see innocent people that look like them -
their mother, father,
best friend,
nephew,
auntie,
grandfather or grandmother -
get verbally abused,
spat on,
physically assaulted,
in public places
in the light of day
by bigots, xenophobes, white supremacists, and neighbours.

I fight for those who had to see people that look like them
get their culture get stolen,
buried, hidden,

and beaten out of them
by colonizers and white supremacists.
Whether it be their land and resources,
their children and community,
their language and their dance...

I fight for and alongside those who've lived experiences where their humanity was taken from them.
I fight for the ones whose identity is seen as dangerous or threatening.
The ones who are seen as criminals by simply existing.
The stories told and the ones we'll never hear.
I fight for the the people who were those people
and the ones who didn't make it to see tomorrow.
I continue to fight for them every day because the enemy of change is complacency.

I'm not going back to my bubble of ignorance ever again.
Now that you've had no choice but to look into the mouth of the beast,
What will you do?
I'm not going back to my bubble of ignorance in a few months when things get "back to normal".
Will you?

Don't suffocate the fire inside your eyes.
And the hunger inside your heart.
You can feel it in your gut.
It's what make you get the hell up
on a really, absolutely, dogshit awful
worst day of your life kind of thing;
Determination.

Keep going.
Get up and get going in whatever way you can!
Because we have so much light to share

and so much love to radiate.

It's warm like a hug from someone you deeply love.
Making change is never easy, that's why things have been the way they are for so many generations.
But no one can make you care about the lives of others.
Empathy is up to you.
You've got this.

Don't forget to love yourself, okay?
You deserve to rest when you need it.
Don't let them take that away from you.
You've got this.

Even when it gets really hard.
You've got this.

Caitlyn wrote a stream of consciousness. What are some keywords that you would use to describe your state of mind during coronavirus?

MCFARLANE, ANITA

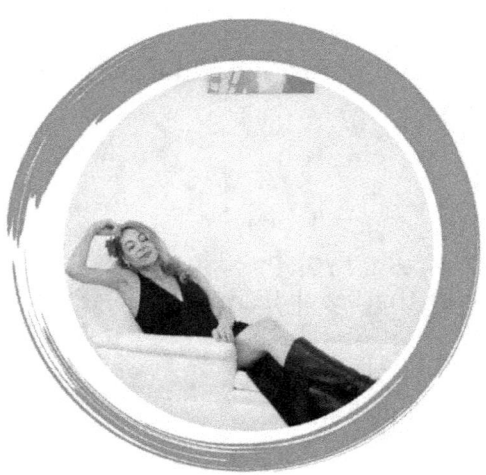

Anita McFarlane. Since returning to Canada after a fun 14-year stint working in Ireland and New York City, Anita has channelled her extensive dance and theatre experience into a lifelong passion: *CircusYoga: The Human Art of Play.* "Teaching and coaching allows me to engage and activate positive energy in others -- to spark the divine through drama, movement, mindfulness, music and laughter." A member of *Actors Equity Association* and the *Screen Actors Guild,* Anita was a founding member of *Twin Cities Theatre Company* and *Horizontal Eight Theatre* whose first short film *Viennese Oedipus* was featured at the short film festival in The Hague. Her three one-act plays *Grappa, The Spiders' Feast and Potato Prayers* were produced professionally in Toronto and published in Canada's Theatre Magazine *Theatrum.* Her play *Daisyworld* was produced at the *Vineyard Playhouse* on Martha's Vineyard. Her short play *Around Midnight* was chosen for *The Black Cat Cabaret Short Play Festival.* As an actress, audiences have enjoyed her performances in plays by *Chekov, Pinter, Shakespeare, De Ghelderode, Strindberg, Wilde,* and *Camus* in Toronto, Dublin, Edinburg, Moscow, and New York. Anita was also a contributing choreographer with her unique dance theatre pieces for

Built On Stilts Dance Festival on Martha's Vineyard (10 seasons) and taught for *Way Off Broadway*, a children's musical theatre school in New York (8 seasons). She is the recipient of over 20 arts council grants in Canada, the U.S. and Ireland. She provides *CircusYoga: The Human Art of Play* classes and sessions in schools as 'Mindful Fun', in businesses and corporations for 'Team-Building', as 'Professional Development' workshops for school districts, the *Association of British Columbia Drama Educators*, and to interested individuals who are looking to reconnect with their own dramatic possibilities, talents and dreams.

And Then We Danced

For far too long the Darkness had been unbearable.
It kept us apart from each other.
We could not see each other.
We could not find each other
to hold each other.
Inexplicably, the Darkness also made us deaf.
We could not hear each other.

And so, we wanted to embrace **their** promises of a
"Brilliantly Bright Inclusive New Future!"
But we wondered, would **they** hold true to their promises?
Would **they** ensure the rebuilding of our Communities?
The lifeblood that keeps us whole and alive?

"Trust in us!" they proclaimed. "We know what is best for all."
We listened.
But we had our doubts and our suspicions.

And so, we turned to those sublimely strange and
mysterious creatures, the Artists.

"Don't trust us!" the Artists exclaimed. We don't know what we are doing. We are surrounded by the same Darkness as you."

"And yet you dance."

"What?"

"And yet you dance!"

"It's the only thing we can do together."

And so, we danced with them.

And we danced.

And we danced!

And we danced!

Together we danced!

And whispers of Light began ribboning throughout the Darkness shredding it into a thousand million little black shards that dissolved into, and became One with, the Light.

And there we were.
We could see each other.
We could hold each other.
We could hear each other.

We could dance with each other!

Well, we could always do that.

Anita described her journey through an artistic dance piece. What artistic luxuries did you have during this pandemic?

BRAIN BREAK

~UNSCRAMBLE~

1. NGIS
2. FEPRRMO
3. PDICMENA
4. RKEFCIL
5. DICVO
6. MZOO
7. ENNOIL
8. SLILKS
9. TAEHRTE
10. DCIMEAPN

MICEVSKI, MASON

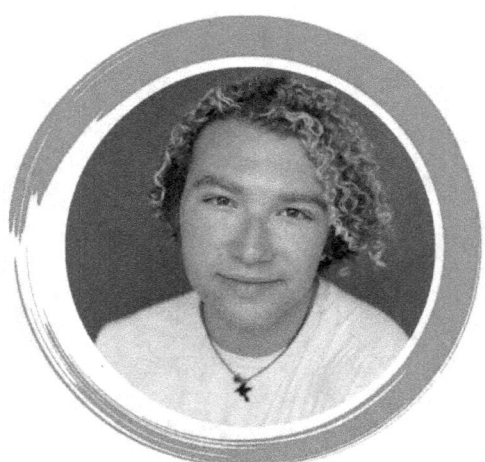

Mason Micevski is constantly thinking of ways to keep artists working. He brings his dedication, determination, and ALL OF HIS ENERGY to his role as Co-Founder and Co-Artistic Director of Emerson Arts. Mason was born and raised in Hamilton, Ontario, to an aggressive Eastern European family. He didn't in fact go downtown Hamilton, until he was 19 years-old because it scared him.

A graduate of Randolph Collage of the Performing Arts, Mason is a triple-threat performer landing roles throughout the golden horseshoe at theatres such as The Lower Ossington Theatre, Oh Canada Eh? and Warner Bros. Studios to name a few.

At the tender age of 18 years of age, Mason began ballet lessons. Just a few years later he would perform with the National Ballet of Canada in their annual performance of 'The Nutcracker'.

Through years of training and performing, he has developed his skills as an extremely effective vocal director and choreographer, working with several companies in the greater Toronto and Hamilton area.

RULES TO PLAY

Mason Micevski's experience during coronavirus.
The follow are the official rules to the Emerson Arts original board game '2020: The Game' This is also the detailed recounting of Emerson Arts Co-Founder Mason Micevski's first year in a coronavirus World.

Start

To begin the game all players must partake in a ROCK, PAPER, SCISSORS tournament. If it ends in a tie, the two players *must* BATTLE in ROCK, PAPER, SCISSORS, **SPLIT -** match to determine the winner.

Or… House rules.

Late February 2020, I de-boarded a flight from Montreal to Toronto, ending a life changing trip (I'll tell you about that later). The passengers departing are spotted with individuals in medical masks. Toronto's great 'Pearson Airport', empty. It was like a zombie movie, and I thought it was HILARIOUS!
My best friend Emily greets me at the pick-up zone in the early afternoon, with news that March break may be extended because of some virus. To which I reply, "They would have never done that when I was in school. Kids today have it so easy." Not truly understanding the gravity of that statement. I'm glad I didn't know, because I had a crash course in life over a short period of time. Things got serious, quickly.

I hope you enjoy reading or playing through my life in a COVID-19-World!

The Events to follow/ Game Tiles are not in chronological order, but the order they appear on the board

REPEATING TILE RULES
Things that happened, daily, weekly, monthly. Things that were constant during my coronavirus experience.
*Each one of these tiles repeats and has a different rule, mini game or challenge! *

Complete A Video Game
You learned the rules and memorized all the buttons, YOU BEAT THE GAME! CONGRATULATIONS! But you didn't do anything productive in three days... You receive no reward or punishment, **STAY ON THIS TILE.**

For the first month of 'LOCKDOWN' When the ENTIRE WORLD SHUT DOWN... I mean no economic growth, all bills and any financial matters paused until further notice... stores had limited capacity, new, aggressive, rules came to be, and everyone was masked up. So, I stayed in and played Dragon Age: Inquisition and beat it four times. I replayed my all-time favourite game series, FABLE, including the 3rd one and the weird one for the X-Box Connect... This was something I was longing for and loved to do, but my determination and dedication to my career as performer kept me from. That is why I view this as positive and negative experience. I feel like it's a bit of a loss of time, but it opened my mind and allowed me to think like a kid and expand my creative mind which, really didn't need any expanding...

Online Play Reading
You participate in an 'online play reading'; you get to assign the 'cast'. **Swap locations with the player in the lead.**

In the early days of the pandemic, everything was shut down and we were all working from home. I was so fortunate, the year prior to the pandemic, to work with 'Flush Inc. Productions' in Ontario's 'IMPACT THEATRE FESTIVAL', an international play festival. There, I met an American playwright name Dwayne Yancey. He writes the most fabulous, whimsical, and out of this world plays, of which I had the honour of reading multiple times. I played a talking rooster, a magical cat, The North Star and so many other zany roles. This was a blessing I never understood until I started talking about it. I got to explore and play in crazy ways with people from all over the world, actors participated from Canada, America, and Australia, allowing me to work on cold reads, creating a character, having a history and so many other skills. I now have two binders full of Dwayne Yancey original plays, a new friend, and some hilarious memories that I will take with me in my life.

Brighten Someone's Day
You are at the drive-through window at work, and you compliment a customer on something basic, "Cute earrings!", "Thanks for wearing your mask!" **MAKE A TOAST TO ANOTHER PLAYER.**

Through the pandemic I faced a lot of challenges. I was an over worked, underpaid 'Front-line Worker', a phrase I would soon LOATHE. I was a barista at an 'international coffee chain'. We baristas went through so many trials and tribulations over time, from customers cussing us out over chocolate drizzle to people wanting 'Secret Menu Items' that they don't even know how to make and neither do I... and now it's my problem. I got through the day by singing to myself and to the customers, I also told jokes or made connections with random people, who over the months, I would get to know about and would become like family. I mean I knew their SECRETS! We're talking insurance scams, theft, affairs, you name it, I knew someone doing it in the area. It was my mission to make sure people felt supported and loved in my community, because when your day starts with a joke or friendly voice, you can choose happiness that day! I looked at it like a system of kindness that began with me. It was a glorious feeling, and it made all the other 'baggage' worth it, for my soul. I also told EVERYONE who would listen or had to wait for their order, about Emerson Arts!

Sing A Song
You just found a new artist to obsess over on your car rides. **SING A VERSE And/or CHORUS** of any song.

Singing... How can I come up with the words to express the way I feel when I sing? It's like flying, inside my body. It feels familiar and safe. It's like going numb and focusing on one sensation. It's like the best orgasm ever. But when I say 'sing', I mean hum, talk sing, random riff, sing an order, sing to the radio, harmonize with beeps, alarms, beatboxing or making any musical noise... It all fills my body the same as singing the lead in a musical. It's all the same to me, I can't explain it and it's always been this way. Literally, since I was three... Imagine being my mom!? Singing makes everyone smile, giggle, feel good. I just assumed it was magic. In my local area I became known as, 'The Singing Barista'. For a while I posted song fragments on Instagram under a similar pseudonym. If I was angry, happy, mad, sad, annoyed, giddy, or frustrated, I sang and was back to bringing the pep and brightening people's days. But one day, mid-November 2020, after six-months in a COVID-19-world, it stopped. I stopped singing. I no longer felt good enough. I felt I meant less. The negativity had gotten to me. I needed something to change. I felt alone. I felt like I was the only person feeling this way... What an arrogant thought! I missed performing, teaching, making art, human connection... Then I woke up in the middle of the night and BAM- I had a GREAT IDEA! This book! I quickly realized I knew exactly how to give a voice to people who were feeling like me. My people. Performers and artists who, even in the face of the pandemic haven't given up. This book was needed to help artists feel appreciated, supported and that they are NOT alone. Then brain blast #2; I contacted Pandamonium Publishing! I had met and dazzled Lacey L. Bakker - Owner, Publisher, & Author, during my time as a barista. After a conversation with Lacey and *Emily*, my best friend, I found it, my voice! I started singing again!!!! The feeling came back. I could fly again! I was able to give the world my heart all over again! But this time, I would soar!

Plugged-In
Host the online talk show, 'Emerson Arts Presents: PLUGGED-IN'.
INTERVIEW ANY PLAYER ABOUT ANY TOPIC FOR 30 seconds.

Plugged-In is a Facebook Live talk show we created as a way for us at Emerson Arts to give exposure and raise awareness about local artists. Our videos have a combined online audience of five thousand people. We feature local talent, interview people of note, and put on a killer show! We were able to run it for very little cost. This idea came about when I was trying to feel connected to the world again. It was a lot of work. At the end of it, I felt like... no one cared. All that hard work was for nothing... Then I had another brain blast! I was able to stop, assess and look around. EVERYONE was fed up with *'online'*, art, learning, and events! It was now too much and there was too much pressure to participate. Everything felt like WORK- and nobody wanted to pay for anything online... I quickly accepted that I would not be getting paid much for my online creations, but I took the opportunity to learn from these experiences give-back to the community through our show. Now we are changing the structure to make it stronger and will be back in 2022! If you want to be featured, check out our website EmersonArtsCanada.com

Write A Play
Wake up. Pour a black coffee. Put on a playlist you don't know the lyrics to, but that has a sick beat. Zone-in and write a play in a day.
FILL IN THE BLANKS: The_____went into the_____to conquer_____. All other players must rate the sentence out from 0-5, if you score higher than 50% move forward.

When we began the process of FRIGHT NIGHT the first time, I wrote my first play, called "Three Witches?" It's a one act, 10-minute play, about two witches, in the woods, looking for their friend. I wrote it in about 30 minutes and spent the next two weeks deep diving and fixing it up to make it perfect. We ended up staging it for FRIGHT NIGHT that year! Afterwards, I wrote a bunch of ideas down. Lockdowns have provided me the time to write them out, think them through and even do a couple of readings of some of them! I have written a full-length graphic novel, a movie, and a teen fiction novel about magic and bloodlines. I am now on my third 'idea book' filled with TV show pitches, intros to scripts, character sketches, new heroes and villains and SO MUCH MORE! Maybe a musical...? The idea for this book, the one you are currently reading, is also in one of those 'Idea books'! Completing that first play changed my mindset about what I was capable of and since then I have realized, I'm unstoppable.

DANCE
You woke up feeling down, BLAST your favourite album, loosen your joints, and shake your booty! **HAPPY DANCE FOR 30 seconds**.

Just before the pandemic began, I was lucky enough to begin my career as a choreographer and it was life changing! Helping people succeed, physically, was a rewarding feeling like I had never experienced. It forced me to be creative like I had never been before and made me expand my mind to create adaptations for those who 'choreographically' challenged! The first show I choreographed was THE WEDDING SINGER: THE MUSICAL and I learned so much! I pushed my skills and fuelled my creativity. There was a zombie dance, a hip-hop dance, musical theatre, contemporary- anyway- I have done a few other things since then, but this was so magical because the cast was so unique! We even had a man who was struck by lighting and had short-term memory loss. I had the most fabulous dance captain/ assistant choreographer, Jasmine Headly, a true saint. Dance and creating dances became a major outlet for me during coronavirus. Dancing in the back yard really fed my soul, however my neighbours really didn't get it. Someone once said to me, "Mason, first you act- tell me the story, you only sing when the emotions are too much to say, you only dance the emotions are too much to sing." I took that as 'Dancing is movement and energy flow- people will feel your emotions on a primal level. It's an art form which needs no language. Singing is the succession of notes which even if you don't know the words, you can feel the emotion through pitch, tone and intention. Acting is a planned path of how you wish to express yourself / character.

MEMORY CARDS
Think back to the days just before the pandemic and reminisce, feel grateful, and sit in the feeling of being lucky! **YOU HAVE IMMUNITY TO THE NEXT PURPLE TILE,** then return the card. This card does not need to be played right away. If all three cards are held by players and a non-card holder lands on this tile, they can take a card from any another holder who must go back to the next MEMORY CARD tile.
There are three Memory Cards, FLORIDA, CUBA, and QUEBEC

Florida:
In late October 2019 I received a call from my cousin Alyssa who lives in Michigan, USA. Alyssa calls and says please tell me you are free for Serbian Christmas! Do you have plans? (January 7th is known as Orthodox Christmas.) My mom is Serbian and Dad, Macedonian. My mom immigrated with her whole family to America and my dad to Canada. They met through the church, my grandmas knew each other, or some such gossip. Anyway, I was like, "It's just me, Jesus and some vodka" and the next thing I know I am planning our first 'cousins' trip 'to our grandparents' condo in St. Pete's Beach on the coast of Florida. We left on the 2nd or 3rd of January, seven adults from 19-25 years of age, piled into a tiny, two-bedroom condo. We all had a BLAST! We all did our own thing, did small activities in small groups, and we all intermingled equally. We did things all together most of the time, but there were no cousin cliques! We had all agreed to make it a yearly tradition, not knowing what was to come!

Cuba:
I know I have mentioned my best friend Emily a bit, and I'm sure

I'm not done- but I just love her so much... She HUSTLES! She is a single mother of two, who takes heat so the father of her children can be seen as normal... anyway she's a saint on earth to say the least. Leaving out her community service, sitting on the board at a local community theatre, donating her time and so much more, I could just go on and on. I decided it was her time for a break! So... for Christmas, humbly, I bought her an all-inclusive 4.5/star Cuban, resort vacation! SURPRISE! We went the last week of January. I had one-week home in-between this and my cousins' trip to Florida. I had THREE WEEKS OFF from work! In Cuba we had one of the most memorable times of our lives; we met an 'alien', sang with the resort band, brought the *party* to the 'foam party', and we did a whole bunch of things I will never admit to... but the best part was making friends with some pretty great people who just happen to live in various provinces across Canada. It's been fun to send updates about what we are experiencing. We all like different things so we had a lot to share and talk about!

Quebec:
I was a tour leader for a Toronto based tour company. I LOVED IT! I was sent all over Canada with grade 7 & 8 students on their year-end trips. The season is dense from March through to the end of June. The following year, after doing a smashing job the summer before, I was asked to come on as a winter tour leader and take on the more grown-up tours! The day after we landed from our trip to Cuba I was called by my boss and asked If I could lead a tour of international students ranging from 13-19. My travel partner was a friend from training and the tour season the year before. Obviously, I said HELL YEA! For this tour, these kids were from ALL over Europe and had come to Canada to learn about Canadian culture for one year. I taught them a lot about Canadian history as well as a few life lessons, but they taught me so much more. They were an awesome group of kids! It was also the first time I had been dog sledding! Quebec is my favourite Canadian city.

To all the people in any country who open their homes to others, from other countries or to people from other walks of life. You are a gift unto this world. Your heart and understanding, compassion and love is something magnificent to see, thank you!

PURPLE TILES
Purple tiles represent things that held me back or things that I think should hold someone else back in the game. They can be challenges or just a string of bad luck.
Land on a purple tile, go back two spaces- keep an eye out for mini-games

Re-Watch 'The Office'
MINI GAME: Circling clockwise through the group, each player must quote 'The Office'. Continue until one player cannot say a new quote. That player must **MOVE BACK TWO SPACES**.

I can't count how many times I have seen Michael Scott and his ignorant, arrogant, hilariousness. Almost every night since the beginning of the pandemic Emily and I fell asleep on the couch in each other's arms, laughing, crying, or getting totally offended when Michael said the F-word... but seeing his growth and feeling safe, relaxed, and normal, with Dwight, Pam, and Jim, too. Maybe it's something to do with the ordinary, mundane quality of the show, or how they are truly just people, but The Office has been a constant of comfort during the pandemic. For example, I know someone who behaves like almost every character in this show. It's not that far from reality! Some of the funniest characters were brought to life on that show – the best for me, it's Prison, Mike! If I had to say who I was most similar to on the show...I think I'd say, I'm a combo of Dwight and Andy, just insane but can sing. "Ri-di-Di-di-di-Doo" -Andy Dwyer – Mason Micevski.

Gain 5lbs
Eat so much you can't move. *Purple Tile* **MOVE BACK TWO**

SPACES.

My weight has always been a topic of conversation in my life. As a male performer, there is an unspoken expectation to look slim, strong and sexy... But when you smoke weed and LOVE Taco Bell, it's hard to maintain those expectations. As a child my father was obsessed with being the strongest and sexiest man in the room. And truthfully, he often was. But for me, that put high expectations on me. I didn't even try to compete with him. I felt inadequate all the time. Now, as an adult, I continue to struggle with body image and personal expectations. This bled into my career and personal life as well. I am either VERY REGIMETNED or have no rules. When isolation began, I decided to have fun but always seek balance. This token represents the weeks that went by where I chose to overindulge.

Car Gets Side Swiped
Your car gets hit a bunch of times while you're at work. *Purple Tile* **MOVE BACK TWO SPACES**.

During my tenure as a receptionist at a local music school, my car was 'side swiped'. I use quotes because it looks like someone backed into it, 30 times. My boss had security cameras, but they were only on the inside. So... guess who looks like a 'Schleper' as The Nanny, Fran Fine, would say. This was the point of the pandemic when I binge-watched The Nanny. I returned to my old childhood friend, to ease my pain after this incident. On a more positive note, this awesome couple, who came through the drive-through daily, and happened to own a body shop, offered to help me get my car fixed, and not get screwed over! It was magical! Good people are out there.

Sleep All Day
You don't work today! Don't set an alarm and do NOT get out of bed. You waste the whole day and re-watched your favourite movie... *Purple Tile* **MOVE BACK TWO SPACES**.

Some days I didn't even make it to the living room, never mind do something productive. This behaviour was something I was conditioned as a child never to do and literally never EVER do now, as an adult. I never get out of bed past 8am. I have worked through countless hangovers, silently. I LOVE working hard. I love learning new things and growing in different environments. I believe you can learn from every single other person on this planet. I know a LOT of people stayed in bed for a lot of coronavirus and this is no shade to them- we all had to survive. I get it- but that's not me... I get extremely disappointed in myself and hyper critical. This would only happen a handful of times over the year.

Stress Leave
Your supervisor harassed you and then slandered your name. He continues to work while you are sent on temporary leave from your position at your day job for an unforeseen amount of time. Purple Tile* **MOVE BACK TWO SPACES**.

When I was a barista, I was friends with a supervisor. He manipulated and twisted our friendship and said some horrific things against me. One day I show-up to work; I was mistreated, bullied, and talked down to by all the other staff, but had no clue as to why. Imagine, you are a social butterfly who is always making jokes at work and then one day, no one will even look at you? Lucky for me, I have a few great friends who were at this company and they eventually filled in the gaps for me... turns out this guy had been saying all kinds of crazy lies and spreading awful rumors. It was all slander but thankfully, the truth came out. I was given almost two months of paid leave, which sounds cool but was hard for me. Then shortly after I quit - but we'll get to that later.

Lose It on A Customer
Time has passed and you have had it! If Dave comes in without wearing a mask again, you're gonna FLIP OUT. Dave came back.

You flip out. *Purple Tile* **MOVE BACK TWO SPACES**.

I came back from 'temporary leave' and my first shift back is with that dirtball supervisor... The one who slandered my name and never had any repercussions... Can you believe it? He was working as my SUPERVISOR on my FIRST DAY BACK! At this point my brain couldn't handle it, and I let EVERYONE know about my discomfort. That's when everything changed for me. I switched restaurant locations and began working as a barista at a drive-through. It was awesome at first. The fast paced, action-packed days went by quickly and were fun with a rotating door of staff, each from different walks of life with a beautiful story. It was never ending laughs! But soon people were nearing their wits end. There was no more smiling after the joke or giggling to the songs I sang. It was like mental warfare- the 'friends' who I had met at the drive-through window, who were once full of life, secrets and gossip, were now gray and distant. The world had changed. I was not strong enough to take it and should mention, I'm VERY PRIDEFUL! My life motto is 'Fool me once, shame on you, fool me twice, never gonna happen.' I also happened to be at *MY* WITS END.... So, I may have put a couple of privileged white people in their place, and definitely reminded a lot of people that kindness is a two-way street. It totally came back to bite me in the ass... But I am human! And I learned from it, isn't that all that *really* matters?

Marvel Marathon
MINI GAME: Put on your comfies, grab a big bag of dollar store snacks and cuddle with your bestie. You watch all the Disney Marvel Movies in chronological order, together. **MOVING CLOCKWISE AROUND THE CIRLCE, EACH PLAYER IS TO NAME A MARVEL MOVIE UNTIL A PLAYER CAN'T ANSWER**. Once someone fails to name a movie title, that person must **MOVE BACK 2 SPACES**. If this tile is landed on and all the movies' names haven't been exhausted, simply begin naming heroes & villains.

Emily took a few days off from work and I took a few days off, too.

We put on matching track suits with our pictures ironed on all over them and cuddled for days as we binge watched all 21 superhero movies! I grew up with Marvel. I have all the VHS tapes of the X-Men cartoon from 1994, had all the action figures, games for X-box, and so many costumes! I love so many heroes, I have to break it down for you. I have two favourite male heroes and two favourite female heroes. Dr. Strange & Ant Man, The Scarlet Witch & Captain Marvel. You can only imagine my excitement as an adult with all the hype around these heroes! My brothers and I used to play 'Marvel: The Ultimate Alliance' on the X-Box. I played as Dr. Strange or Capitan Marvel, who we would call 'Lucky Charms Girl' because her powers were the colours of the rainbow! I was so grateful Emily watched all these movies with/ for me. She knew it meant a lot to me, and she got *invested*. She watched, laughed, cried, participated in the world- she's the best. It was an unforgettable time for me in my life. I know how long these movies are, how she hates violence, and how these were mostly explosions. She could have just slept through them. We re-watched the intro to Guardians of the Galaxy three times because I fell asleep and then she stopped the movie so we could watch it together. THAT'S LOVE!

Followed to Work, Fist Fight
Get followed to work and punched in the head.
Purple Tile **MOVE BACK TWO SPACES**.

So, here's the tea... I was getting onto the highway and a guy cut me off, so I gave him the finger... I drove across town to work only to find he had followed me! When I parked, he whipped open my door and punched me in the face before I even knew what was going on, or that he had even followed me. It took me a second to realize what was going on. I am a pretty a big man, so I always must think about how fast and hard I move. I don't believe in violence unless for defense. So, he gets me, but I don't even blink. I push open the door throwing him nearly 3ft from the force of the door. I can now see him. He was a 5'10, 175lbs, bald, thin, pale European man. I noticed he had a can of spray in his left hand. I noticed it was bear spray. I caught or blocked a few of his punches, only enhancing his rage and desire to see me bleed. I pushed him back again, as he tried to advance on me. He began waving around his hand with the spray, trying to distract me. It worked – he got another hit in, but I was unphased. It was like a baby had hit me. Once he saw how he had punched me twice, and I didn't even react, he ran back to his car so fast! He looked like he was MESSED up on drugs... like coke or some serious shit. It was a rough day... really shook me up... I am now a calmer driver, I leave extra time, and mind my own business on the road. Road rage is a waste of energy.

LIFE CARDS
LIFE CARDS are awarded for standout moments in my corona experience and grants the user a bonus. Move forward 2 spaces...

Start Emerson Arts
Begin your journey of entrepreneurship and start your lifelong, dream company with your best friend. **Draw a LIFE CARD.**

In early August 2020, I convinced my best friend Emily, whom I am continually mentioning, to start a for-profit, professional grade, theatre company -whose main focus would become, creating paid work for artists in as many ways as possible. Within its first year of life, Emerson Arts has contracted, employed and paid just under 50 artists! In *one* year... With *no* money... *Or* help... **Just Em and I...** We hustled... This was a big moment for me, my life had meaning again. I have faced a LOT of adversity in my life, from obvious and unexpected people, in a 'game changing' variety of ways, and it's usually because people think I can't do something or tell me 'no'. I immediately feel obligated to prove them wrong. So, I started a company when theatre was banned, and put on a show outdoors, when coronavirus cases were low. It was a controlled 25 people per show, masks mandatory. We were safe and successful. I could now feed my soul even more through creating. I was creating under *my* new banner **Emerson Arts**! And creating is exactly what I did. Day and night, filling my 'Ideas Book', which I purchased at the dollar store, to hold all my outlandish and unrealistic ideas. Over time Emily would refine and make these ideas possible. This was a big turning point in my life. I was more confident when I felt I was representing something bigger than myself. Knowing I had a goal and that I wanted to help others achieve their dreams, really helped *me* have clearer focus. I also have unstoppable work ethic and am determined to do what I say I'm gonna do. Emerson Arts gave me a cause to focus on and fight for- paid work and recognition for artists.

FRIGHT NIGHT
An Emerson Arts original series of short one act plays, in late October set to a Halloween/ horror theme. **Draw a LIFE CARD.**

I came up with the idea for FRIGHT NIGHT: An Evening of Horrors after participating in a similar style of theatre with 'Asphalt Jungle Shorts' produced by 'Flush Inc Productions'. This was a series of hilarious and random plays, strung together loosely with a host or tour guide. I wanted to produce something similar. It seemed affordable and fun. Halloween, my favourite holiday was fast approaching. I knew to be successful we needed to tap into a niche market. Then everything fell into place. We were able to hire six actors, pay 10 playwrights scattered across North America, and put a small amount cash into an account for Emerson Arts' future endeavors. **We had successfully put on a show during the pandemic!** It was October 2020, we had created Emerson Arts just two months earlier, in August of that year, held auditions in mid-September and opened the show on October 22nd. It was a fast and powerful turn around, with a magnificent final product! FRIGHT NIGHT: An Evening of Horrors now runs annually in late October.

Learn Piano
Take advantage of your surrounding resources as a receptionist at a music school, learn piano on your own and get feedback from friends and staff. **Draw a LIFE CARD.**

During my 'leave' from the international coffee chain (remember that story?), I was able to finish writing a graphic novel I've created called 'The Light Of Day', and began writing another about Emily, my bestie, and I called 'The Red Witch & White Knight'. I then began to play video games and play and bond with Emily's daughters twelve-year-old, Page and Ava, who is nine. Weeks passed and I began to wonder if I would be going back to work at all. I had worked almost every day in my life since I was 14 years old. At one point in college, I had three jobs. I'd worked the entire pandemic but, after two weeks off I was itching to get back to work, back to dazzling. I then got a job at a local music school as their receptionist and accounts receivable. I quickly began to create my own systems of operation and really cleaned up the filing system and back-end of the company, all the while fulfilling myself by being kind to the students and parents of the busy school. It was awesome. By November I was heavily involved in running the daily operations of the company, working very closely with the owner. Soon I was the first one in and last one to leave. I started going to work a half hour earlier and began to play around and try to write music. I then bought a piano lesson book at a local music store for 'Beginner Adults' and stared learning! After a short while I was able to breeze through beginner lessons, filling in for some of the teachers when they were running late or had an emergency. I'm by no means a 'good' player but I can, in fact, play.

I feel the need to mention, I'm good at theory. I had private lessons before college and have a great understanding of it, which helped me a lot in learning the piano. I'm not Jimmy Neutron... I also made a bunch of new friends with the teachers of the school. Sometimes they would come in early, I would play and ask for them for tips or suggestions to be better. That combo fast tracked my development!

Get Dis-Owned by Your Brother
You fight hard for love, and never give up. Your father teaches you 'BLOOD IS THICKER THAN WATER'. Not everyone listened to that lesson. Get dis-owned by your brother. **Draw a LIFE CARD**.

During coronavirus my brother disowned me for the second time. He will never get that opportunity again. My life motto is 'Fool me one shame on you, fool me twice, never gonna happen.' I let it happen. But it wasn't all bad because this was the last, in a series of unfortunate events. It was the push I needed to take full ownership over my life, to stop living for others and worrying about what others thought. One last thing- I'M GAY.

JUMBO FOOD
Happy Birthday to you! Your best friend made JUMBO FOOD! An 8LB hamburger, fries the size of your arm, a single Oreo made from an entire box... and so... much... MORE! **Draw a LIFE CARD**.

For my 'COVID-19 Birthday' I turned 26, what a weird age to be. My best friend was 41 and I was slowly becoming a type of father-figure or fun-uncle for her two incredible children. This was one of the biggest blessings of coronavirus. Page, now 13 years old and Ava 10 years old, would quickly become my new best friends and the loves of my life. The four of us all isolated together, Me, Emily, Page and Ava, what a magical experience. It was hard *for sure*, but so worth it! Back to my birthday, Em made JUMBO FOOD all day long and the girls and I had a feast that lasted a week! It was GLORIOUS! More over- she got me *my favourite childhood movie* "Spice World" on DVD and paid WAY too much! But the memories she gave me and reminded me of were worth so much more.

CAR HUG 2020
Travel to a string of Canadian cites in Ontario named after European Cites/Countries including but not limited to, London,

Dublin, Paris, Prussia, Saville, and Oxford. **Draw a LIFE CARD.**

For real, there were so many cities on this tour. We sang and recorded a song at every city welcome sign. It's on Instagram, somewhere. For Christmas 2019, Emily and I had a $10.00 gift limit, which I just blew so far out of the water, with that trip to Cuba. But she did too, her gift to me was 'Car Hug 2020' which was a mapped-out city tour with stops at wineries, breweries, and candy factories! Unfortunately, when we began Car Hug, the world was completely locked down, so our plans had to change. Regardless, we were determined to have a great day! We were COVID-safe, only getting out of the car to sing except for our stop at a local restaurant in Dublin, ON where we ate outside on a bench. It was a magical day, fun in the sun, with my most favourite person on the whole planet, Emily Bolyea!

Get A Puppy
Get a cute little baby girl, the sweetest puppy of all time. **Draw a LIFE CARD.**

We got a dog! Page, Emily's daughter spent her days doing school online and her nights looking at the cutest puppies our local neighbourhoods and shelters had to offer. She found a little baby girl, half Cairn-Terrier, and half Shih-Tzu. She is stunning and smart, energetic, and fun. Once you look into her eyes you can feel her soul. It's warm and loving, like the mother of your childhood best friend. Her name is Willow, and she has become the glue of my new little family. She smiles and we all melt. She ends fights, brings joy, and now knows how to sit, shake a paw, and go potty on the puppy pad! She is a defender and protector; she reminds us how pure our love for one another is and how we would do anything for each other!

Quit Your Day Job
After years of hustling, it's time to work for yourself, FULL TIME! **Draw a LIFE CARD.**

Let's go back to when I was working at the drive-through at this unnamed coffee chain. I've lost my cool, got it back and am singing the day away. But things quickly flip all over again. coronavirus spikes- much stricter precautions are put in place. We closed the coffee shop due to multiple staff members testing positive for coronavirus. We open for one day and close for two weeks, for the SAME REASON! We planned to open the coffee shop again. My manager calls me and says only 10 people are eligible to return to work because the rest risk possible exposure to coronavirus. I'm one of the 'lucky ones' who can still work. She asks if I am willing to work two weeks straight, from open to close, although we had modified hours. I foolishly agree to do it. After the first day, we leave optimistically with a jar full of tips. I was on the drive-through window and was KILLING IT! I was keeping the morale up on the floor and customers calm at the drive-through window as their orders took up to 13 minutes to be made, due to the overwhelming volume of customers and to us being short staffed. We all agreed to ask for danger pay or over-time for our bonus hustle. I should add, after the first three hours one girl left in tears because it was too much for her. We were told we weren't working any harder than normal- so why should we get paid more? A few weeks later, I had a meeting with my boss. I got my annual raise! It worked out be something like 30 cents... I knew immediately that I had to quit. It was too much for my heart. I had very high expectations put on me because I was able to thrive in this setting. But now my behaviour was getting out of control and the pressure put on me was growing. A new supervisor came from another store and literally told me "I *will* micromanage you, that's the only way I know you will succeed." By now I think you know how quickly I wrote my resignation letter.

The reason I think of this a positive is because it was the first time I didn't explode or lose my cool, I saw the growth I had achieved in my choice of behaviour and also it was the push I needed to jump-in, feet first, and dedicate all my time to EMERSON ARTS!

I am a small business owner! I am a MOGUL.

Overview:
During coronavirus, I learned a LOT. I created a business, came into my own, and started participating in the raising of two beautiful girls. I really learned how to relax! I have changed and I am still changing. I made SO MANY mistakes. Coronavirus has taught me, that we are all in this life and on this earth *together*. We must work and live *together*. **All for one and one for all!** I also found out what I want to dedicate my life to- the growth of paid work and sustainability in the arts. I want people in the arts to be able to work full-time hours and earn a living wage. I want people to take performers as *seriously* as they do doctors, businesspeople, or teachers. Why do I receive less judgment when I say I work in customer service than I do when I say I'm a singer? THAT is what I'm fighting for. That is my purpose in this life. This is the world I want to see, the world I want to live in, the world I *will* live in!

You purchasing this book is helping my dream come true. THANK YOU!

Mason shared moments in his life that were constant and moments that fluctuated. Did you have a similar experience?

NG, TIMOTHY

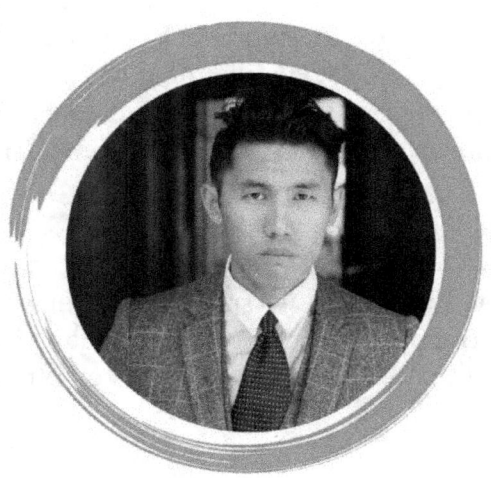

**Timothy is an award nominated actor. His credits range from Off-Broadway to Netflix to HBO.
He can be seen in CBCs Canadian reflections "May Flowers" and Netflix's Jupiter's Legacy just to name a few.**

2020: shitshow.

January 2020.

Just got news from relatives in Hong Kong that a new virus might be coming to North America.
Not worried but ordered masks anyways. A whole 20 boxes.

February 2020

The calm before the storm. Still not as worried. However, Wuhan has now been hit hard. They plan to hunker down and lockdown. Meanwhile, here in Toronto, joyous laughter, happy faces, people without a care in the world. I was in the midst of over 1000 people crammed into one building on the same floor. Talk about how easy of a breeding ground that could have been.

March 2020

This is where everything goes to shit. We hear news. Good news. And bad news. But mostly bad news. My Birthday coming up. Looking forward to All You Can Eat sushi to top off my 29th Birthday.
TOILET PAPER.
We got news of the virus and it touched down in Canada. The month that everything changed.
RIP BREONNA TAYLOR.

April 2020

Seemed quiet at first. Virus still new so we took precautions and still took to the streets for our essentials.
My first case of racism. I came out of my dental appointment greeted by teens walking by and feigning coughing. Then laughing. Because simply the fact that I am Asian.
My agent retires. I am no longer represented.

May 2020

RIP GEORGE FLOYD.
Black Lives Matter.
Asian business owners were being harassed when customers were asked to wear a mask.

First case of Asians being attacked because ignoramus' thought we carried the virus.
Posted about awareness on Facebook and weeded out "friends" who did not align with me. Black Lives Matter and always will matter had more than half my friends list delete me. I had no problem with that. The rest that agreed, stayed.

June 2020

It was calm at home. Started doing push up trends thinking this would be a good way to stay healthy and on top of things. Learned how to bake bread, as most of us learned to do. Started playing a lot of video games.

July 2020

Restrictions eased a little bit. We went out for the first time in a long time. Finally got my All You Can Eat for my Birthday. At this time, I was actively agent searching. All my friends had gigs. Turns out the industry had not really shut down.

August 2020

RIP ELIJAH MCCLAIN
Hanging out with friends again. Outdoors. Masked. Social distanced. And those in our bubble were allowed inside. We built our collection of board games. We played a lot. Outdoors. Indoors. We just played. It was a vice to get our minds off the lockdown.
I learned how to make pizza.
Got wind of many more Asians being harassed in the streets.

September 2020

I finally get an Agent. I sign and was already on my way to my first gig of the year. A commercial. I was feeling hopeful. I was feeling strong. I was feeling unstoppable. A family member passed from COVID-19. It sets a reminder for us to be very careful. Asians still being attacked on the streets.

October 2020

Highlight month of the year.
Given a challenge to write short screen plays and read them over Zoom.
Self-tapes. LOTS of them.
Joined a self-tape class.

November 2020

My fiancé's birthday month.
We celebrated with a few of our bubble friends.

December 2020

A hopeful end. We are hopeful this lockdown would end. 2021 will be a new year and looking forward to what it will bring.
Celebrated a low-key holiday with bubbled friends.
Zoom fatigue set in.

Is this it? What will 2021 bring?
(Upon writing this, it's the year 2021)
Will we finally end this lockdown once and for all? Will vaccines finally be available?
Will we be able to dine in again?
Will I be able to return to work before my employment insurance ends?

And finally,

Will the anti-Asian racism stop once this pandemic end?

Timothy asks, 'Will the anti-Asian racism stop once this pandemic ends?' Throughout the past year and a half, and the months leading up to March 2020, increased incidence of overt racism have been on the incline, despite positive, peaceful activism from groups like Black Lives Matter. How can art and artists contribute to ending racism in this current climate?

PIERCE, ERIN BREE

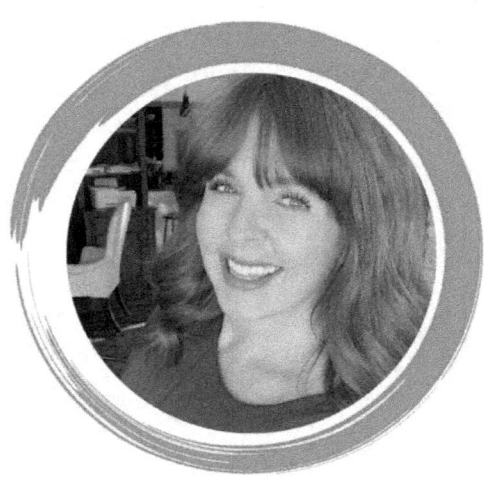

Erin Bree Pierce graduated from The University of Western Ontario with her degree in Voice Performance. She keeps up her vocal studies with Thomas Schilling in Hamilton and holds her own voice studio and company, right in the heart of Brantford ON. Her past stage work has ranged from leads in Gilbert and Sullivan to Musical Theatre to Choral and Solo Classical Works. Erin Bree sang with Opera Mississauga for three seasons and continues to present Operatic works in solo recitals and with fellow musicians. Recent Theatre roles include Donna in *Mamma Mia*, Miss Hannigan in *Annie*, Princess Fiona in *Shrek The Musical*, Sister Amnesia from *Nunsense*, Magenta from *Rocky Horror Picture Show*, Ronnette from *Little Shop of Horrors,* Golde from *Fiddler on The Roof*, Eliza from *My Fair Lady*, Kate from *Kiss Me Kate*, Babette from *Beauty and The Beast,* Mrs. Johnstone in *Blood Brothers*, Aunt Em/Glinda in *The Wizard of Oz* and the Fairy Godmother in *Cinderella*. She has directed many shows including Les Miserables, 13 The Musical, Rent, Cinderella, Snow White, Aladdin, Annie, Wizard of Oz, Alice in Wonderland, Grease, and High School Musical, along with directing and singing in many Musical Revues. If she's not teaching or performing in a show, she just may be performing concert works with

with her dad, Frank Pierce. Erin Bree continues to thank her family, for all of their support and encouragement in her busy career.

A Performer, keeping the passion and art alive during a Pandemic.

I would consider myself a theatre girl through and through. I come from a classically trained background and have a degree in Voice Performance in Opera. But the truth is, I sing all genres of music and perform a lot of character roles. THIS is my passion.

My involvement in teaching voice and directing has always been very present in my career. I love coaching and I love the opportunity to direct.

COVID-19 put a halt on these things, didn't it?

From the get-go of the pandemic, I told myself I was going to continue what I do ... and that is, sing every day. I didn't want to get rusty. I encouraged others to "keep up your craft" because when the doors open, we want to be ready!

So... that's what I did. I sang every day. I challenged myself with new repertoire, I sang through the entire role of Donna from Mamma Mia, which was the last show I did before the world changed ... and I believe, it has changed in many ways, forever.

It wasn't always easy to get up off the couch and do a 2-hour vocal "workout" but when I did finally get up off the couch, it reminded me of the joy this brings not only to myself but to all of the people we have performed for. It was important for me to "keep up my craft". I have always been like this. Consistent with my technique and keeping my singing healthy. It's something I believe in strongly. And COVID-19 wasn't going to stop me from that.

Don't get me wrong ... some days it was sad. Really sad. Remember those dark COVID-19 days? I think we all do. But nothing said, "I need a pick me up" like a good vocal workout.

I had friends I did remote songs with and mixed them and created some nice YouTube videos and that kept us going. I created 2 videos for a "Theatres United" remote project and that lifted our spirits. It kept me busy. It kept me singing. It kept the music alive in my own heart and soul. This was and is so important to me.

Thing is ... music is in everybody's lives, and I think music saved a lot of people during this pandemic. How many times when you were stuck in quarantine not seeing your family or friends, did you turn on the music? I would bet music was a source of comfort for many.

As artists, it's important to keep it alive ... even if the stage is dark.

Erin Bree trained daily to keep her voice in peak-condition. What actions have you taken to ensure you are ready for the stage when theatres open?

PINTO, CHRISTABEL

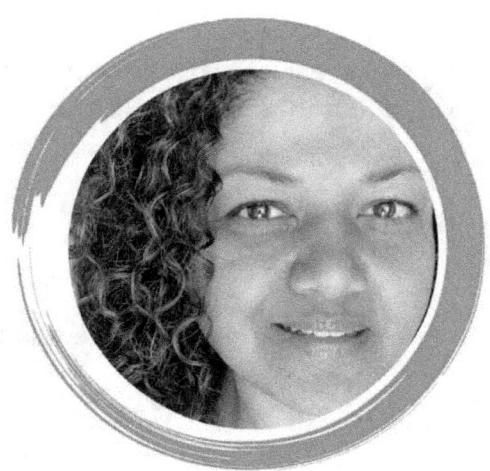

Music is Christabel's life!
She is a much sought-after Music Director and Collaborative Pianist who accompanies and coaches for many string and voice studios.

Christabel has been the Organist and Music Director at Stoney Creek United Church for 30 years. She plays for ballet classes and coaches voice at Sheridan College. She obtained a B.A. in Music from McMaster University, and a B.Ed. from Brock University.

Christabel is the recipient of several awards, including: The Lee Hepner Award, The Margaret Oswald Memorial, Intermediate Finalist for the Hamilton Kiwanis Festival (3 consecutive years), and the winner of the Reginald Bedford Gold Medal.

Christabel loves to volunteer at St. Patrick's church, help seniors with groceries and spend quality time with her two teens, Kambria and Crispin.

I will never forget – Thursday, March 12th, 2020...
I was teaching the Boiches piano. Gema, the mother, came home and said the March break has been extended due to the "coronavirus."

I then went to my choir rehearsal that was held in my church, and everyone was talking about this new virus. The church was closed the next day.

I was excited at first for an extended break from work and to spend quality time with my kids.

However, the extended break turned out to be way longer than expected.

All of a sudden, the United Church Conference, Hamilton Music Festival, lessons, weddings, funerals, exams, concerts, and auditions were gone. Everything was gone.

I coped by filling my time with lots of volunteering... making calls to members in my congregation, singing hymns over the phone by request, visiting the lonely and taking them meals and groceries.

I was fortunate to have recorded every week with a small group from church and play for livestream services at St Pats with Joe Allain. I even taught my 4-year-old neighbour piano/voice/art everyday. Because of all the activities aforementioned, I was able to keep my music alive in my heart and soul and spread it within my community.

I feel blessed that I can safely share my gift of music under these circumstances!

Christabel says she will always remember the events of March 12, 2020. Is there a specific date or time that you can remember when your life changed due to the outbreak of the coronavirus?

PORTER, JENSEN

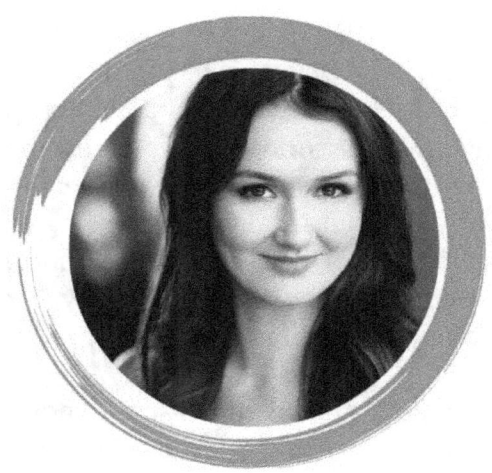

Jensen is a Toronto-based actor, dancer, and creator! She graduated from the Randolph Academy ('15), prior to that she was a competitive dancer and studied at the Quinte Ballet School of Canada. From screen, to theatre, to dance festivals, Jensen has dipped her toes into many creative waters, including being published by the Canadian Poetry Institute. She has had the opportunity to perform in the New York and Toronto International Dance Festivals, premiere a web series(Gay Mean Girls) at TIFF Next Wave, and perform on many stages across Canada. Jensen has worked under the direction of Thomas Carter (American Gods), Robin Bicknell (Paranormal 911), Heyishi Zhang (Gay Mean Girls), Rosanna Saracino (Little Pricks, Suitcases, Rosencrantz, and Guildenstern are Dead), Linda Garneau (Spring Awakening, Suitcases), and Victoria Fuller (Echo Productions). Jensen is thrilled to be apart of this writing collective, cheers to the artist's journey in uncharted waters!

Hey you,

Congratulations.

I'll say it again. CONGRATULATIONS. Whatever the trick is to surviving as an artist during a global pandemic, you are doing it. If you are reading this — looking for insight, comfort, inspiration, advice, or just out of sheer curiosity — you are fighting to make sure you have that spark flaring, no matter the circumstances. From my perspective, having that spark, knowing what ignites it, and hanging on with both hands is the most important thing when experiencing the ebbs and flows of this industry. In or out of a global pandemic.

My name is Jensen Porter, and I am an actor. I primarily grew up a dancer, getting into acting and singing later in my high school years. In hindsight, it was the opportunity to tell a story through any art form that really stole my heart. I was the kid busting out a full school schedule, rehearsals for the school play, 25+ hours of dance every week, and a part-time job. I truly only knew how to function on a constantly moving schedule. I later went on to graduate from Randolph College for the Performing Arts Triple Threat Program, and here I stand today: riding the magical, rough, brutal, and refreshing waves of an artist.

Let me start off by saying that I don't naturally have the personality that thrives with being an actor and artist in complete normalcy, let alone in a pandemic. My personality is classified as type A; I love a plan and being in the know, I overthink and make sure every inch of control that I have is maximized. I love to know what's coming next, which doesn't always mesh well with this industry. As every moment passes (in or out of acting), I feel myself considering "what could I have done differently?" to an obsessive degree. What could I have done more of? Am I listening? Paying attention? I aggressively articulate the "th" in "clothes" and "tt" in button because that level of specificity makes me feel just about as warm and happy as a freshly baked oatmeal chocolate chip cookie. That being said, I've had to train myself every day for the past 20+ years of being a performer to accept that I only have so much control. YOU only have so much control. Yes, Jensen. Be prepared. Work hard. Improve. But once you've done your part, pat yourself on the back. Reflect. And then delete whatever space you're creating to try and beat yourself up. It isn't productive. Besides, a global pandemic could hit at any time, so what's the point?

The beginning of 2020 was probably the best I had felt in my career — mentally, creatively, and physically — in a long time. I was starting to feel like the hard work was paying off. In fact, I felt so good that I actually took some of my hard-earned money and gave myself permission to step away from the auditioning game to take a month-long Euro Trip; see some of the world, find some inspiration, and dance down new streets. Then, the reality of a global pandemic came smacking us in the face like a brick wall. My points of income disappeared, auditions vanished, my pre-paid trip was cancelled, and people evaporated into their homes. Doesn't it always work out that whenever you're at the pinnacle of contentment, the pendulum has to swing the opposite way? Don't get me wrong; I am extremely lucky and grateful to have had a home to quarantine and stay safe in. But for the sake of this book, I'm going to shed the niceties and address how it felt, the experience I had, and how I dealt with it. So, here goes.

Reality is, this put an extreme halt on my life that I was in no way ready for. I deal with anything and everything, good or bad, by trudging forward. I give myself a limited amount of time to feel something, understand it, address it, and then I refocus and push through with my to-do list. This was no longer a viable option. For the first time in my life, I had zero plans for the foreseeable future. No distraction. Nothing to trudge forward to. Truth be told, COVID-19 made me question my choice to be an actor for a hot minute. The pity looks and tones of "oh, you're an actor…

how are you doing?" started to get to me. My shield of busy, hustle, and productivity wasn't there anymore. I was always proud of the intricate balance I meticulously carved out for myself, and how it sheltered me from the storm of other peoples' opinions. This now felt difficult. The stillness, combined with the ever-critical third eye creeping in and criticizing, along with the external sea of hustle culture and "what are you doing to further your career in a global pandemic?" made me want to disappear. Let me tell you, if I had a nickel for every time someone (who generally speaking, wasn't asked) gave their opinion about what you should be doing to further your career or get closer to their version of success, I would have enough money to start my own production company and create my own films (with COVID-19 safety and all!). Don't get me wrong, your colleagues and peers are an incredible tool in this industry. Use them. If you know someone who is achieving things that resemble accomplishments that you aspire to have and they are willing to share, one hundred percent seek advice and feedback. However, don't measure your success with rulers that aren't your own. If there is anything that I can recommend always, not just during a pandemic, it is to block out the noise. Easier said than done. This is something I'm working on every day. The thing is, we have one life, and what isn't adding to our equation is subtracting. I'm a big advocate for "cost vs. reward". This pandemic experience really put that into action. I don't know about you guys, but when the pandemic hit, I didn't have anything left to subtract. Anything that I was going to jump into had to feel really damn good.

Inevitably, the sleepless nights and depression-nap-filled days started to creep in, filling the nothingness. It got to a point where I became painfully aware that this quality of life was not one that I was interested in living. Without an end date, I needed to fixate my eye on a point. I needed something to get me through a time and state that was completely foreign to every inch of my person. I fixated my eye on being human and experiencing it, no holds barred. It sounds simple but was foreign to me. I tried to shed all expectations, filters, and judgements I had for myself and just do what felt good, despite how hard that proved to be. I focused on what I love, what I hate, and why, protecting my boundaries, my energy, and surviving. Hopefully, leaving the experience a more fleshed-out human being.

I struggled with virtual. A big reason why I got into this industry was for the human connection. Looking into a scene partner's eyes, reactionary beats, and a sweaty, heated vibe with tons of bodies breathing in a dance class. I found that Zoom sucked the love out of a lot of the reasons why I became an artist. Virtual learning cut human connection off at the knees for me; it felt fragmented from how the industry would continue to operate, pandemic or not. For that reason, I personally had trouble forking out money (with no income) for Zoom classes, workshops, etc. which felt like they were costing a lot; not only monetarily, but also mentally and emotionally. I didn't want this to mean that I couldn't do these things at all for the foreseeable future, so I found a few outlets that worked for me as an artist and human. I said no a lot and frequently. I was extremely picky as to what I exposed myself to, but in hindsight, I think I made choices that served me. My roommates and I started picking scenes to rehearse and film for fun in our home. I wrote a short film and made it with an iPhone. I submitted scenes to showcases and got feedback from industry professionals to keep the machine oiled. I received journaling prompts every day to keep the creativity flowing and have a moment to check in. I watched a lot of amazing films, TV, and murder documentaries (If you need a recommendation, I'm your girl!). I did a lot of listening to podcasts, meditations, music, and peoples' perspectives throughout the world. I moved my body with stretching, yoga, HIIT and barre. I rested when I needed to. I played cards and kicked butt. I took a course on Indigenous Canada. I started cooking fancy meals. (I hate cooking, so this was a big one for me.) I drew some boundaries with people in my life and connected deeply with others. I turned my home into a perfect oasis. I cried a lot. Laughed a lot too.

Like I said, I'm constantly pushing through my life, jumping from one thing to another, trudging through. I think the pandemic forced me to sit in the shit a bit. Feel it. Let everything I had skimmed over in the past several years catch up with my physical body. It sucked and I hated it, but I think as much as I resent that time period, I needed it. My perspective shifted a lot. I learned a lot about myself, and I can still feel myself shifting. I visited crippling doubt and then came back home to certainty a million times over. The rose-colored glasses have completely come off, which can sound depressing, but I think it makes me a more sure, more empathetic human; more in tune, a person who loves deeper, lives by their own compass, and cares less about the external noise. It's like the dentist: annoying, slightly painful, you can taste the blood and you leave resenting the cost — but also understanding and feeling what it gave you. Ultimately, I was fortunate and privileged to make it through COVID-19 healthy and safe. My experience isn't one-size-fits-all by any means. Only you know what you need to survive something like this. I'm surviving it, and I'm riding the magical, rough, brutal, refreshing waves of an artist and performer. Overall, I wouldn't change my path for anything, pandemic or not. So, cheers, to simultaneously loving and hating what we do, and trudging forward. Keep hanging on with both hands, my friends.

All my love,
Jensen

Jensen talked a lot about working hard and the 'hustle'. Do you view the 'hustle' as positive or negative? Why?

SHIELDS, TRÉ

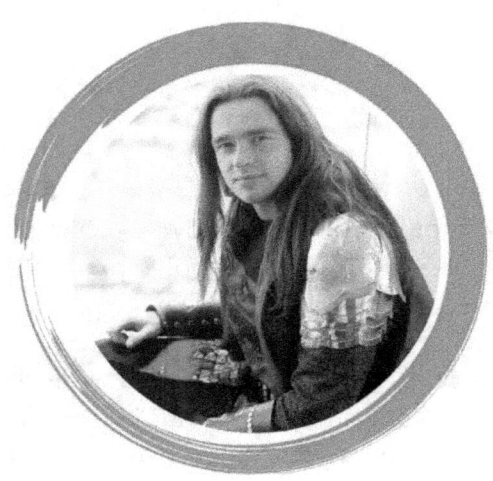

Tré Shields is a triple threat performer from Timmins, Ontario. He grew up dancing, teaching, and co-running his own dance school with his mom in Iroquois Falls. He was accepted into the private post secondary institution, Randolph Academy for the Performing Arts in Toronto. He is now a Randolph Alumni. Aside from performing, his free time consists of writing music, playing video games, and playing hockey. Currently you can catch him as one of the Knights at Medieval Times Dinner and Tournament in Toronto, ON. He hopes to see you there!

Taps microphone... Am I on? Testing 1-2-3. Okay good! Let's get started. For those of you who don't know me, my name is Tré Shields. I am twenty-five years old, and my STAGE LIGHT has been flickered. For any of you who have reached my page, I am going to give you the low down of how the COVID-19 pandemic has affected the art of performing, as well as myself personally, in both a negative and positive light. In order for you to truly graspthe entirety of the situation that actors like myself have experienced, I need to take you through my journey from the beginning....

****

It's New Year's Eve 2019. The Castle's rockin' and I am playing the role of the Champion in a sold-out show which my family was able to be a part of. To give you a closer look into my life, I am a Knight at Toronto's *Medieval Times Dinner and Tournament.* The lights were on and burning hot, flowers were thrown, crowds were roaring, lances were breaking, swords were clashing, sparks were flying and only one stood victorious in front of over a thousand guests, me, the Green Knight. The show is over, but the New Year's Eve Festivities are just beginning. I'm dancing with family and strangers alike, balloons cascading around us, champagne sparkling as we welcome the New Year and expect it to be even greater than the last. We were *ignorant of what was to come.* January rolls around and I'm still doing my thing five days a week, seven to fourteen shows, body sore and tired from the almost finished, but busy holiday season. We're all feeling it and most of us jokingly say to each other, man, we need a vacation. The old saying, "Be careful what you wish for," has never been more relevant. ...*Lights flicker.*

****

NEWS RELEASE
Ontario Confirms First Case of Wuhan Novel Coronavirus Extensive Protocols in Place to Detect and Contain Cases

January 25, 2020
TORONTO — Today, Dr. David Williams, Ontario's Chief Medical Officer of Health, announced Ontario's first presumptive confirmed case of Wuhan novel coronavirus in Toronto.

On Thursday, January 23, 2020, Sunnybrook Health Sciences Centre admitted a patient brought in by paramedics who presented with fever and respiratory symptoms. The patient was screened, recent travel history to Wuhan, China, was confirmed and the patient was immediately put under isolation. The hospital and paramedic service took all necessary precautions to ensure the safety of staff and other patients.

Diagnostic testing was conducted, and specimens were sent to the Public Health Ontario Laboratory to confirm the diagnosis. On Saturday, January 25, 2020, the Public Health Lab confirmed the case as a presumptive positive case.

"All appropriate infection prevention and control measures were followed by both paramedics and the hospital," said Dr. Williams. "Toronto Public Health is conducting case and contact management and Ontario is in touch with our federal counterparts to help determine exposure to other individuals on the flights."

Recently, to strengthen the province's ability to monitor any coronavirus cases, the Ministry of Health added novel coronavirus as a designated disease reportable under Ontario's public health legislation. Because of this, and other protocol and procedures that Ontario has in effect, the case was quickly identified and protocols for protection of health care workers and the public was immediately enacted.

"Although there is now a presumptive confirmed case of novel coronavirus in Ontario, I want Ontarians to know that the province is prepared to actively identify, prevent and control the spread of this serious infectious disease in Ontario." said Elliott. "I want Ontarians to know that their health and well-being is my top concern. Ontario has robust processes in place, skilled clinicians, and dedicated health workers to identify and manage this and any future cases safely and effectively. We have specialized units within our hospitals to deal specifically with these types of cases when they arise."

The ministry has been and will remain in constant contact with the Public Health Agency of Canada (PHAC) and other jurisdictions to monitor the developing situation and safeguard the health of all Ontarians, as well as to ensure our shared efforts to protect the public are coordinated and effective.
To help educate Ontarians about Wuhan novel coronavirus, how they can protect themselves and what to do if they suspect they may be at risk, the province has launched a dedicated webpage.

Moving forward, each weekday this web page will be updated with the most up-to-date information on the number of cases under investigation and those that have been confirmed.

It's crazy to think how often we turn a blind eye to world issues that aren't affecting our personal proximities. A spotlight needs to be shone on the shortcomings of humanity when it comes to these issues. I'm referring to the cliché term, "It won't happen to me." This is how many of us felt as China was suffering from a virus that North American didn't seem to take seriously until it consumed our borders and our lives. Its name, COVID-19 ...Blackout.

****

It's now March 2020 and we've received word from the company that we are no longer doing shows until further notice. Most of us got our wish, a small vacation if you will, which turned into the longest vacation of all. We had just survived the Christmas Holiday rush and were about to embark upon the March Break, the two busiest seasons we have at Medieval Times. We were sent home without the March Madness upon us. At first, most of us were relieved. We were all sore and exhausted by the constant flow of eat, joust, sleep, repeat. What originally began as a lucky two-week break from the everyday turned sour as fourteen days turned into the unknown. This is where the negative decline of my personal life has its curtain call. I didn't realize how much performing gave to me before it was taken away. In order to explain my reality to you, I will clarify in three acts entitled: Physically, Mentally and Emotionally.

Act 1: Physically

Physically, I was in the best shape of my life. I was doing multiple shows and giving each one 150% each time. I was riding high. On top of that I was working on a Fan Film Project as a Power Ranger. So, you could say my plate was full. With all of this going on and eating well to sustain the vigorous physical demands of my Knighthood, my younger self's goal was achieved...I got abs. You may think this is funny or a meaningless goal, but as a male actor wanting to thrive in film, a strong physique is an asset. I was more confident, more driven, and more motivated to continue my fitness journey than I had ever been before. I had a system and when that system was taken away from me, I found myself back in old habits: sleeping less, eating more, and consuming carelessly.This resulted in a relapse of the progress I was making and the physique I was proud of. I don't want to blame all of this on the pandemic as I think it's important to take responsibility for your own actions, but when restrictions were made so harshly in Ontario where I am residing, the options were narrowing and narrowing every month on ways to continue my fitness journey. And when it comes to being committed and staying on course, your will and mental well-being are put to the test.

Act 2: Mentally

Mentally, I felt like I was starting anew. I was moving on from a bad relationship. I became more focused on performing and fitness. Life was simple and everything that I did was routine and for the most part organized. I was piecing myself back together and just as I spent all that time rebuilding, the pandemic hit me like a wall, and it felt like it reset my progress to zero. I felt lazy. I was bored. I felt lonely from isolation where my only form of interaction was through online gaming or by phone with family or friends; it wasn't enough. Because of my lazy decline, I stopped being active which led to weight gain, which then led to insecurity and frustration. This brings me to my final Act.

Act 3: Emotionally

Emotionally, I was sound in the beginning. Everything was going according to plan. I achieved my childhood dream of being a performer in the big city, a Knight at Medieval Times. I was happy with the progress I was making to better myself physically and mentally. I was hopeful to carry and continue that momentum into the New Year of 2020. When the pandemic hit us hard, and I lost the ability to perform, see the smiling faces of the audience, spend time with my colleagues and take part in enjoying the realm of the arts like movies and live performances, I realized how much my soul is connected to the stage and the life the audience brings to it. Not only was the happiness that I had found from the arts dimming, but also in my personal life with the loss of normal, everyday pastimes like social gatherings, eateries, and human interaction. All the aspects that make up for a healthy human life were restrained.

****

Not only was performing at Medieval Times affected by the World Pandemic, but also my other endeavours which consist of performing in theatre, musicals, and film. About the audition process, let's discuss live dance calls and auditions for theatre and film. I thrive in the audition room. I feel I have a charismatic demeanor about me which I think makes me likeable and memorable. This lasting impression is difficult to leave in a virtual setting where most self-takes are subject to time restraints. This topic will be dealt with in more detail in a later chapter. Touching back on dance calls, the thing I miss the most is seeing familiar faces from previous projects worked on together or reminiscing with classmates from college. The industry is "a small world."

Going to an audition is a stressful experience since actors take their profession seriously and really want to get the parts. There are many applicants and very few roles to go around. Therefore, seeing colleagues and friends who are experiencing the same feelings and challenges is comforting and takes a weight off one's shoulders. When you're auditioning with friends and colleagues you've worked with in the past, there's a mutual love and respect for one another and we are all sincerely rooting for each other. A great example of this is evident when you're in a dance call and you're separated into smaller groups to perform the final routine. This creates an audience of audition applicants. More often than not, there will be a familiar face in that audience whispering words of encouragement, flashing a comforting smile and giving you insight into how you performed. This gives the actor a sense of accomplishment and builds strong confidence as he moves forward into his or her career and into future auditions, regardless of the outcome of the day. Getting words of affirmation from respectable people in the industry like yourself is rewarding and comforting, assuring you that the work you're putting in is paying off.

Comparatively, when turning in auditions virtually, the camaraderie of traditional auditioning and the easing of tension from that format are transformed creating a more cold and confusing experience. Also, the underlying fear of the unknown, whether you've got the role or not, or whether you've impressed or not, is amped up by self-takes since you've got no live audience to give instant feedback regarding how your performance is going. The artist then becomes more self-critical and second guesses his or her take, not knowing whether it should be submitted or not. This virtual process feels like it becomes more about getting the perfect aesthetic take, as opposed to letting the art flow through you naturally. It's important to trust your training, your experiences and to celebrate the fun you have with the process that you embarked on right from the beginning of your performing arts journey. This happens naturally in a live environment, but when delivering art virtually the famous saying, "Dance like no one is watching" takes on a literal meaning and isn't as positive as it suggests. Virtual auditions feel more mechanical than organic. In my opinion, a self-take feels more strenuous than auditioning live. I also feel like the panel expects more of a self-take because you have a chance to film several attempts rather than one. It's more stressful because you're constantly dissecting your product since you know everyone will be doing the same with his or her own submissions. Sometimes how you handle a mistake in a raw audition or how your personality shines through can get you in just as much as nailing the audition itself. Often the spontaneity of an actor is very creative and fed by a live audience that laughs, claps, and otherwise reacts to the artform. With live auditions, the work is fresh and authentic. With virtual auditions, this perk is absent from the process. We are all human as well as the panel and they usually don't expect you to nail the audition perfectly when it's live. On the other hand, a submitted audition could be viewed several times, and perhaps critiqued more closely.

When you're filming scenes for a self-tape audition, you're also facing new challenges and uncharted waters that did not exist prior to the World Pandemic. If you are someone who has roommates, it can be quite challenging to find a chunk a time where it's quiet and you're not feeling like you are inconveniencing the people around you. Having a scene partner in the audition room, who knows the script and knows how to respond to your lines, can be very helpful when staying in character and really diving deeply into the role. I found myself, many times, having trouble staying in character because I've been alone and had no reader. Therefore, I would often set aside a slot of time where an imaginary someone would be speaking or replying to what my line was. Living alone and having no one to read the scene partner's lines is the worst. Fortunately, my roommate's cousin lives in the same building as I do and is willing to help me when I call upon her, but it's just not the same as having a partner in the field. The people doing the asides in the audition room know the script, know the characters and they're there to help you portray your best version of the character that you have taken on. If I were to expect the same outcome from a volunteering friend, I'd have to have that person commit his or her time reading and understanding the character and how that character would respond to mine. It would take a lot of time which isn't fair to my reader and the result wouldn't be as professional regardless of the time spent and genuine commitment, in most cases. All these requirements to make the scene work are like another language to someone who isn't trained in theatre or film.

Not only is it a challenge to be working with non-trained readers, but it's also an obstacle to be acting in an environment which is not conducive to the artform, namely one's personal dwelling. Normally, the panel wants you to succeed which is the biggest secret out there. When you walk through the door, they are hoping that you are the person they are looking for. However, due to COVID-19, panels are seeing more of actors' personal lives than they normally would which, at times, can bring about more judgement. For example, I watched a viral video of a director belittling an actor, because of how his apartment looked while he was auditioning, and I wondered why one's dwelling and financial status would be a factor in getting the role or not. It seems like the regular criteria and standards of the audition went out the window here. In school we were taught about audition tactics and ways to be more noticeable such as dressing according to your character's personality, and financial status. After seeing this prejudiced video, I feel like the key aspects of an audition, focusing on performance, aren't as important as they once were. It is my hope and belief that not all panel members would be so quick to judge based on one's personal environment in this unfair manner. The pandemic has allowed for a more intimate look into actors' lives and dwellings which unfortunately could make them more susceptible to criticism. This is out of their control most of the time and even more so during a Pandemic such as COVID-19 which hit the entertainment industry hard. The world of the Arts was non-existent in live form during the height of COVID-19 and going dry. Ironically, the Arts were one key ingredient that we all needed so much to lift our spirits, feed our souls, and help to make life worthwhile. No stage lights were shining, no music was playing, audience seats were vacant, and costume racks were collecting dust.

If you, the reader, have made it this far and you're still with me, I promise there's some light at the end of the tunnel for every story has a silver lining. In my case, I have been explaining how COVID-19 negatively affected me and my craft, but now I think it's a good idea to explore the upside of this pandemic. Being a Knight at Medieval Times and a consistent show performer daily makes it very hard to have time off to visit with family and friends that live further away. I was born in Timmins, Ontario and my hometown is Iroquois Falls, a small community of approximately 4200 people, situated eight hours North of Toronto. This Northern Ontario community is home to my parents, siblings, and maternal grandparents, not to mention childhood friends, teachers, coaches, etc. The point I'm trying to make here is I rarely get home even once a year. My hectic schedule causes my family to travel to me more than I can travel to them. As wonderful as these visits are, it's not the same as returning to where I grew up, the town where my journey as a performer began, grew, and awarded me with the opportunities I have today. COVID-19 provided me with time and time is precious, and irreplaceable. It's so delicate and no one knows how much of it he or she will have. During the World Pandemic of 2020, I travelled home for some much-needed time with my family.

In March of 2020, around the same time that Medieval Times was on a hiatus due to the early stages of COVID-19 in Ontario, I received upsetting news from back home that my grandmother was diagnosed with an advanced stage of rectal cancer which had travelled to her lungs. We were all upset and unsure of how this journey would transpire. More testing would be needed in order to put a plan into action to provide my grandma with more time and hopefully a cure. This emotional time for the world was also a time of turmoil for my little world. Due to the severity of my grandmother's diagnosis, we didn't know how much time we'd have to support her and help her fight the disease. COVID-19, as terrible as it was and is, did provide me with time to go home and support my family in our difficult journey. I flew home and was greeted by my mother and grandmother's open arms. I was welcomed back to my childhood home which I hadn't entered for a few years. As I crossed the threshold, I was in awe of my family dwelling and mentioned how beautiful it was. It was a sight for sore eyes as they say and being back under one roof with my parents and siblings was priceless. Waking up, after my first night back, felt refreshing and like I had never left. What I assumed was going to be a few weeks grew into months as COVID-19 cases were spreading at an uncontrollable rate. However, at home, I felt safe in more ways than one for I was with my family but also in a small community where no cases had been reported. I was living far from the outbreaks of COVID-19. It was a good thing too because we had more immediate family issues to deal with and more important battles to face, namely my grandmother's disease.

I know, I know...not much of a silver lining yet for my readers, but I'm getting there. I went from a hectic workload to a rollercoaster of emotions with my family life. However, even with my grandmother's illness, good was evident all around as many family suppers were had, bonding was taking place and time as a big brother to my younger two siblings materialized. There's more than a decade of time between me and my siblings and as a result of this, I had very little time to be their big brother under the same roof. COVID-19 provided me with the gift of sibling bonding which would have never been possible in a normal lifetime. That was truly a remarkable gift which strengthened my bond with my kid brother and sister. I was present for both their birthdays which I hadn't been able to attend for the past seven years. Also, I was able to celebrate my birthday, a little early, but at home surrounded by my family who were going through so much.

Being at home allowed me a chance to help out in a great time of need. For example, my grandmother underwent intense radiation for a week and 10 months of chemotherapy. I accompanied her on some of those medical trips, but other times I stayed home and watched over the house and my younger siblings. Another positive experience that came from COVID-19 was the fact that my grandparents decided to sell their starter home, a home that I lived in from the ages of 9-15 and I decided to buy it from them. This strengthened our bond and gave me a business venture as well as a forever home in my hometown. The longer I stayed with my family and experienced the comforts of home and the simplicity of restrictions, compared to Toronto, the more I questioned whether I should stay and pursue a job at home since there were more opportunities at that time due to lower COVID-19 cases. Brief moments of questioning my current life in the city and occupation in the Arts, flooded my mind as I wondered whether my life would ever return to normal. I questioned whether my life would be simpler, happier, and more productive in COVID-19 times, if I stayed home. The loneliness I had felt in the big city was a lot to deal with and the contrast of the warming embrace of family was tempting me to leave my life in Toronto behind. I was feeling somewhat of a lack of motivation connected to my life as a performer since the Arts world was uncertain and seemed to be declining. I wondered if performing would ever open up again and financial concerns went along with these thoughts. There was very little employment in a field I loved so much and one that I put my heart and soul into for so long. At home, there were more job options that were available during COVID-19. As nice as the time was at home, it was also scaring me into exploring other career paths which would take me away from my dream. Choices had to be made "career life" versus "home life." I felt like my life was on pause and this feeling wasn't unique to me alone. The whole world was experiencing uncertainty and questioning everything. The irony here is that there was no stability in acting, but performances and home entertainment was what the world needed to lift spirits, and mentally motivate the populace. The world needs the Arts to embellish the good times and to illuminate the skies and landscape in times of darkness.

During this internal struggle of not knowing whether I should stay home or go back to Toronto, I naturally decided to follow my instincts and return to a career that was and still is such a driving force in my life. I had faith that the situation would improve and that everything I had worked towards would not be in vain. I was Toronto bound with my family's concerned blessings. COVID-19 is what took me out of the city and now I decided to face it head on and take my performing life back. Even though I wasn't returning to work just yet, I was determined to go back to the industry I was born to be a part of. I was aware I wouldn't be able to work just yet, but I was mentally prepared to get a call any day from my manager at Medieval Times. In the meantime, I decided to venture into an atmosphere I had always had a taste for, streaming video games. As a pastime, I play a lot of video games and some of them I can play quite well. I won a few gaming contests as a teenager. Since performing was taken away from me, I decided to venture into an aspect of performance that the world couldn't wipe out.

My bedroom became the stage, and my headset, the microphone to connect with my audience. Lights, Camera, Action. At first, when streaming video games comes to mind, you think you can just turn on your camera and viewers will tune in, watch you play and cheer you on. However, it's actually way more complex than that; you have to decide which games you will play knowing that your choices will affect your fans. You should pick peak times that people will tune in the most. You must consider scheduling, the content, your wardrobe and what the audience is seeing and hearing. You must build a following; you have to be entertaining and charismatic. It's an Artform. We're coming on to April and I've been streaming for about three months. I was making some money from it which encouraged me to keep going and then it happened; I got the call. We're back baby, back in the saddle. We weren't doing shows yet, but I was working in the job that I loved, going through the necessary steps to bring the castle back to its original glory. It was wonderful and yet challenging to return to work. It felt like a bootcamp. I hadn't been as active as I once was, for over a year. Riding horses, going back to the gym, and running circuits in the sand overwhelmed my body. About two weeks in, I started experiencing severe spinal pain when riding, to the point where I had to dismount immediately. This was a scary moment, for my mind started to wander and wonder about my future as a Knight. I promptly went to see a doctor to be assessed and to hear what my options were. There were differing views about the severity of my situation which caused me to be concerned. One chiropractor suggested an x-ray, due to his professional opinion that I could be suffering from early onset Scoliosis. This was alarming to me and would not only affect my regular life, but the riding in my professional career. I went to get an x-ray and due to COVID-19 restrictions, this experience was a lengthy and complicated process. What would normally have taken 1-2 hours took me a whole day. I got the results back and my spine was perfectly normal. The pain I was feeling was chalked up to a pinched nerve which healed after medication, rest, and light duties for a week or so. After time passed, I started getting used to Knighting again and began to see the fruits of my labour. I noticed improvement in my stamina and observed the betterment of my physical appearance. I can now fully appreciate the challenges that actors go through when gaining and losing weight for certain performances and when they suffer and heal from injuries.

Fast forward to July of 2021. We are hitting stage three in Ontario, and we have been given the green light to do shows again. This time, it's different. We have masks and certain parts of the show are altered to accommodate COVID-19 Protocols. Let me tell you firsthand that knighting with a mask on the entire performance sucks, but the show must go on and we at Medieval Times Dinner and Tournament are committed to bringing our guests back to a safe, and fun environment. **The light flickers no more** as I ride out with the spotlights on and burning hot. The crowds were roaring as usual, like music to an actor's ears. I was pleasantly surprised because I didn't know what to expect with COVID-19 being a fear in the back of people's minds for the past two years. Hearing their laughter and chanting was so welcoming and made it feel like COVID-19 was no more. Familiar sounds of lances breaking and swords clashing filled the arena. Aesthetic visuals return with hair flying, sparks glowing, and vivid colours filling the arena. Being a Knight again was exhilarating and nostalgic, a rush for which I had been longing. Being back in the show allows me to continue to live out my childhood dream to be a Knight. Working in the field of my choice enables me to inspire young and old. The younger generation dreams of becoming the powerful Queen or the strong Knight. The older generation watches in awe as they remember more limber days. I also hope to encourage budding actors to become performers and to pursue their dreams despite the extra challenges brought to the industry by COVID-19.

In retrospect, COVID-19 has restricted our art and taken away the means of expressing it. We are destined to create, perform, and enjoy the arts so I tell you, if you are an actor and your light is flickering, replace the bulb because we need you out there. Be a bright, resilient star in the darkness. COVID-19 has taken away a lot of things, but in my personal experience, it has also provided me with time to heal physically, moments to bond with family emotionally and time to reflect on my life mentally. This brings me to a strong quotation from the Bible, as God's word has helped millions through this pandemic. I hope by sharing it with you now, you can draw parallels and find peace within the pages of the text:

A Time for Everything
3 There is a time for everything, and a season for every activity under the heavens:
² a time to be born and a time to die,
a time to plant and a time to uproot,
³ a time to kill and a time to heal,
a time to tear down and a time to build,
⁴ a time to weep and a time to laugh,
a time to mourn and a time to dance,
⁵ a time to scatter stones and a time to gather them,
a time to embrace and a time to refrain from embracing,
⁶ a time to search and a time to give up,
a time to keep and a time to throw away,
⁷ a time to tear and a time to mend,
a time to be silent and a time to speak,
⁸ a time to love and a time to hate,
a time for war and a time for peace.

Ecclesiastes 3: 1-8

At this time, I want to thank the readers for investing in our stories. A special thank you to Emerson Arts for giving me the opportunity to share my story and a final thanks to my mom and grandma for helping me through this writing process. Here's to a new chapter of the Arts where we rebuild, grow and come out swinging harder than ever before. Get ready because we're coming back to a theatre, stage, or arena near you.
Mic. drop.
    (Tré walks away.)
Backstage Crew: Tré, you left the stage lights on.
Tré: They stay on.

fin

Tre says he was in his peak physical condition just as the pandemic hit. What has your daily exercise routine changed during COVID-19?

SPENCER, DARLENE

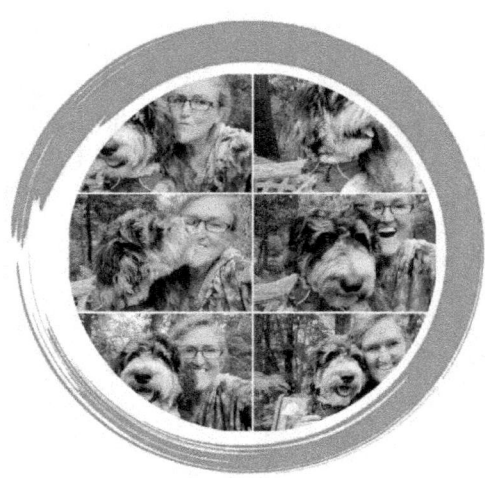

Darlene Spencer, M.F.A. (she/her) is a Canadian born actor, director, and educator. She adores storytelling and all aspects of making theatre. She has jumped, back and forth, from one side of the table to the other over the past 35 years. She has learned so much, from so many, during her times as a teaching artist at the University of Waterloo, Wilfred Laurier University, York University, and the Randolph College for the Performing Arts (former Artistic Director). Currently, she lives amidst the cicadas, on the Stillwater River in Ohio, with her remarkable partner Michael, four cats (Rrrnold, RuPaul, Nina, and Django), and an aussiedoodle puppy (Harley, as in Davidson).

REMEMBERING
(a mnemonic acronym for these apocalyptic times)

Paranoia. Prayers for protection keep me up at night.

Alarm. Theatres go dark. Recording studios close. Film sets shut down.

Numbness. My "neighbors" fight for their right to NOT wear masks. I am enraged. I won't let myself feel the magnitude of this insane choice, a choice which affects (and may well infect) us all, because I will surely implode.

Despair. I can't possibly celebrate the long-awaited green card which I receive in the mail. I hold my breath for the upcoming election. I haven't a vote.

Engage. Find online Equity workshops, CAEA and AEA. Stream the theatre festival offerings. Binge watch every series of interest. Tune in for the "lives". Zoom with the kids, my as-yet-unmet grandson, my siblings, my bff from high school, my gang from the university drama department, my forever ago friends from kids camp. Attempt to Zoom with my octogenarian parents who can't figure out how to unmute, so we laugh and mime hand hearts and arm-wrapping air hugs. Don't learn to bake sourdough bread but eat all of my guy's attempts during his weekly trials until he succeeds and moves on to chocolate babka.

Mourn. The loss of life after life. After life. After life. Obsessively check the news graphs which calculate the number of new C19 cases in our township, our county, our state, our country, our continent, your city, your province, your country, your continent. Astounding numbers. Not numbers, souls. Lost souls. I can't bear it. I cancel our cable. My feeble attempt to shut out the devastating reality.

I stare into the brown-with-a-patch-of-white-walker-blue eyes of our now fully grown puppy and make quiet apologies: for his third puppy class being cancelled, for my bumbling attempts at YouTube learned training prompts -- through a mask -- on our outdoor walks, for his need to bark at other dogs because he just wants to play and for being that owner who respectfully insists we stay 6 feet away, for making him "sit/stay" for copious numbers of photos in an attempt to satisfy my crushed creative spirit, for crate training every afternoon in preparation for that day (which may never come) when I go back to work, for the closed Canada/U.S. border keeping him from being reunited with his birth pack and me from mine, for the poop that gets caught in his paw because it was not picked up by idiot dog owners who don't care a crap about community, for my craziness in making an Instagram account in his name @WhereIsHarleyTheAussiePoo, even thought I know exactly where he is -- in quarantine -- in the middle of a stay-at-home order and there is nowhere "away" to go, for the extra pounds we both gain because treats make the pain go away, for checking and rechecking for fleas and ticks and poisonings and chills and coughs and fever because we really aren't sure if dogs can catch or carry the virus and NOBODY is gonna die on my watch, for confiding things to him (which no dog should have to know) in non-stop babble (which no dog should have to listen to), for yelling at him when his bark startles the black teens because I'm afraid they will think that I taught him their lives don't matter, for being afraid of the vandals who douse a local Vietnamese-Thai restaurant in gasoline and racist graffiti, for a culture that bold face lies about EQUITY and buries all EVIDENCE when inequitable EXPERIENCES come to light, for making home in a place where the voting majority believes that a selfish-fearful-vainglorious person will lead a country to greatness by making money matter more than lives and who vomits hate and violence and riot-inducing vitriol ON-THE-DAILY, for being born in a country that stole children from the families of its first peoples -- in the name of GOD -- abused and then discarded them in unmarked mass graves, for not knowing what to say, to think, to feel. Except grief. Profound grief. I apologize to my puppy for holding him too tight and for crying when we cuddle because even though he is right here, I have separation anxiety, because he and my guy and the cats are my only family nearby. I apologize for the times I've been casual with my power – made ignorance my excuse – taken privilege for granted – been overwhelmed and under-involved because... because...because...GOD-grant-me-the-serenity-to-accept-the-things-I-cannot-change-the-courage-to-

Change. The things I can. I can't. I'm so tired. I don't have the energy. The endurance. The know how. The. The. The. Then ... though I can't explain how, and I believe not by coincidence, I am guided to:
- *We: A Manifesto for Women Everywhere* (book by Gillian Anderson and Jennifer Nadal)
- *The Body Keeps the Score: Brain, Mind, and Body in the Healing of Trauma* (book by Bessel van der Kolk)
- *White Fragility: Why It's So Hard For White People To Talk About Racism* (book by Robin DiAngelo)
- *The Book of Joy* (book by 14th Dalai Lama, Desmond Tutu, and Douglas Carlton Abrams)
- *It's OK* (song by Nightbirde)

And I am gifted grace and forgiveness and healing and hope. And serenity, by moments, to face an uncertain future.

AN ADDENDUM
(because, the delta variant)

God grant me the wisdom.

Still a ways away. I am a slow study, a late bloomer, an experiential learner. So... I wash one dirty dish. Take a hot shower. Do a load of laundry. Write one sentence. Make sweet potato and black bean chili. Self tape an audition. Go for a wade in the Stillwater River. Play a game of Letterpress. Make an amend. Take Harley on a hike. Look down at my feet. Breathe into the soles. Feel my connection to the earth. Right here. Right now. Exactly as I am meant to be. Grateful.

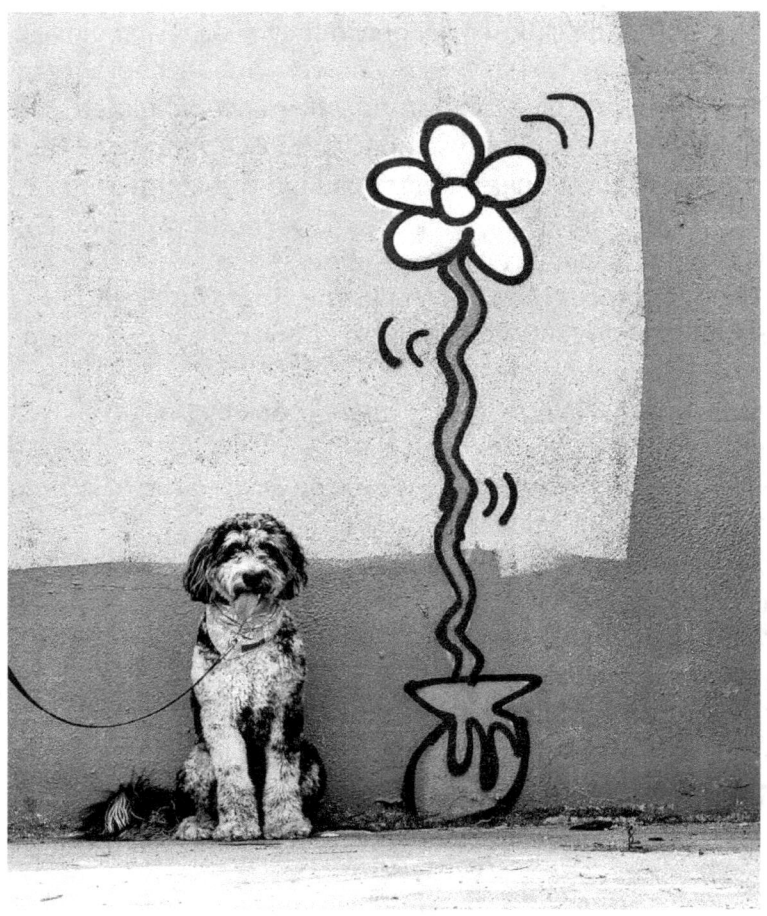

Darlene became obsessed with daily COVID-19 numbers during the early days of the pandemic. When things were at their worst, how did you manage the emotional roller coaster of loss and lockdown?

WILSON, TOM

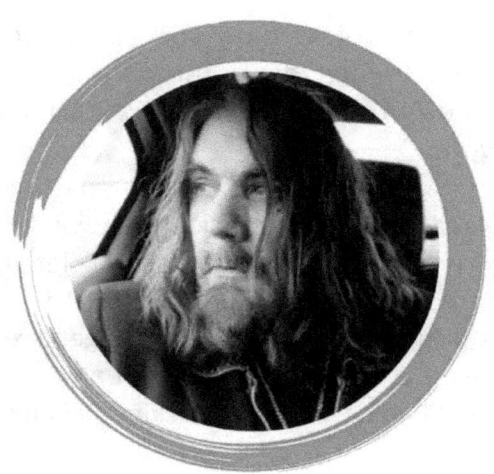

Tom Wilson (Junkhouse, Lee Harvey Osmond, Blackie and the Rodeo Kings) is a veteran of the Canadian music scene with years of experience in several different genres of music. His first performing group The Florida Razors was a popular band in Hamilton, ON, producing Beat Music, his first full length album. In 1989 Tom became the founder of Junkhouse. Most recently, Tom and June Award winning iskwē released their new single "Blue Moon Drive" featuring trumpeter Chuck Copenace with Red Music Rising in what has been called collaboration, community, artistic eminence, and Indigenous excellence.

Portrait of an Artist as an Old Dog by Tom Wilson Tehohah'ake

From time to time, I get asked to travel around lecturing at universities and colleges about writing, art and creating. As I ramble on and on in these lecture halls and classrooms, I consider my good fortune from a lifetime of hard work. Yes, that sounds boring or maybe I sound like some old - er man, which I am, but hard work is all I've got.

Most of the time that answer, 'hard work', is not what people expect to hear me say when they ask stupid questions like, 'So Tom...How did you write your first book'? Well, I tell them... 'It was just hard work.'

They freeze because they don't consider that what we [as artists] do, what we are trying to do as artists as work, let alone hard work, but that's really what it comes down to. To sit down and write, to block out the noise of the world, to get a few words arranged in a way that may engage a reader and inspire a fresh idea in someone...Yeah... that's hard fuckin' work my friend...

Hard work separates the pros from the amateurs, and it gets the job done most of the time. The rest of the time we are conjuring spirits, cleaning up puke from the yellow brick road and hammering nails into crosses trying to find our way to injecting some poetry into our work...

I've somehow managed to get myself into the rare and delicate position of being able to do whatever I want to do, whenever I want to do it... creatively that is. It's been a long haul that has come with plenty of trips from the middle of the road (where no artist should ever be) straight into the ditch. The ditch is where you may end up if you take your hands off the wheel, stop paying attention or forget your destination. The ditch is where you go when you've lost focus on your artistic goal.

I've learned what I've learned the hard way and I hopefully still have a long way to go...Even the ditch has served me well because as I lay there in the dirt, filled with hopelessness, staring up at the night sky with the traffic whizzing by me, I managed to get inspired from a perspective that I may not have gotten from the safety of the road.

I'm not saying you must crash and burn and go to rehab to be enlightened. I'm just saying that as much as those experiences hurt me deeply, I still managed to keep humming away at the next song I was wanted to write. The desire to create never died. In fact, it may have changed my direction and gotten stronger. The desire beat the odds and kept me going. I got inspired enough to pull myself out of the shit and aim my crosshairs at greater goals. Creative goals. Goals that came into focus from the desperation that comes with personal failure.

COVID-19 has been our collective ditch. COVID-19 has been the line drawn, where the world lost control and created the opportunity for artists to flourish. When the world slows down, when nights are still and the buzz in the air dies down, we take off.

As the world shut down and business opportunities died down, tours got moved into an unknown future. I woke up and set a schedule that would take on some new creative possibilities. My mornings were and are spent writing a second book for my publishers at Double Day. Then, I'm writing songs for several projects including Blackie and the Rodeo Kings, Serena Ryder, iskw'e, as well as soundtrack for a play I wrote and a film documentary, both due out next year. The song writing, or co-writing at least, had to be done via Zoom and by sharing files of developing ideas.

It was different, and horrible at times, but it all came down to content and creation and I found that as artists, we adapted probably better than the general public because as artists, we make it up as we go along. Here we we're finding ourselves in a situation where our fundamental skills were put to good use. I sat and did the work and although the book is not completed, I found that it was easier to focus on my creative work with the noise of the world turned way down.

My afternoons were spent in my art studio which is housed in an ancient factory called the Cotton Factory. When the sky clouds over and turns the old bricks of the building grey, the Cotton Factory could become a set from 'Peaky Blinders'. In fact, the site is used as a backdrop for film and TV. I settle into my studio to continue developing an exhibit on residential schools and to work on consignments that have come in regularly as COVID-19 marched on.

I'm lucky enough to have been able to work for people who needed art because instead of hopping on planes and taking vacations they decided they needed to fill that space above the fireplace or perhaps they needed some colour added to their home renovation. It was like shooting fish in a barrel and as a result I found that I could have survived the year and a half just from my art revenue.

But... I'm lucky. I know it. I've cut my path and I'll live or die from my decisions. For this period of time, I was able to live. But this isn't about money or success. It's about the art. It's about what drives us despite what is going on around us. We have worked outside of the lines and rules of what is considered sensible society, only to find ourselves living healthy creative lives. We, the artists, have become the cockroaches of the pandemic, surviving on own terms.

We have a responsibility to ourselves and everyone around us who will pay attention to our work that there is an alternative to the world that is breaking down our front doors and bombarding us every day. A world that is trying to crush us with power and ego and control.

We as artists can prove that we can live outside of the realm of those churches that killed children, governments that divided us and corporations that lure us and control us with shiny shit that has no lasting value. You may think I'm over-stepping my position as an artist here. I'm not and I'm not a conspiracy guy by any means. I'm someone that is just trying to create a balance of colour and words and sensibility for the planet. I hope you're doing the same.

I start my lectures by telling people that "if you don't have to do this .... Don't!...
I mean it. If you don't wake up with a burning desire to create something that didn't exist yesterday, then just don't bother because what you're doing is indulging yourself in an exercise with results being sub power.

So...give'er.

Tom is living a successful artistic career despite the pandemic and attributes his success to the simple concept of hard work. Do you believe success is based off of talent or hard work?

WINCZA, VITEK

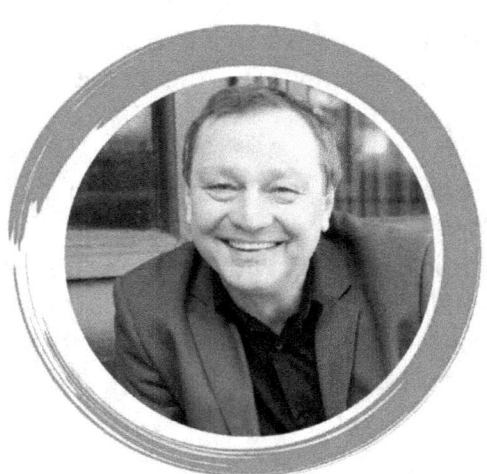

Vitek Wincza graduated as a professional dancer from the State Ballet School in Gdansk, Poland. He has performed for the Musical Theatre of Gdynia, Poland; The Grand Opera; the Ballet Theatre of Lodz, Poland; and the National Dance Company "Mazowsze" where he toured throughout North America. After several successful performances in Hamilton Place, he decided to stay permanently in Canada. In 1982, after his defection, he ran and operated his own dance school in Burlington and Hamilton area.

In 2001, he founded the HCA Dance Theatre, a non-profit organization which is dedicated to professional artists and the creation of new innovative works in dance, music, drama, and visual arts. Performances include Robert Desrosiers' original choreographed "Circus Dream", as well as "An Evening with Michael Ondaatje" featuring the work of Oscar-nominated Canadian writer Michael Ondaatje ("The English Patient"). Wincza's realization of Ondaatje's prose was interpreted by dancers and musicians in a truly unique and unforgettable multi-disciplinary performance.

He was honoured with an award from Hamilton's Vision 2020 (1998);

Honours from Moscow's Diagliev Foundation (2003); City of Hamilton Dance award (2004); and the WNED Canadian Artist Award (Buffalo, NY, 2004).

In 2009 his critically acclaimed production of "Displacement" featuring Christos Hatzig and Robert Glumbek was honoured as one of the top ten dance performances in Ontario.

Mr. Wincza was the recipient of the City of Hamilton Community Arts Award in 2011 and was nominated as RBC Citizen of the Year for Hamilton in 2013.

-with Allison Warwick

In early March 2020, I pulled my staff into the office to discuss the growing threat of COVID-19, and how it might impact us. One of my daily rituals is tuning into the local evening news, and I was alarmed to hear of the rising cases of this highly contagious illness hitting Canadian lands. There were rumours of Ontario school boards extending March Break, murmurs of a complete shutdown in our province. After almost twenty-five years as the Artistic Director of Hamilton Conservatory for the Arts and its two charitable organizations, I had never faced something like the COVID-19 pandemic. Navigating it would prove new territory, uncharted waters. Later that month, our building - whose historic hallways are usually enlivened with the hustle and bustle of students of all ages rushing to classes in visual arts, dance, theatre, and music - shut down. I didn't know if we would be back in a few weeks or a few months, or what the world would look like a year into the future. But this wasn't the first time that I faced uncertain circumstances in my life. My past flooded back to me, along with the sense of resiliency and perseverance that I had built up and sported over the years like plate armour. *'We can survive this as a community,'* my instincts told me, *'We can emerge better and stronger.'* Throughout my life, I have learned to cope by embracing the unknown, rather than fearing it. I thought back to almost 40 years earlier when I faced one of my biggest challenges.

Easter Sunday, 1982. The streets of downtown Hamilton were deserted. With only $2.50 in my pocket, I stood at Stelco Tower on King Street West, awaiting an immigration officer after exiting the stage doors of Hamilton Place following a performance with Poland's national dance company, Mazowsze. After our final show ended, eleven of us from the ensemble had chosen to defect from our communist home country. I was filled with uncertainty, my thoughts churning like the waters in the Hamilton Bay on a blustery day. *'If I return to Poland, I will go to jail,'* I thought. My mother would be investigated back home by government officials and I didn't know when I would see her again. I didn't speak English. I had no friends or family in this country. As an artist from a distant place, I had no money or way to make a living in Canada. I could end up on the streets of a country that was foreign to me, tossed back into the sea of poverty that I was trying to escape. I had no choice but to trust my instinct that even though I had no idea what would happen in the future, I would be alright. I would find my way. I would not waiver from my mission of being an artist. I had to leap into the unknown. Like a fish in the sea, I had to keep moving despite choppy waters. I would continue swimming against the tide and survive.

The poor have to overcome obstacles and fight for their continued existence, visibility, and survival each day. I was born in Gdynia on the Baltic coastline of Poland, behind the Iron Curtain. My father left my family when I was seven years old, and I was forced to grow up quickly, helping my mother - who worked three jobs to keep us afloat - and taking care of my younger brother. I never stopped dreaming of a better life for my family. When I was nine years old, my neighbor brought over a newspaper advertisement announcing auditions for the State Ballet School in Gdansk, with a photo featuring a young boy flying through the air in mid-jump. I longed to be that child, to experience that weightlessness and joy. I had never gone to the theatre. I didn't know what an audition was before that moment. But I tried out for the school and was one of fifty boys out of hundreds to make the cut. It was a turning point, a door swinging open to my future. I was provided room and board and was also given a stipend due to my poor economic circumstances. At ballet school, I could alleviate my mother of the financial pressure to support one of her children. After three years at the school, I finally began to learn how to perform a *Grand Jeté*. I was taught to leap like the little boy in that newspaper ad. I felt like I was no longer bound by gravity. When I was up in the air, I felt free. Leaping gave me a new perspective. I knew that dance would help make my dreams come true; I could leap out of poverty and hopelessness and into a better life.

After completing my formal ballet training and as one of only a handful of people to graduate, I danced in different professional companies and was eventually accepted to Mazowske, the country's national dance company. It was my ticket to leave the country, to see the world. At that time, Poland was under Martial Law and the average citizen was not granted the right to freedom of movement. Tanks and soldiers with guns flooded the streets. I didn't know what would happen next and felt uncertain about my future in Poland. The ensemble members of Mazowske were given special permission to leave the country and embark on a performance tour across North America. There were tanks surrounding the Warsaw airfield, and we boarded a plane that would take us to Switzerland - a free zone from which to fly to North America - and then to NYC for our first tour stop. As the plane lifted and I peered out the window, I felt that same sense of freedom and weightlessness that I experienced when I saw that boy leaping in the newspaper ad and after I learned to *Grand Jeté* myself. I could leave my old life behind. The tour took us to many places, but Hamilton - the only Canadian city we visited - would be the most fateful stop, the one that would change the entire direction of my life. Eleven of us from the company decided that we would not be returning to Poland, to our old lives that offered no sense of possibility or freedom. We would walk out those Hamilton Place stage doors, leave the tour and everything we knew, and remain in Canada.

Life was not easy for me after defection. The first years as an immigrant artist were very tough. I vowed to continue my work as an artist in Canada, no matter how difficult that path would be or how much sleep I had to sacrifice for my dreams. Despite the obstacles I faced and the overwhelming feeling that the odds were against my success, I felt propelled forward. In 1997, I learned about the existence of 126 James Street South in downtown Hamilton. It was a three-story building with a storied history as the Hamilton Conservatory of Music, which opened in 1897, but had stood derelict and neglected since its closure in 1980. As I stepped through its doors, I saw possibilities past the cobwebs, fire damage, and dust. Coming from a poor background, I developed the capacity to dream and see challenges as opportunities. This would be a school for fellow dreamers - those who wanted to follow their passions and learn dance, music, theatre, and visual arts. During the day, my friends and I worked on restoring the building, little by little, room by room. Since I couldn't afford rent for an apartment, I slept on the building's third floor at night. Exactly one hundred years after the Hamilton Conservatory of Music opened, the building was reborn as the Hamilton Conservatory for the Arts. The school eventually grew to welcome hundreds of students each year, with a full concert series and the establishment of two charitable organizations, employing over seventy artist-educators in our city.

Everything came to a halt in March 2020. In the arts world, none of us could have imagined or prepared for a scenario like the COVID-19 pandemic. The beautiful part of live arts classes and performance is the ability to create together, learn together, share special moments together in the same space. Suddenly and unexpectedly, that physical togetherness had the potential to spread a terrible new illness. COVID-19 threatened to separate us all. Hamilton Conservatory for the Arts and its two charities are built upon fostering community connections. We consider our students part of our family, with hundreds of people of all ages and cultural backgrounds coming together to take arts classes. Our charitable organization HCA Dance Theatre aims to bring the community together and make the art of dance visible, accessible, and inclusive for all. Our other non-profit Culture for Kids in the Arts (now Arts for All) provides low-barrier accessible arts, delivering no-cost arts programming to over 60,000 since its inception in more than twenty neighborhoods in the greater Hamilton area. How would we sustain our connections? What would the future look like? How could we continue our community-building while a devastating communicable disease tore through it? I had so many questions and no answers, but propelling forward in the face of adversity is second nature to me - from the days that my father left, and I became the man in the house at seven years old to the moment that I decided to defect from my home country with nothing to my name. Everything I faced in the past prepared me for the unknown future presented by the pandemic. I had no choice but to leap with the faith that we could not only survive the struggle but thrive. As a leader, even if I was uncertain, it was important to remain calm. I vowed to motivate others by maintaining a sense of optimism and enthusiasm despite any setbacks and tribulations. I envisioned success and saw challenges as opportunities - dreaming of a better future is the only way I've been able to move through hardship in my life.

Right before the pandemic hit, our non-profit Culture for Kids in the Arts (CKA) successfully applied for a grant from the Ontario Trillium Foundation to transform our old Recital Hall into a state-of-the-art black box theatre. I envisioned a dedicated performance space for the local community that would present ambitious high-quality arts presentations and workshops in music, theatre, and dance. During our shutdown, working within the boundaries of restrictions during the pandemic, we actually had the time to almost complete renovations. We were able to plan for a rebranding and revisioning of CKA after twenty years; it was something that we wanted to do but never had the time to accomplish, and the pandemic provided a chance to complete this work. I witnessed the negative mental effects of the pandemic on our community - young children separated from their friends, parents struggling to keep their kids engaged with online learning, many losing their livelihoods or dealing with sick family members, front-line and essential workers putting themselves in danger on a daily basis and experiencing severe burnout. While Hamilton Conservatory for the Arts paused our normal programming in Spring 2020, we created a Pay-What-You-Can model of online classes. Despite my initial fears of our community being separated, we were still able to bring people together through the arts and allow our students to maintain and build connections throughout the pandemic's initial shutdown. CKA contributed our programming to essential worker families with free arts programming through our childcare partners. We were determined to contribute to the well-being of our community, in whatever form we could. When I learned to leap as a boy in ballet school, I experienced pure freedom. I knew that during the pandemic, we could provide the same sense of freedom to others through our arts programming. The arts enrich our lives and give us a sense of purpose and meaning. Despite all odds, our arts organizations persevered and provided community to those who needed it most. With so many artists struggling with their livelihoods taken away by the pandemic, I also wanted to ensure that we provided them with resources for the future - prepping our facilities to engage artists that lost so many opportunities to perform and create during the pandemic. Our Black Box Theatre is primed to become a new venue to share with the artists in our community - an incubator for creation.

While no one truly knows how long COVID-19 will continue to

impact our community, as an arts leader and creator, I carry with me so many plans and aspirations for the future. I've always been a dreamer - and like Don Quixote in *Man of the La Mancha*, I often follow what others see as 'The Impossible Dream.' But from my poverty-stricken boyhood in Poland and my determination to live a better life in Canada to navigating the arts world during COVID-19, I have never stopped moving forward - despite setbacks, challenges, and fears. This sense of strength and resiliency, cultivated through my background and life experiences, has allowed me to accomplish so much during the pandemic. I encourage artists everywhere to keep dreaming and refuse to give up hope. This pandemic is just one chapter in a story that's still being written, and I can't wait to discover what happens next.

Viteck built an artistic empire fuelled by his complete dedication to bringing quality artistic experiences and programs to our community. His devotion to foundational instruction for longevity of the arts is the basis for the Hamilton Conservatory for the Arts. Do you share in his certainty and optimism for the future?

WYDER, HOLLY

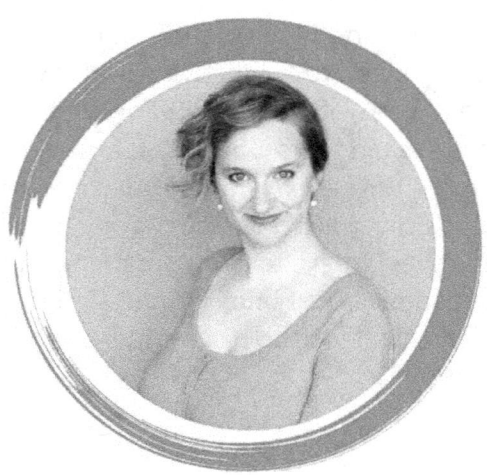

After living and working in Toronto for the last 10 years, Holly Wyder has dipped her toe into a variety of artistic cesspools. Beginning with her diploma in Musical Theatre - transitioning into live improv/sketch comedy and eventually falling in love with writing she has developed a multitude of work that she is very proud of. Her main goal as a creative being is to use her art to allow our society to understand romantic vs sexual attraction in its entirety. As an asexual (a term which many reading this are lifting their eyebrows at still), Holly has used her own personal experience to create a web series (Female Therapy, YouTube), perform an award-winning solo show (Drink of Choice, Toronto Fringe 2019 and Factory Theatre), and is currently working on transitioning the entirety of her art into a comedic, half-hour, television series (Aced It, TBD).

"If you get tired, learn to rest, not to quit" - Banksy

~~THIS WAS GOING TO BE~~

~~MY YEAR'S WORK~~

~~BUT INSTEAD IT'S JUST~~

AN UNTITLED SCREENPLAY

Written by

HOLLY WYDER

did I?

Based on ~~surviving~~ 2020

Address: anywhere the wind blows
Phone Number: nothing really matters

Emerson Arts   The Stage Light Flickers   Pandamonium Publishing

INT. HOOLS APARTMENT - BEDROOM - DAY

Sun peeks out below unevenly cut blackout curtains into a Toronto-size tiny bedroom, fitting hardly more than a double bed and a side table, with very little decoration on the walls aside from a whiteboard that reads 'today is another day'

[handwritten: The]
[handwritten: says that I'm poor? Or lazy?]
[handwritten: foreshadow?]

An ALARM blares as a human size lump in the centre of the bed begins to shift, a GROAN from underneath it.

            HOOLS (O.C.)
      Stop.

The alarm stops. LOLA PEANUTBUTTER, a tortoiseshell round cat, jumps on top of the bed and crawls awkwardly on the lump. The top of the comforter gets thrown to reveal HOOLS, a long-nosed, mousy blonde haired, female appearing, adult with an undercut and a top knot glares at Lola, who blinks.

            HOOLS (CONT'D)
      Hey Google, good morning.

            GOOGLE (V.O.)
      Good afternoon.

The overhead lights spark on from the prompt.

            GOOGLE (V.O.)
      The time is 12:30pm, in Toronto it
      is 22 degrees, with a high of 26
      and a low of 15. Have a good one.
      Today's news.

[handwritten: this could be written more accurately]

            NEWSMAN (V.O.)
      Good day, it is still a pandemic.

The covers are thrown back over Hools head.

INT. HOOLS APARTMENT - KITCHEN - DAY

Hools drags herself through her bedroom door into the kitchen.

CHIK-CHIK-CHIK, the sound of turning on a gas stove to heat the hot water for the kettle.

BRRRRK, freshly ground coffee beans.

Hools pours the hot water over the filter full of grinds.

Holding a cup of coffee with the words 'YOU ARE FUCKING AWESOME', Hools opens the fridge door.

She pulls out a large tub of lime yogurt, sniffs it, then dunks a spoon into the whole thing.

INT. HOOLS APARTMENT - LIVING ROOM - CONTINUOUS

Hools walks into her living room area carrying both the coffee and the tub of yogurt. It's a tight space with very limited furniture. Lola follows behind.

[margin note: will I ever get to a point in life I live by expiry dates?]

Hools plops herself down onto the couch, slightly spilling her coffee.

              HOOLS
  FUCK ME.

Lola hops onto the coffee table and stares at Hools' misfortune.

            HOOLS (CONT'D)
  Thanks for the help.

Clearly not much of a big deal, Hools licks any of the drips off her hand and finds a kleenex to dab the drops on her oversized sleep shirt, not doing much of anything.

While absentmindedly shoving yogurt into her mouth she scrolls through Instagram, double tapping photos she has hardly glanced at. It all begins to blur together the faster she scrolls, happy faces of people posting just for the likes. [margin note: everyone is fake!]

[margin note: Bo Burnham joke, not out in 2020, I'm stealing content]

She opens up the 'stories' tab and snaps a quick photo of her smiling with her coffee, adding the caption 'go to pour my coffee, missed my mouth, OMG that is just my luck'. She smiles at her own cleverness of faking a hilarious online persona.

Hools moves over to her tiny corner desk, on it sits a laptop. She turns it on. After inputting the password the opening page appears as a blank word document, the cursor blinking at her. After a bit too long for comfort she opens up a web browser to the news. All headlines are focused on the pandemic "Stay inside, stay alive", "Stay at home order in effect" "Trudeau promises to keep citizens afloat with CERB".

Hools spins on her chair and grabs a notebook sitting on the coffee table. She cracks open the cover, it's blank. She grabs her pen and writes "May 27th, 2020, just another day scrolling the pages of the internet when--'

[margin note: BZZT → Consistency]

Her phone buzzes. A text comes up from 'BOYFRIEND <3'

                    BOYFRIEND (TEXT)   → remains nameless
               Morning my love.

Hools puts down the notebook and pen, she picks up her phone
and smiles. She responds.

                    HOOLS (TEXT)
               I'm going to get some writing done
               today!

                    BOYFRIEND (TEXT)
               You got this boo! Xo.
                        → I hate that pet name
Putting the phone down she turns back to her laptop, already
forgetting her notebook, and exits out of the news browser.
The blinking cursor returns, blinking harsher somehow. Hools
taps the keys with her fingertips, not pressing hard enough
for words to appear.

Instead she opens a new internet browser to facebook. Videos
of facebook friends appear, doing cool things while in   Is this too
lockdown. Silly home cooking shows, streaming video games,   niche for
dying hair blue. She stops at a 'sketch comedy' video,   the general
glaring at the likes and comments with envy. She throws a   public to
like on the video and then exits the page.   understand?

Slowly she spins her desk chair around until she's facing a
camera on a tripod collecting dust in the corner. How long
has it been since she's even tried to make something. She
stands and moves over to it. As she moves the tripod, a plume
of dust injects into her nostrils causing her to sneeze.

                                                    CUT TO:

INT. HOOLS APARTMENT - LIVING ROOM - LATER
                          → pandemic joke maybe?
Now sporting a paper mask and rubber gloves, Hools sprays
down any surface she can see, then pounces with her cloth to
wipe it down.

                    HOOLS
               Hools: 1, dust bunnies: negative
               25!

Lola struts by.

                    HOOLS (CONT'D)
               You know most of this is your own
               dead saliva covered hair's fault.
               You're lucky I love you.

4.

Hools grabs Lola into a hug aggressively, a sight to behold as Lola squirms in the rubber gloves, not too happy about the debacle. Hools catches a glimpse of the charade in a wall mirror, then notices her hair length. *then Hools*

She puts Lola down, who jolts out of the room, ~~and~~ walks closer to the mirror. She pulls at the ends of her undercut, seemingly too long for liking then exits the room.

Her reflection still there, lifts up the notebook from thin air and tosses it into the abyss.

INT. HOOLS APARTMENT - BATHROOM - DAY *→ is this location necessary, could be done in bedroom to cut back on locations if filming*

Hools has an electric razor to her head as her muddy blonde hair falls around her. Lola walks into the bathroom and starts to lick the hair off the floor. Hools takes notice.

                    HOOLS
          Oh my god, stop! You weirdo.

BZZT!
While distracted Hools shaves a little too much off the left side of her scalp. She looks at it in the mirror and decides to match it on the other side.

INT. HOOLS APARTMENT - LIVING ROOM - DAY
How many times can one person flop?
Hools flops down onto the couch. Lola hops up onto her lap and lies down. Defeated and tired Hools decides to grab the TV remote and turns on some random Netflix show.

                              ↳ Ⓒ   CUT TO:

INT. HOOLS APARTMENT - LIVING ROOM - NIGHT

A few hours later Netflix asks 'continue watching?', at which point Hools notices the dark outside, her entire day has been eaten up, and therefore no writing will be done. *→ mental state, not reality*

She clicks 'yes' on the tv. The show continues to play.

BZZT!
Her phone chimes and she looks at it.

                    BOYFRIEND (TEXT)
          I hope you had a wonderful day! Xo

                    HOOLS (TEXT)
          Yeah, got some things done, off to
          bed now. Night.

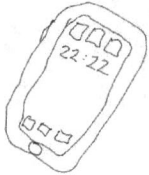

She puts her phone down, but stays immobile on the couch.

                                               FADE OUT.

INT. HOOLS APARTMENT - BEDROOM - A NEW DAY

A lump under a comforter moves just as an alarm goes off.

                    HOOLS (O.C.)
               Stop.

[write a better action]

The alarm stops. Hools appears from under the comforter, her hair that was buzzed, now seemingly returned. Lola jumps on top of her and licks Hools' nose.

                    HOOLS (CONT'D)
               Hey Google! Good morning!

                    GOOGLE (V.O.)
               Good Afternoon.

The main lights on the ceiling spring on.

                    GOOGLE (V.O.)
               The time is 12:30pm, in Toronto it
               is 22 degrees, with a high of 26
               and a low of 15. Have a good one.
               Today's news.

                    NEWMAN (V.O.)
               Hello Toronto, we are still in a
               pandemic.

Is it a new day? Or is it just repeating itself? [why bother commenting]

INT. HOOLS APARTMENT - KITCHEN [DAY? NIGHT? WHO EVEN CARES]

Hools repeats the movements to making her coffee and grabbing her yogurt. This time she smells it and decides to toss it out. Her fridge now completely empty. Shutting the fridge door--

INT. HOOLS APARTMENT - LIVING ROOM - CONTINUOUS

--opening the living room door, coffee in hand. The place a little bit more of a mess than before. Clothes strewn, a few empty cups sit around, beer cans that have been crushed.

Hools stares for a moment, sipping coffee, then decides to start cleaning up.

INT. HOOLS APARTMENT - LIVING ROOM - LATER

Standing in the midst of a tidy living room, Hools sits down and turns on her laptop, determined to get some writing done. Her laptop opens to the blank word document. Staring at it she starts to zone out. Suddenly words begin typing in red 'what the fuck is wrong with you, you lazy stupid bitch'.

(handwritten: Is that really how I feel?)

Hools looks down at the keyboard, did she write that? She rubs her eyes and suddenly the red words are gone. Shaking it off she opens up instagram and scrolls the familiar patterns.

She stops on a picture of a cute girl holding flowers. The caption reads: 'So nice to have such a supportive partner to be with during this crazy time, she pushed me to finish my final draft which I just found out today is in the top 10 of 500 entries of the NewPlayWrites competition. Love you so much babe.'

(handwritten: Could be a better made up name)

Hools glares at the post and rolls her eyes. She double taps the photo - then writes a comment 'so happy for you darling, you deserve all the love and happiness, miss you!!'. Send. She tosses her phone on the couch.

BZZZT. An incoming message. Hools goes to read it.

(handwritten: I'm so two faced, how do I have any friends)

                  BOYFRIEND (TEXT)
            Morning my love.

Hools sends off a quick heart emoji then goes to find her notebook, which has been placed under a few other books on a high shelf. She goes to pull it down and in the process ends up knocking a Nintendo switch controller onto her head.

                  HOOLS
            MUTHERFU--

Hools picks up the controller, she tosses the notebook aside and goes to turn on her gaming console.

                                        CUT TO:

INT. HOOLS APARTMENT - LIVING ROOM - MUCH LATER

(handwritten: LAZY LAZY LAZY)

The entire day has vanished. Hools' eyes are reddened from staring at the screen all day, a pizza box with only the crust left over sits beside her.

BZZZT. Hools startles from the noise outside of the game. Finally re-entering reality she looks at her phone, which reads 10:00pm.

                    BOYFRIEND (TEXT)
            I hope you had a wonderful day! Xo

                    HOOLS (TEXT)
            It was a Skyrim filled adventure!

                    BOYFRIEND (TEXT)
            Hah, been there! Did you slay a
            dragon?

                    HOOLS (TEXT)
            Many!

Hools begins to text 'sorry for being so distant lately' but instead decides against it.

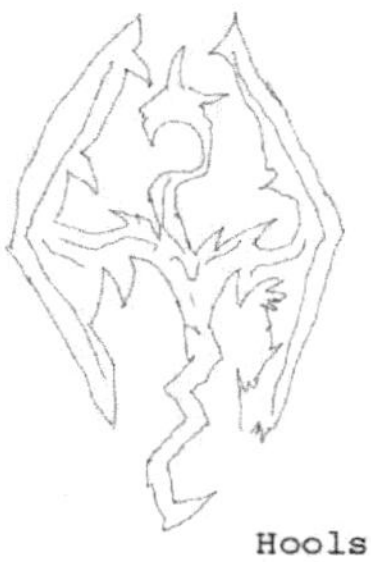

                    BOYFRIEND (TEXT)
            Done any writing lately?

                    HOOLS (TEXT)
            Noooo! I'm the worst!

                    BOYFRIEND (TEXT)
            You are most definitely not! You'll
            do it when you want to do it.

                    HOOLS (TEXT)
            I miss you.

                    BOYFRIEND (TEXT)
            So write about that!

Hools puts her phone down. She turns off the Nintendo switch and walks slowly over to her laptop. When she turns it on the glare of the screen lights up her face in an eerie way. She sits down and begins to type, late into the night.

INT. HOOLS APARTMENT - BEDROOM - THE NEXT DAY

On cue, an alarm goes off, this time Hools is wide awake, waiting for it.

                    HOOLS
            Stop!

The alarm stops. Hools gets out of bed.

INT. HOOLS APARTMENT - LIVING ROOM - DAY

Hools enters with a cup of coffee. She excitedly walks over to her laptop to turn it on. It opens to a blank word document. She freezes.

Handwritten annotations:
- "I seriously don't deserve him ♥"
- "What is my spark of inspiration?"

                    HOOLS
          What?

Hools puts her coffee aside and begins typing frantically in her document search bar, trying to find the file she wrote last night. Nothing is coming up. Did she forget to save? Or did she really even write?

She whips open her phone and scrolls to 'Boyfriend <3'. She presses call. Without even a ring she begins to spiral.

                    HOOLS (CONT'D)
          I can't do this anymore. I don't
          want to pretend that I'm okay. I
          wrote fifteen pages last night, or
          at least I thought I did. I don't
          know, maybe I'm going crazy, or
          maybe I am just not meant for
          greatness, and the world is just
          giving me constant signs. I hate
          this so much. Not being near you
          hurts, not performing live hurts,
          see people only through a screen is
          torture.

                    BOYFRIEND (V.O.)
          I'm sorry.

                    HOOLS
          It's not your fault. I don't think--
          That's a joke. I'm spiralling.

                    BOYFRIEND (V.O.)
          Breathe. I haven't actually heard
          your voice in over a week. So,
          thank you for calling. I want you
          to be okay, I want to drive three
          hours to you and hold you for days.
          But I don't know when the border
          will be open again. You are
          brilliant. I'm sorry I can't make
          things better.

                    HOOLS
          I've been so out of it.

                    BOYFRIEND (V.O.)
          I love you.

Hools has slumped onto the floor. A beat.

                    HOOLS
          How are you though?

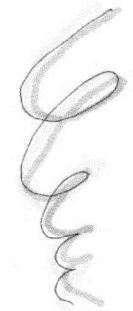

[handwritten annotations: "Too wordy & I'm so ANNOYING"; "It's not funny..."; "do I really actually care? am I a narcissist?"]

A pause.

> **BOYFRIEND (V.O.)**
> Not great. I miss you. But, this is what it is. It's not a forever.

> **HOOLS**
> Yeah.

A moment of realization as Hools understands what that means.

> **HOOLS (CONT'D)**
> You're right! Hey, I am going to do some writing, I love you!

> **BOYFRIEND (V.O.)**
> Okay. Have fun!

Hools hangs up and starts to write. [handwritten: notebook or laptop? → Is there a metaphorical difference? Am I just thinking too much about it?]

The sun slowly goes down.

INT. HOOLS APARTMENT - BEDROOM - THE NEXT DAY

Hools wakes up before her alarm. She hops out of bed, ready for the day.

INT. HOOLS APARTMENT - LIVING ROOM - CONTINUOUS

Hools enters the room without a coffee, wanting to get right to work. She opens her notebook to see no words but instead of worrying she starts to write again.

Begin montage:

--writing frantically, Hools forgets that she needs to use the bathroom, waiting until the end of sentence to run out of the room

--multiple cups of coffee surround her as the morning turns into night

-- the next morning, opening her laptop, she starts a new draft. Lola hops onto the laptop and she moves her out of the way to keep writing.

-- Hools sees Boyfriend calling, she ends the call and sends off a quick text 'in the groove' to which he replies a smiley face and a thumbs up.

-- late into the night, she saves the work as 'another day'

[handwritten left margin: no one cares about the process only the final result]

[handwritten: full circle]

-- opens the laptop with no saved file. She continues to write.

END OF MONTAGE

INT. HOOLS APARTMENT - BEDROOM - NIGHT

Hools speaks excitedly on the phone with her boyfriend.

                  HOOLS
But in this version, the girl doesn't know she's been alone this whole time until the end when it's revealed!

[handwritten: Too meta? or just dumb?]

Boyfriend laughs.

[handwritten: I miss hearing this sound]

                  HOOLS (CONT'D)
What?

                  BOYFRIEND (V.O.)
It's nice to hear you this excited.

                  HOOLS
I guess I haven't felt good about writing in a long time, I forgot it could be fun. And being alone actually has been great, no distractions!

A long pause, before something that has been unsaid for too long.

                  BOYFRIEND (V.O.)
Are we going to make it through this?

Hools has known the answer for a while.

                  HOOLS
I don't want to lose you.

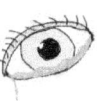

                  BOYFRIEND (V.O.)
You never will. Maybe when things open up, we can see what we can do... try again? And, I'll always support you.

[handwritten: way too good for me]

                  HOOLS
You're a good person, and I love you a lot.

Emerson Arts   The Stage Light Flickers   Pandamonium Publishing

11.

>   BOYFRIEND/FRIEND (V.O.)
>   I love you too. And I'm so freaking
>   proud of everything that you are.
>   Good night.
>   HOOLS
>   Good bye.

Hools hangs up. A moment as she takes in this turn in her life.

INT. HOOLS APARTMENT - BEDROOM - THE NEXT DAY

An alarm goes off. Hools wakes up slowly.

INT. HOOLS APARTMENT - LIVING ROOM - DAY

Hools goes over to her laptop to turn it on, when she opens her documents suddenly she sees a folder of the past year of work that has appeared. Instead of opening any of it, she begins a new draft.

The cycle has ended. Or had it ever really started?

- What am I trying to say?
- Does anything I say matter?
- Accepting change allows for new opportunity
- Will anyone even care?

never enough...

In Holly's piece her protagonist experiences COVID-19 as a sort of Groundhog Day – living the same day repeatedly. How did you manage this feeling?

ZAMMIT, ANN-MARIE B.

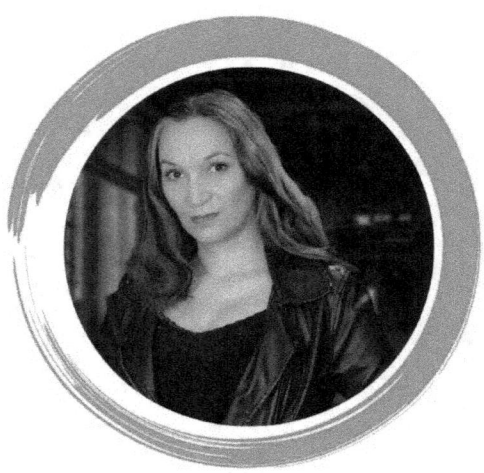

Ann-Marie B. Zammit is a seasoned theatre performer, who was most recently seen as Rosie in MAMMA MIA! for Linus Hand Productions. She has been fortunate to be part of many exciting music theatre projects in the Niagara Region, including roles with Garden City Productions, her favourites being Miss Hannigan in ANNIE and Fruma-Sarah in FIDDLER ON THE ROOF; performing in an original rock musical, based on the biblical story of Job as Wife in JOB AND THE SNAKE (CubeCity Entertainment); and writing and performing original music for THE HANGMAN'S GAME, a Halloween-themed murder mystery show (Cloak and Dagger Productions). AMZ, as she is affectionately known, spent two seasons on the stage at Oh Canada Eh, in their historic (and sadly final) 25th season of their award-winning musical show that celebrated everything Canadian. She spent her summer months entertaining thousands of tourists from all around the globe who had stopped in to catch a show after experiencing the majesty of Niagara Falls.

While at OCE, Ann-Marie put on a top hat and stepped into the tall boots of The Ring Master, in their winter season carnival-themed rock'n'roll musical THE SHOW MUST GO ON, featuring songs of the 1960s and 1970s. AMZ is also a playwright. Her first full length play, IS THIS THING ON?, in which she also performed and directed, was produced for the renowned Toronto Fringe Festival.

She wrote, directed, and performed in IN THE WINGS – A CABARET for Something- Something Productions in historic Niagara-on-the-Lake. She is currently writing her next full-length play entitled CLICKED, about a high school teacher and his former student finding each other on Facebook thirty years later. She is also writing her first feature length screenplay BETA IS BETTER, about a fellow who collects X-rated beta tapes (oh my!).

Ann-Marie also has extensive experience off stage in several production capacities. She co-produced LEND ME A TENOR for Firehall Theatre in Niagara Falls. She has been on the production teams for Canadian Idol (CTV), Gemini Awards (Global), and five seasons with Royal Canadian Air Farce (CBC). She also served as line producer for THE CONSPIRACY SHOW (Film One Media) and segment producer for THE ROMEO REPORT (YourTV Cogeco). She is currently producing, editing, and co-hosting a web talk series, THE BOB & ANNIE SHOW, which can be found on Facebook at

@RomeoRadioOrg. https://www.facebook.com/RomeoRadioOrg

The production she is most proud of is her family – husband Bob, daughter Catherine-Jane, and puppy Rosie. Without their unconditional love and support, AMZ just would not be.

Dots… the universal understood symbol for trailing off…and waiting for what's next. The dots below represent my life during COVID-19, from March 15, 2020, until June 24, 2021, my first day back on set.

Some dots represent gigs that were cancelled, birthdays of my husband, Bob, daughter, CJ, and other loved ones, my first dose of the vaccine (April 21, 2021), and rehearsals for a play in which I had been cast.

March 15, 2020

inhale . . . .

. . . .

. . . .

. . . .

. . . .

. . . .

. . . .

. . . exhale

June 24, 2021

Four Sixty-Six
By: Ann-Marie B. Zammit

WE GOT THIS!

The performing arts industry was one of the very first industries shut-down by COVID-19. Theatres were closed, seats were empty, stages were abandoned – sets and all, as entire casts and crews were sent home to help control the outbreak of a new mystery virus. We were gifted with copious amounts of unexpected and unfamiliar time. No place to go, nowhere to visit. We finally had time. Time to work on new projects, imagine, re-imagine, and re-charge. But the economic impact of this new virus has had severe implications on those already struggling to bring their best, find a gig, and pay those bills. It is estimated that Broadway's closure alone lost over $35 million per week. It's been a hard road, and there are still a few kilometres to go.

The common thread running through these pages is of passion and love for a gruelling industry. We could not stop creating because it runs in our veins. For many performers, the vigorous recognition of the Black Lives Matter movement had a massive impact on the type of art being created. The time for thought and reflection during the pandemic gave new energy, renewed strength and expression for the importance of representation on stage and in the media. Representation matters.

We have seen multiple examples of how the artists have persevered through it all, no money, no work, no place to go. There was sadness, fear, and frustration, and yet, we countered this with new ideas, new methods, new platforms and learned new skills. As usual, we made the best of it. There was a true appreciation for the slowdown, although, we would have rather shared our talent and passion with the world. Afterall, why else would performers do what they do? It's not easy.

As we slowly begin easing restrictions and the stage lights continue to brighten, we must ask ourselves, are we truly ready for things to be back to normal? The hustle is real. Performers are forced to live a gig-to-gig lifestyle, with very little respect and appreciation outside of the theatre walls. Although we have a $50,000 education, MBAs, and special training, like our friends in other industries, it's only the arts where the work is demanded, but the skills are not appreciated. We are often asked to perform for 'exposure'. But I don't pay for my groceries in exposures!

Keep in mind, what you see on stage is not an automatic magic-maker! Audiences are witnessing months of rehearsals, long-hours, physical and mental extremes. Musicians spend years learning their instrument. Playing a difficult character on stage for two hours can be as draining as ten-mile run. It drains you of every bit of energy in your body. It's a skill that takes years to hone. It's hard work, but we love it. We want this experience. We want to share ourselves with the world.

It's wonderful to see, that for each negative experience during the shutdown of live entertainment, for most, there was some sort of unexpected positive. Whether it was spending time with family, or taking time to finish a project, or the awesome luxury of binge-watching a mind-numbing show, as we awaited the lifting safety regulations. Through these pages, we hope you have connected with the stories and emotional ups and downs experienced by each one of the performers.

During the pandemic the world relied on the hard work, talent, tenacity, and creativity of artists of all kinds. It is our hope that thisnew learned appreciation will translate into better paying jobs, with job security and overall artist appreciation. If we don't take care of the artists, art will become fleeting. Live performances are part of the final stages of re-opening the economy after all these lockdowns. And as usual, we'll be ready, so long as we're still here.

Ann-Marie artistically demonstrates her anxiety and the feeling of holding her breath until her exhale moment, when she finally was able to perform again. Did you feel anxious and unsettled during this time, or did you welcome the new normal a global pandemic provided?

Group Discussion Questions

Discuss the paradox of time as a giver or as a taker during the coronavirus.

How do you feel about the current climate of the performance industry?

Do you feel like you have a place in this current theatrical world?

In your opinion, what makes a professional performer? Has coronavirus changed your view?

What was your biggest struggle during lockdowns and the uncertainty of the coronavirus?

Do you think performers and artists were more prepared for the feelings of uncertainty and the unknown than their counterparts from other industries? Why or why not?

What was your biggest take away from the book?

In five words, describe your COVID-19 experience?

Which piece affected you most? Why?

What role did social media play in your experience during the pandemic? How did it affect you?

What behaviour did you learn to change with the rise of Black Lives Matter?

How has COVID-19 affected, inspired or changed you, your art, your outlook on the arts or your career?

How have you been filling your time? How did you cope with the closures?

What are some tips & tricks you have picked up to keep your passion, creativity, or drive/ motivation high?

What do you think the future for your industry is to become?

How have you been mentally, spiritually, physically and how have you kept the arts alive your heart?

What do you hope will affect your industry positively because of COVID-19?

How have you kept afloat, finically/ mentally?

Personal reflection:

Have you learned a new skill over Coronavirus? If yes, do you plan to continue this new skill once theatre resumes?

Do you enjoy your lessons/meetings/ performances/ rehearsals via Zoom or in person? Why?

Did you truly feel isolated and alone during isolation? Why or why not? If yes, when did your feelings of solitude end?

Did you ever feel like no one else feels the same as you?

Who did you most identify with? Why?

Did you take issue with anyone? Why?

Could you cast yourself in Paddy or Holly's plays? Which character would you be?

What was the biggest emotion you felt while reading this book? Why?

Did your art turn into activism?

Do you consider yourself an activist?

Did you cherish your time or wish it away during the numerous lockdowns? Why?

Did you have creative blocks or feel a new sense of artistic freedom?